Last Things in Shakespeare

Last Things in Shakespeare

Harry Morris

UNIVERSITY PRESSES OF FLORIDA
Florida State University Press
Tallahassee

UNIVERSITY PRESSES OF FLORIDA is the central agency for scholarly publishing of the State of Florida's university system, producing books selected for publication by the faculty editorial committees of Florida's nine public universities: Florida A&M University (Tallahassee), Florida Atlantic University (Boca Raton), Florida International University (Miami), Florida State University (Tallahassee), University of Central Florida (Orlando), University of Florida (Gainesville), University of North Florida (Jacksonville), University of South Florida (Tampa), University of West Florida (Pensacola).

ORDERS for books published by all member presses of University Presses of Florida should be addressed to University Presses of Florida, 15 NW 15th Street, Gainesville, FL 32603.

Library of Congress Cataloging in Publication Data

Morris, Harry.
　Last things in Shakespeare.

　Bibliography: p.
　Includes index.
　1. Shakespeare, William, 1564–1616—Religion and ethics—Addresses, essays, lectures. 2. Eschatology in literature—Addresses, essays, lectures. I. Title.
PR3011.M58　1985　822.3'3　85–1453
ISBN 0–8130–0794–1

Contents

Illustrations

vii

Preface

xi

Introduction

The Images of Last Things

1

1 *Hamlet*

And Is It Not to Be Damned?

12

2 *Othello*

No Amount of Prayer Can Possibly Matter

76

Contents

3   *King Lear*

The Great Doom's Image, I

115

4   *Macbeth*

The Great Doom's Image, II

163

5   *Romeo and Juliet*

Some Shall Be Pardoned

205

6   *A Midsummer Night's Dream*

So Quick Bright Things Come to Confusion

232

7   The *Henry* Plays

Prince Hal, Apostle to the Gentiles

255

8   *As You Like It*

Et in Arcadia Ego

289

Appendix

The *memento-mori* Lyric

311

Index

342

Illustrations

1. Four last things, St. Mary the Virgin, Great Snoring, Norfolk   2
2. Title page, *La grant danse macabree des hõmes & des femmes*   6
3. Disasters in the sun and moon, *Queen Elizabeth Prayer Book*   35
4. Signs, *Queen Elizabeth Prayer Book*   37
5. "Flights of angels sing thee to thy rest," *Queen Mary's Psalter*   57
6. *The daunce of Machabree*, John Lydgate   66
7. Patience, *Queen Elizabeth Prayer Book*   124
8. Pelican misericord, SS Peter and Paul, Lavenham, Suffolk   149
9. Copy of chancel-arch Last Judgment, Guild Chapel, Stratford-upon-Avon   158–59
10. Doomsday painting, St. Peter's, Wenhaston, Suffolk   161
11. Possession and exorcism, Pierre Boaistuau   177
12. Signs preceding doomsday, *Queen Elizabeth Prayer Book*   179
13. Signs preceding doomsday, *The book intytulyd the Art of good lywyng & good deying*   181–83

14. (a) Doomsday trumpet raising the dead, *Hore presentes
ad vsvm Sarvm.* (b) Dead rising from the earth, St. Peter's, Wenhaston, Suffolk.   188–89
15. The Four Horsemen of the Apocalypse, Albrecht
Dürer   191
16. Dying man, *The craft to liue well and to die well*   203
17. Title page of *The glasse of vaine-glorie*   209
18. Funerary monument, Church of St. Mary, Bottesford,
Leicestershire   211
19. Death and the lover, St. Mary Magdalene, Newark-on-
Trent, Nottinghamshire   215
20. Foolish virgin, Lincoln Cathedral   218
21. *Patientia* and *Ira, The boke named royall*   222
22. West portals of St.-Denis   225
23. Wise and Foolish Virgins, Hans Eworth   228–29
24. Frontispiece, *A Midsummer Night's Dream*   234
25. West front, Lincoln Cathedral   275
26. Old man, Dance of Death, Hans Holbein   279
27. All shall die, *The boke named royall*   281
28. (a) Salamander, Garden of Eden, Hugo van der Goes.
(b) Salamander poisoning fruit tree, *Queen Mary's
Psalter.*   282–83
29. Souls in Abraham's bosom, *Hortus Deliciarum*, Herrad
of Landsberg   285
30. *Respice finem*, Heinrich Aldegrever   286
31. Soul in the bosom of God / Abraham, Percy chantry,
Beverley Minster, Beverley, Humberside   287
32. Et in Arcadia Ego, Giovanni Francesco Guercino   292
33. (a) Et in Arcadia Ego and (b) detail, Nicolas
Poussin   299–300
34. Putto with a death's head (Three Ages of Man),
Vicenzo Cartari   304
35. Putto with death's head, Church of St. Thomas of Canterbury, Clapham, Bedfordshire   305
36. The seven ages of man, *Batman vppon Bartholome*   307
37. *Memento-mori* skull, Geffrey Whitney   308

38. *Memento-mori* iconography of death and implements
    of burial   316–17
39. Fool, Dance-of-Death alphabet, Hans Holbein   334
40. "To this favor she must come," *Hore presentes ad vsvm
    Sarvm*   336

These hymns of praise are offered as Christmas carols
to St. Anne

Preface

The first four essays in this book are more closely related to each other than they are to the last four; yet all are approached from the same starting place: to ascertain what in these plays treats of last things—of eschatology and how eschatological themes illuminate the larger drama. To find so much of death, judgment, heaven, and hell in the gay and golden comedies of *A Midsummer Night's Dream* and *As You Like It* might prove shocking; to find the behavior of the universally beloved children, Romeo and Juliet, held up against a theology that should judge them damned might prove disturbing; to forget the wit, joviality, and expansiveness of life in Falstaff in order to consider the plight of his soul might be irritating; and yet all these things these essays do, because these things I believe Shakespeare to have included in the plays here considered. Last things hold these essays together, and last things hold the book together.

Earlier versions of four chapters and the appendix have appeared as follows: chapter 2 (on *Othello*) as "No Amount of Prayer Can Possibly Matter," *Sewanee Review* 77 (1969): 8–24; chapter 4 (on *Macbeth*) as "*Macbeth*, Dante, and the Greatest Evil," *Tennessee Studies in Literature* 12 (1967): 23–39; chapter 7 (on the *Henry* plays) as "Prince Hal: Apostle to the Gentiles," *Clio* 7 (1978): 227–46; chapter 8 (on *As You Like It*) as "*As You Like It*: Et in Arcadia Ego," *Shakespeare Quarterly* 26 (1975): 269–75; and the appendix (on the *memento-mori* lyric) as "*Hamlet* as a *memento-mori* Poem," *PMLA* 85 (1970): 1035–40. The version of "No Amount of Prayer Can Possibly Matter," which first appeared in the *Sewanee Review*, is in copyright 1969 by the University of the South and is reprinted by permission of the editor. The version of the appendix printed in *PMLA* is reprinted by permission of the Modern Language Association of America. Other reprinted material has appropriate permission to reprint.

I would like to remember Irving Ribner, who, though he had no part in this book, is a man with whom I argued Shakespeare during the five years we were colleagues at Tulane University. The original of the essay on the *Henry* plays was intended for a festschrift in his honor; since the project did not materialize, I would like to dedicate this essay to his memory. For labors on the manuscripts, typescripts, and proofs, above and beyond recompense, I would like to thank Daphne Williams Liedy and Carol Gray. Finally, I want to express my gratitude to the staffs of Florida State University Press and University Presses of Florida for their fine work in the production of this book.

Introduction
The Images of Last Things

Speculation on last things in Shakespeare raises the specter of a medieval poet, the sort of Shakespeare that almost all existing commentary tries to prove this poet is not.[1] He is irrefutably a Renaissance man, more modern than any of his contemporaries except Ralegh and Marlowe. But Shakespeare is not only all things to all men, he is also all things to himself. Nothing in the sixteenth century that caused the intellectual man to focus more on the world and less on heaven led him to blot out heaven altogether. No one more attentive to the new Humanism was less likely to ignore his obligation in faith than Sir Thomas More, no one more caught up in the jostling, worldly London of his day more fearful of judgment than John Donne. Clearly, the violent, sometimes fanatic, turbulence we call the Reformation prompted many men to exam-

1. Notable exceptions to the view of a purely Renaissance Shakespeare are Willard Farnham's two books, *The Medieval Heritage of Elizabethan Tragedy* (New York, 1936) and *Shakespeare's Tragic Frontier* (Berkeley, 1950). Other important writers who see significant medieval elements in Shakespeare's plays include Roy Battenhouse, *Shakespearean Tragedy: Its Art and Its Christian Premises* (Bloomington, Ind., 1969), and Bernard Spivack's *Shakespeare and the Allegory of Evil* (New York, 1958).

1

Fig. 1. Four last things. Painted board, sixteenth century. North wall, nave, St. Mary the Virgin, Great Snoring, Norfolk.

ine their beliefs with a closer scrutiny than men had done earlier throughout most of the Middle Ages, and no part of belief concerned a man more than his part in heaven. Even a free-thinker like Marlowe who, with many another overbright and overnaughty sophomore, engaged in atheistic talk both for novelty and shock-effect, in *Faustus* subjects his protagonist, a Renaissance man if ever any was, to retribution as medieval as that meted out to evil souls by Tutivillus in the judgment pageant of the Wakefield Plays.

Shakespeare, if less saint than More, was less sinner than Marlowe, and like them both gives the most disturbing issues of religious belief sharp focus in many of his works. The epitaph in Stratford provides ready evidence of a truly medieval fear about the disturbance of his remains:

> Good frend for Iesvs sake forbeare,
> To digg the dvst enclosed heare.
> Bleste be ye man y^t spares thes stones,
> And cvrst be he y^t moves my bones.

Well known, however, is the doubt over the authenticity of these lines as Shakespeare's. Better instead is to take the testimony of all that he wrote, a better epitaph itself, the "monument" without the "tomb." As medieval as the church inscription may be, no more is it so than the eschatology of the plays. No disservice is done Shakespeare to assert this element in his work. His Humanism is the establishment of four hundred years of comment and scholarship. The few writers who bring our attention to the thought of the Middle Ages that permeates his work are merely rounding out the picture.

Most eschatology of the medieval Christian world has a far more immediate existence in the visual arts than in the written (fig. 1). The concerns that prompted both Romanesque and Gothic church builders to put forth the Bible in stone in order that the illiterate devout might nourish their faith through their eyes as well as through their ears were the same that led those with the talent to supplement the encyclopedias of the Middle Ages with pictures. Not enough were the tongues, books, and sermons in trees, brooks, and stones. Those who could not read, whose ears closed

3

to the monotonous drone of the homily, needed something other than the church fathers or the familiar, boring priest. Augustine, Jerome, and Bernard, even the encyclopedists like Isidore of Seville and Vincent of Beauvais provided grist only for other learned churchmen and, fortunately, for the very illustrators who could make their thought comprehensible to the unlettered. Visionaries like Herrad of Landsburg or the unknown painter who put the first Dance of Death on the walls of the cemetery of Holy Innocents in Paris, artists whose gifts worked more comfortably, more strikingly in graphic images, these brought the good news to the apprentice, the tradesman, to the peasant, the farmer, to the salt of the earth.

Some themes, ultimately becoming conventions of the pictorial encyclopedia, had their origins as early as the fourth century: the *Psychomachia* of Prudentius, for example. Others developed as late as the fifteenth century, like the Dance of Death. Intervening years saw the emergence of more and more pictorial treatment of last things, gradually building an iconography that changed little from century to century. Then in the same way that vast compilations of widely varying, though always religious, materials were gathered together by Isidore and Vincent, illustrators like Herrad and the anonymous artist of the *Holkham Bible Picture Book* assembled predictable drawings of a spiritual nature in well-established modes of presentation. The penitent in any of the northern Gothic cathedrals and churches who lifted his eyes to the stained glass and scanned from light to light, who studied the stories in stone atop the pillars of the nave, who, if his eyes were good enough, read the wooden tableaux of the roof bosses, would encounter from church to church the same *legenda*: a Tree of Jesse, a Christopher and the Christ Child, a Vision of Paul, a Visitation, Annunciation, Birth, Crucifixion, Assumption, Resurrection and so on. Similarly, another devout, capable only of turning from picture to picture, if he might somehow lay his hand on an illustrated manuscript or book, would find from volume to volume representations of the Battle of the Vices and Virtues, the Triumph of Death, the *Ars moriendi*, the parables especially of the Prodigal Son, the Wise and Foolish Virgins, or the Beggar and the Rich Man, a History of Antichrist, a series of the Signs that Pre-

4

cede Doomsday (usually the Fifteen Signs), a Judgment panel, the Joys of Paradise, the Seven Deadly Sins, the Ages of Man, the Three Living and the Three Dead, and the Dance of Death.

Fritz Saxl has given us a convenient title by which to call these books generally. Describing the rediscovered Wellcome Manuscript and comparing it with a similar fifteenth-century work in Rome, the Casanatensis Manuscript, Saxl lumps them with the encyclopedic tradition of Isidore, Hrabanus Maurus, Vincent, and Bartholomaeus Anglicus to call them spiritual encyclopedias, but he details an important offshoot that is distinctive because of pictorial accompaniment. Illustrative materials seem to have been included in a significant manner for the first time in the *Liber Floridus* of Lambert of St. Omer in the first quarter of the twelfth century. But the *Hortus Deliciarum*, later in the same century, becomes the prototype for later compilers. Herrad, Abbess of Hohenburg (1167–95), in her grace and charm, encompasses "everything from the creation to the Last Judgement, and everything had to be illustrated."[2]

Some two and a half centuries separate Herrad from the Wellcome Manuscript, and although the latter was rediscovered in England, Saxl's authority is sufficient to tell us the work is German. Apparently no English pictorial encyclopedia confined to spiritual themes develops in England until shortly after William Caxton's death. In 1490 and 1491, Caxton translated from the French and published on his press in Westminster two short pieces in the *Ars moriendi* tradition but lacking the famous illustrations that accompany the work on the continent. Wynkyn de Worde, the printer's former apprentice, reissued in 1497 the second of Caxton's two translations, still without woodcuts. In 1506, however, the third edition of this same pamphlet was set forth with two illustrations: a frontispiece of the Three Living and the Three Dead and one block imitating its conventional counterpart in French and Latin *Ars moriendi* across the Channel. Meanwhile, in an English translation in 1503 but coming from the Paris press of Antoine Vérard, was a work entitled, *Art of good lywyng & good deying*, illustrated

2. Fritz Saxl, "A Spiritual Encyclopaedia of the Later Middle Ages," *Journal of the Warburg and Courtauld Institutes* 5 (1942): 117–19.

A grant danse macabree des hōmes ⁊ des femmes hystoriee ⁊ augmentee de beaulx ditz en latin.

Le debat du corps ⁊ de lame
La complaincte de lame damnee
Exhortation de bien viure ⁊ bien mourir
La vie du mauuais antechrist
Les quinze signes
Le ingement.

Fig. 2. Title page, *La grant danse macabree des hōmes & des femmes*. Press of Nicolas le Rouge, Troyes, 1496.

with a complete set of excellent woodblock prints. The work was encyclopedic in the sense that added to the *Ars moriendi* were additional tracts commonly found in works like the *Hortus Deliciarum* and the Wellcome and Casanatensis Manuscripts: "the cūmyng of antecryst," "the xv syngys or toknys that shal cum befor the iugement general of god," "the iugement general," and "the ioyes of paradys." Especially fine is the set of fifteen woodcuts complementing the fifteen signs. Excellent also are full-page illustrations preceding the tracts on "the iugement general" and "the ioyes of paradys." Vérard vies with Guyot Marchant as the earliest printer of a Dance of Death, both publishing in Paris in 1486 dual processions of *La Danse Macabre des Hommes* and *La Danse Macabre des Femmes*.

Wynkyn de Worde found, apparently, that Vérard's English edition of the *Ars moriendi* was a work with which he could compete. In 1505, hiring A. Chertsey to make a fresh translation from the French, Wynkyn published *The craft to liue well and to die well*. He imitated the illustrations found throughout Vérard's work but obviously was unable to get a craftsman with skill equal to the Frenchman's. When Wynkyn reissued his book the next year, the fifteen illustrations of the tokens preceding judgment day were decreased to eight. Compensatory additions were made by increasing illustrations of the *Ars moriendi* itself as well as of the Coming of Antichrist and the Joys of Paradise. Clearly, Wynkyn was developing something like the spiritual encyclopedias by this time common on the continent.

The epitome of the pictorial spiritual encyclopedia in France may be seen in a volume from the press of Nicolas le Rouge, published in Troyes in 1496. Capitalizing on the contemporary popularity of the Dance of Death, Nicolas titles his folio *La grant danse macabree des hōmes & des femmes hystoriee & augmentee de beaulx ditz en latin* (fig. 2). But the male and female processions are only two of several eschatological picture stories contained in the book. Bound in with the Dance are the following: "Le debat du corps & de lame," "La complaincte de lame damnee," "Exhortation de bien vivre & bien mourir," "La vie du mauuais antecrist," "Les quinze signes," and "Le iugement." Saxl, commenting specifically on Well-

7

come and Casanatensis, explains perhaps the success of these disturbing *memento mori*:

> our 15th century writers aim at fighting vice and avoiding the pains of hell. Their interests are varied but there is no unity in this variety. And last but not least they also believe in representing their ideas in pictures, but the pictures are unimpressive except when they touch the deepest fear of these men—the fear of death and the fear of hell.[3]

The grim fascination that these thoughts of the end held on the minds of men of the later Middle Ages had far from disappeared by the end of the sixteenth century. Beginning in 1569, but continuing until 1608, the English printer John Day published a series of Prayer Books which, though they appeared under various titles in the five separate editions covered by these years, were called generally the *Queen Elizabeth Prayer Book*, after the full-page portrait of that monarch printed as a frontispiece. The earliest edition had the fewest illustrations; but by 1581, the complete series of woodblocks, used as a border on all four sides of the prayers making up the text, included an extensive gallery of the Vices and Virtues, twelve scenes of the Works of Charity,[4] a group of the five senses personified, a sequence of eighteen cuts of the signs that precede Judgment Day, a Last Judgment, and a lengthy procession of the Dance of Death, divided after the French fashion into a dance of men and a dance of women. None of these pictures has any direct relationship to the text and, consequently, are essentially a second book, a pictorial spiritual encyclopedia.

The five editions of the *Queen Elizabeth Prayer Book* cover Shakespeare's entire life span. Given the obvious habit in the poet

---

3. Saxl, "A Spiritual Encyclopaedia," pp. 119–20.

4. The Works of Charity are a frequent eschatological convention. They reflect Matthew 24 and 25, concerning the end of the world, and begin at 25.35 with the words "For I was an hungred, and ye gaue me meat" (Geneva Bible [1560]). All biblical quotations are from this edition.

of voracious reading, he would have perused, probably, whatever from the presses of Caxton, Wynkyn, and Vérard was extant. He would have access to French volumes as well. The on-and-off alliances with different French factions throughout the reign of Elizabeth, and especially the Anjou flirtations, created considerable cultural exchange. The rich Norman and Breton Gothic influence of the Middle Ages hung on longer in northern France than elsewhere, and no doubt some of it made its way across the Channel. Innumerable other works of a spiritual nature appear to make up the greater bulk of all printing done in the last half of the sixteenth century, and many were illustrated. That these graphic materials should fail to influence a craftsman whose work demanded a rich imagery almost as its life's blood is so improbable as not to bear thinking.

In addition to the subliterary world in which the spiritual encyclopedia belongs on the whole, a vast body of serious art exerts a similar influence. Quite allied to the illustrated books are the artworks in almost every medium that glorified the great cathedrals as well as many lesser churches. Although art tied to eschatology was undoubtedly in far greater proliferation all over northern France, Flanders, and Germany, significant representation is to be found throughout England. In church sculpture, in stained glass, in pulpit, choir, and other ornamental woodcarving (misericords, poppy heads, roof bosses), in religious paintings, and in illuminated *literae sacra*, the art of last things is evident from parish churches like Shakespeare's Holy Trinity and the Stratford Guildhall Chapel to great Lincoln Cathedral and Beverley Minster.

Mystery-play cycles all concluded with a Last Judgment, and some had additional eschatological plays that included the Harrowing of Hell, the Resurrection, Pentecost, and the Antichrist. Writers like Rosemary Woolf and Mary D. Anderson[5] have shown the interplay that exists between the imagery and staging of the plays and the iconography, symbology, and emblems of illustrated manu-

5. Rosemary Woolf, *The English Mystery Plays* (Berkeley, 1972); Mary D. Anderson, *Drama and Imagery in English Medieval Churches* (Cambridge, Eng., 1963).

scripts and church art. A play about the Wise and Foolish Virgins[6] performed at St.-Martial de Limoges contains elements in common with the highly dramatic rendering of the parable on the jambs and tympanum of the central portal in the west facade at St.-Denis, outside Paris. Whether play influenced sculpture or vice versa seems impossible to say, but when Lincoln Cathedral employed the Wise-and-Foolish-Virgins motif in its Judgment Porch in the thirteenth century at least one trope had preceded it. No Wise-and-Foolish-Virgins pageant has been found among the English mystery cycles, but that is not to say none once existed. Furthermore, as M. D. Anderson reminds us, "up to the middle of the twelfth century, the Channel was less a distinct cultural frontier than it afterwards became, so that liturgical plays performed in the great cathedrals of France or Germany can be reckoned as a fair indication of what happened in England."[7] Of course, this cultural "barrier" opened and closed after the twelfth century as relations between the nations altered; but even in times of severest conflict, such as the Hundred Years War, ties with Flanders strengthened and invasion of the enemy France gave poets like Lydgate opportunity to copy the Dance-of-Death verses from the walls of Holy Innocents and bring them for the first time to England, where they were recopied on the walls of the cloisters of St. Paul's in London with appropriate paintings.

Lydgate's *Daunse of Machabree* reminds us that a very large proportion of the narrative and didactic literature of the entire fifteenth century as well as a good bit of the first half of the sixteenth—the poetry and prose of Gower, Lydgate, Hoccleve, More, Barclay, and Hawes, even some of Skelton's; the poetry also of most of the Scots Chaucerians—had more than its share in concerns of the last things. Specifically, Gower's *Mirour de l'Omme* is a fusion of the Seven Deadly Sins and the psychomachia, and his *Confessio Amantis* approaches very close to a spiritual encyclopedia without pictures. Beyond Lydgate's *Daunce*, among other things, is his trans-

6. Karl Young, *The Drama of the Medieval Church*, 2 vols. (London, 1933), 1:74–75, 2:361–69.
7. Anderson, *Drama and Imagery*, p. 33.

lation of Deguilleville's *Pèlerinage*, itself as much a spiritual en-
cylopedia as Gower's *Confessio*. Hoccleve has a poem of almost one
thousand lines of rhyme royal plus a prose supplement called
Lerne to Dye, and Skelton, in addition to one of the greatest *memento-
mori* lyrics in the language, "Vppon a deedmans hed," gave to his
contemporaries a poem now lost to us but mentioned in *The Gar-
land of Laurell* as "to lerne you to dye when ye wyll." Sir Thomas
More's *Four Last Things* is another illustration of a great Humanist
and one of the founders of the English Renaissance chained in his
faith to the conventions of the Middle Ages. All the other poets
mentioned above have longer or shorter pieces, of which the finest
representative would be Dunbar's "Lament for the Makaris," as
great a *memento-mori* lyric as Skelton's and more highly personalized.

These elements of his inherited culture could not but affect
Shakespeare, and they did. The readings of his plays herein presented are oriented about these materials and the themes that in-
spire them. Shakespeare is the richest of our playwrights, the
richest of our poets. He is a great Renaissance figure, but he is
also, inescapably, as is the entire Renaissance, grounded on the
bedrock of the Age of Faith.

1. *Hamlet:*
And Is It Not
to Be Damned?

rior to *Hamlet*, Shakespeare had written six tragedies, if we accept three of the history plays—*Richard III, King John,* and *Richard II*—as tragic in the personal downfall of their titular heroes. Although it would seem quite difficult to write a tragedy in which the nature of evil were not considered at all, Shakespeare in these six earlier works was less concerned with the nature of evil, more with the tragedy of character. What is of evil in these plays may be seen as something internal in a man, having its effect on that man and on all around him. With the series of tragedies initiated in *Hamlet* and terminating in *Macbeth,* Shakespeare became more interested in evil as an external force, working its poison upon a person, will he, nill he, who goes to mortal destruction in all cases but who, in half of these four great tragedies, perseveres to immortal beatitude.

One might argue that of these four plays—*Hamlet, Othello, Lear,* and *Macbeth*—the last two are as much studies of the tragedy of character as ever Shakespeare wrote. But if we accept the view that Lear is a man more sinned against than sinning, as well as the view that vast supernatural forces put Macbeth to the test of enormous temptation, then we see in these plays important thematic concerns that continue speculations which Shakespeare had begun in *Hamlet* and *Othello*.

For some time three of the four central tragedies have been regarded—by some writers—as eschatologically oriented: *Hamlet*, *Macbeth*, and *Othello*.[1] More recently *Lear* has been also so considered.[2] I find attractive the idea that these plays constitute a tetralogy, all investigating the theme of salvation/damnation from the four possible approaches. I hope to show that two plays present a man bad at the outset. The possibilities are that a bad man will remain evil and go to the merited end: damnation; or that he will repent, lead a new life, and receive the promised reward: salvation. These plays, I intend to argue, are *Macbeth* and *Lear*, respectively. The two remaining plays present a man good at first. The possibilities are that the good man will resist evil and gain the offered mercy: salvation; or that he will succumb to the promptings of the devil and go to his prepared doom: damnation. These plays are *Hamlet* and *Othello* respectively, and with *Hamlet* we deal first.

Hamlet, as it inaugurates my hypothetical tetralogy, initiates

1. See G. Wilson Knight, *The Wheel of Fire* (London, 1930); G. R. Elliott, *Flaming Minister* (Durham, N.C., 1953); Paul N. Siegel, *Shakespearean Tragedy and the Elizabethan Compromise* (New York, 1957); Bernard Spivack, *Shakespeare and the Allegory of Evil* (New York, 1958); Irving Ribner, *Patterns in Shakespearian Tragedy* (New York, 1960); Joseph A. Bryant, Jr., *Hippolyta's View* (Lexington, Ky., 1961); Eleanor Prosser, *Hamlet and Revenge* (Stanford, 1967, rev. 1971); R. H. West, *Shakespeare & the Outer Mystery* (Lexington, Ky., 1968); Roy Battenhouse, *Shakespearean Tragedy: Its Art and Its Christian Premises* (Bloomington, Ind., 1969); and H. R. Coursen, Jr., *Christian Ritual and the World of Shakespeare's Tragedies* (Lewisburg, Pa., 1976).

2. See especially J. F. Danby, *Shakespeare's Doctrine of Nature: A Study of King Lear* (London, 1949); and also Siegel, *Shakespearean Tragedy*, pp. 161–88, and Ribner, *Patterns in Shakespearian Tragedy*, pp. 116–36.

certain modes and devices for the presentation of themes that recur in the later three. To be expected is a rather tentative or uncertain handling of materials that are used subsequently with sophistication and confidence. In the last of the four, *Macbeth*, Shakespeare achieves his consummate view of evil. Comments of a considerable number of critics are reflected in G. Wilson Knight's: *Macbeth* is Shakespeare's "most profound and mature vision of evil."[3] Support can be given Knight's claim by reference to Dante.[4] Macbeth is guilty of all four crimes punished in the lowest circle of hell: the usurper betrays lord, guest, country, and kin in the one awesome murder of Duncan. When Shakespeare began his investigation of evil in *Hamlet*, then also he was looking for evil in unusual measure. He develops his villain Claudius along lines later to be used again for Macbeth. Claudius kills his king (secular and spiritual lord);[5] he betrays his country, since the usurpation puts a foul corruption upon the realm (something is rotten in the state); King Hamlet is closer in kinship to Claudius than Duncan to Macbeth; and though Claudius does not stand in relationship of host to guest (the crime Dante describes in Canto xxxiii of the *Inferno* and the crime indeed of Macbeth), nevertheless, Claudius, who must be presumed to have had the run of the royal castle, was guest to King Hamlet's host and commits therefore surely an equal though opposite betrayal.

Where Shakespeare weakens his vision of evil in this earlier play is to add incest to Claudius's sins, for the unnatural marriage all but buries the other crimes. First among Hamlet's thoughts at play's opening, that sin still dominates the Prince's mind when he pours venom down his uncle's throat at play's end: "Here, thou incestuous, murd'rous, damned Dane, / Drink off this potion" (V.ii.327–28).[6] Hamlet's reaction is so violent and his loathing of

3. Knight, *The Wheel of Fire*, p. 154.

4. See chap. 4, where the following matters are treated in depth.

5. The notion that Shakespeare makes his assassin guilty of betraying his spiritual lord, partaking thereby of the sin of Judas, is pursued more fully in the chapter on *Macbeth*.

6. Shakespeare's plays are quoted from *The Complete Works of Shakespeare*, 3d ed., ed. David Bevington (Glenview, Ill., 1980).

the sin so deeply embedded that it remains before the Prince and consequently before Shakespeare's audience throughout the entire play; the significance of the greater crimes that Claudius commits is thereby lessened, obscuring the obligations of Hamlet as true king and as restorer of his country's health.

Nor does the fact that Richard III is guilty of all the crimes for which Macbeth and Claudius stand condemned make of that history play a forerunner to the kind of drama I describe here. *Richard III* is more properly a tragedy in which the central figure is indeed evil personified, but the playwright's concern is not so much to look at that evil as to note its existence as a fact and to observe what villainy and destruction that evil produces about itself. Richard acts; Hamlet is acted upon. And although Macbeth acts and evil falls upon all around him, still there is that even closer view of evil itself, evil engulfing a focal character that cannot be found in *Richard III*. In *Hamlet* evil saturates all, and by *all* we mean the universe. Critics refer commonly to the Hamlet universe, the Lear universe, the Macbeth universe. The evil creation into which we look in these four plays includes the gods "that keep this dreadful pudder o'er our heads" (*Lear*, III.ii.50) as well as those spirits lurking in "the dunnest smoke of hell" called on by Lady Macbeth (I.v.39–50). Furthermore, the eschatological matters, which are an omnipresent concern, along with the nature of evil, and which cause us to follow the characters themselves either into heaven or hell, make these plays very different from *Richard III*.

Among the devices that Shakespeare employs in his search for the nature of evil is the supernatural. *Hamlet* proves the least sophisticated of these four plays in that the old ghost of Senecan drama is resurrected, although a very different ghost from forebears in *Richard III* or *Julius Caesar*. But in *Othello* Shakespeare puts a highly polished devil on the stage; in *Lear*, although supernatural forces diminish, constant reference is made not only to the vast legion of Harsnet's infernal regions but also to the retributive justice that Lear calls upon his daughters in the form of a "thousand with red burning spits / [to] Come hizzing in upon 'em" (III.vi.15–16); in *Macbeth* Shakespeare invests with demons the living bodies of Macbeth and his Lady immediately after the murder of Duncan.

Other devices, more familiar, include that of false appearances. Pervasive in the canon, from the earliest plays to the latest, false-seeming is everywhere apparent in these four tragedies as well. But one of the special forms it takes particularly in them is that of the world turned upside down. Perhaps the theme of the topsy-turvy universe reaches its fullest expression in *Lear*, but it exists also in the black-white displacements of *Othello* and the fair-is-foul, foul-is-fair motif in *Macbeth* and is initiated in *Hamlet* through the antic disposition that Hamlet feels impelled to put on in order to escape unharmed in the evil Claudian ambiance.

In three of these four plays the true king is usurped or displaced by a false king, placing at the top of the Hamlet-Lear-Macbeth universe a ruler who is a canker in the state, the cause of its corruption, and the establisher of its upside-down morality. In *Hamlet* not only is Claudius the false king who in an act of fratricide has stolen the crown but also he is a thief who, in a continuing conspiracy of evil, keeps Prince Hamlet from succeeding his father as inheritor of a throne rightfully his.[7] To see Hamlet as true king from the moment of his father's death is the only means of unraveling the knotted skein of the play in the now-familiar scourge-and-minister view.[8]

If the world is topsy-turvy in the sense that evil usurps good,

7. The early and forceful advocate of such a view is John Dover Wilson, *What Happens in Hamlet* (New York, 1935), pp. 26–38.

8. See Fredson Bowers, "Hamlet as Minister and Scourge," *PMLA* 70 (1955): 740–49. Bowers's arguments prevailed relatively undisputed until the challenge of R. W. Dent, "Hamlet: Scourge and Minister," *SQ* 29 (1978): 82–84. Dent holds that *scourge* and *minister* were interchangeable, "one of the play's innumerable pairings of synonyms" (p. 84). Thus no distinctions might be made between Hamlet as sinful scourger and as divine minister. What Dent neglects is Hamlet's own determination to "answer well / The death" he gave Polonius (III.iv.183–84) and the Prince's penitential tears "for what is done" (IV.i.27). Neither does Dent acknowledge that ministerial acts such as Hamlet's role in the deaths of Rosencrantz, Guildenstern, and Claudius are "not near" Hamlet's conscience (V.ii.58) and are mere justice (V.ii.329).

in the sense that the false king usurps the true, and if evil is able to cloak and mask itself successfully for a while—at least until God's great design for mankind restores the good and the true—then concomitant with false appearances must be problems of identification. Shakespeare in a series of utterances laments the honest man's inability to pierce the disguises of his misleaders:

> There's no art
> To find the mind's construction in the face.
> > (*Macbeth*, I.iv.11–12)
>
> . . . one may smile, and smile, and be a villain.
> > (*Hamlet*, I.v.109)
>
> O heaven, that such companions thou'dst unfold.
> > (*Othello*, IV.ii.143)

In *Othello* Shakespeare delineates the destruction of a man—soul and body—because of the Moor's inability to identify the evil creature who assails him.

Similarly, we find problems of identification in *Hamlet*. The plot is set in motion by the ghost's identification of Claudius as his murderer, a fact not perceivable by the people of Denmark through any natural means. The identification of the ghost itself—its nature and origins—has created one of the thorniest problems that face readers and interpreters of the play. Lesser difficulties of identification in terms of the good recognizing the evil are everywhere evident: Hamlet's pains to know his friends from his enemies— Rosencrantz, Guildenstern, Ophelia, even his mother; Laertes' failure, like his father's, to identify Claudius as a false leader, who in the following leads them to their destruction; Gertrude's misplaced love of her second spouse.

Working in the opposite direction, we find that the good man is not always perceived as good. No one, unless admitted to the deception, sees through Hamlet's antic disposition, and all, consequently, suppose him a menace to the King and state.[9] Ophelia mistakes Hamlet. In such a universe almost no one sees his fellow

9. Ribner, *Patterns in Shakespearian Tragedy*, pp. 70, 76.

clearly. The fog and mist of evil make all perceptions difficult. Darkness and cold as human conditions wall out the weak eyes of innocent creatures. Such is the keynote of *Hamlet*; such is the business of the opening act; such is the imagery of the first scene; such are the words that begin the play:

> Who's there?

Suspicion prevails:

> Nay, answer me. Stand and unfold yourself.

Francisco's words, echoed by Emilia in the lines already adduced from *Othello* (IV.ii.143), carry the metaphysical quality that she more clearly gives them. Follows then the dramatic hopes of the kingdom—"Long live the King!"—even as we learn ironically that one true king has not lived out his natural life and his true successor is not easily made out.

The setting of this scene has been noted often: bitter cold, midnight darkness, sickness of spirit, fearful behavior—all the conditions to concretize the cankered state. That some portentous revelation is pending, figured in the meaning of the walking ghost, is evident in the air of frightened expectation, noticeable even in that lowly creature borrowed centuries later by Clement Moore: "Not a mouse stirring" (I.i.10). Loyalties, relationships, obligations are all ambiguous. Identifications continue wary as Marcellus and Horatio join the watch with vague responses:

> Who is there?
> HORATIO
> Friends to this ground.
> MARCELLUS   And liegemen to the Dane.
> (I.i.14–15)

These men are truly loyal to Danish ground, yet Horatio's is an evasive commitment. Marcellus, pressed also to identify himself, finds a formula more interesting: faithful servants to the Dane. In view, however, of the later decision of these men, wherein they impart their harrowing experience to Hamlet rather than to the man who sits on the throne, it would seem at least arguable that they identify the Dane with the Prince.

Their decision raises immediately the vexing question of the true king. Involved are the terms *love* and *duty* as introduced by Horatio:

> Do you consent we shall acquaint him with it
>   [the appearance of the ghost],
> As needful in our loves, fitting our duty?
>   (I.i.172–73)

Throughout the rest of Act I the word *duty* recurs with insistent frequency along with companion terms of *obedience, obligation,* and *bond.* These terms are met elsewhere in the play also and support a major theme, but after the first act they diminish in number. Duty supported by love seems tendered only to Hamlet and his dead father. The Prince exchanges constantly vows of love for his supporters, as they use the word to him. When duty is mentioned by Claudius or in obligation to Claudius, the word *love* does not appear. In I.ii. Claudius cites *duty* to ambassadors to Norway and to Hamlet. The ambassadors and Laertes acknowledge *duty* to Claudius. Hamlet employs *obey,* although through his mother, to the King (I.ii.120). But then, as if to enforce the contrast, I.ii. ends as Horatio, Marcellus, and Bernardo all offer "duty to your honor," which Hamlet corrects: "Your loves, as mine to you" (252–53).

Doubt over the identification and thus the origin of the ghost develops early in the first scene.[10] Although medieval and sixteenth-century treatises on the supernatural indicate a belief in the ability of both angels and demons to walk the earth and to

---

10. The major treatment establishing the ghost as a "goblin damn'd" is Prosser, *Hamlet and Revenge.* Many of Prosser's proofs of the ghost's evil nature are repeated in this essay, but additional materials are also adduced. Other critics who consider the ghost to be demonic include Knight, *The Wheel of Fire*; Harold Goddard, *The Meaning of Shakespeare*

commune with mortals, angelic visits are barely mentioned, and all is the matter of demons.[11] All reference to the ghost in I.i. is made in irreverent or fearful remark, for the probabilities are that the apparition has nothing to do with anything holy. Horatio, who initially does not believe in spirits either good or bad, derides the ghost constantly as *thing* (three times, I.i.21, 148; I.ii.210), *figure* (I.ii.199), *usurper* (I.i.46), *illusion* (I.i.127), and *apparition* (I.ii.211). Bernardo and Marcellus also use *apparition* (I.i.28) and *figure* (twice,

-----

(Chicago, 1951); John Vyvyan, *The Shakespearean Ethic* (New York, 1959); L. C. Knights, *Some Shakespearean Themes* (London, 1959); Virgil Whitaker, *The Mirror Up to Nature* (San Marino, Cal., 1965); Sister Miriam Joseph, "Discussing the Ghost in *Hamlet,*" *PMLA* 76 (1961): 493–502; and William Hamilton, "Hamlet and Providence," *Christian Scholar* 47 (1964): 203.

    Roy Battenhouse, "The Ghost in *Hamlet*: A Catholic 'Linchpin'?" *SP* 48 (1951): 161–92, inaugurated an ongoing controversy over the Catholicity and/or origins of the ghost. He amplified his position in his *Shakespearean Tragedy: Its Art and Its Christian Premises* (1969) and garnered opposition, chiefly from West, *Shakespeare & the Outer Mystery* (1968) and Coursen, *Christian Ritual and the World of Shakespeare's Tragedies* (1976), who conclude that ultimately "We cannot rationally fathom the Ghost" (West, p. 68) and "it is Hamlet's problem—not the critics'—to determine the nature of the ghost" (Coursen, p. 90). Battenhouse's position leads finally to that espoused so fully and so brilliantly by Prosser, *Hamlet and Revenge* (1967, rev. 1971). Battenhouse and West may be forgiven for ignoring Prosser since their work must have been finished in manuscript even if not yet in print when Prosser's book was published. But Coursen, publishing five years after the revised edition of Prosser's book, neglects her arguments on the ghost altogether and dismisses her in a footnote as one to be consulted for recent criticism on revenge.

    11. See for instance *A Treatise of Specters* (1605) or *A Discouerie of Witchcraft* (1584) in which both Pierre le Loyer and Reginald Scot, respectively, devote well over three-fourths of their material to various evil spirits. The remainder—on angels and other good spirits—are for the most part restricted to biblical or legendary rehearsals. King James, of course, in *Daemonologie* (1597), devotes his entire book to the nether world. In fact, King James asserts that "all we that are Christians, ought assuredly to know that since the comming of Christ in the flesh, and establishing of his Church by the Apostles, all miracles, visions, prophecies, & appearances of Angels or good spirits are ceased" (K^{r-v}).

I.i.41, 109). There is talk of "dreaded sight" (I.i.25), "guilty thing" (I.i.148), "fearful summons" (I.i.149), "erring spirit" (I.i.154), "oppress'd and fear-surprised eyes" (I.ii.203), "distill'd / Almost to jelly with the act of fear" (I.ii.204–5), and "shrunk in haste" (as a guilty thing, I.ii.219).

All Hamlet's early responses and actions are like the others'. The Prince's tentative words, "If it[12] assume my noble father's person," echo the unvaried statements of Horatio, Marcellus, and Bernardo who are always careful to distinguish that the ghost is "like" the dead King. At the ghost's first appearance to the Prince, Hamlet cowers in fear and cries for the protection of angels and ministers. After he regains composure and no longer fears for his life, he copes still with a destructive spirit:

> I do not set my life at a pin's fee,
> And for my soul, what can it do to that?
> (I.iv.65–66)

The ghost appears consistently (five times) at one o'clock, "jump at this *dead* hour" (my italics, I.i.65), a time described by Hamlet as "the very witching time of night, / When . . . hell itself breathes out / Contagion to this world" (III.ii.387–89), a time unusual for angels or any heaven-originating spirits to make appearances to men. Where else in literature or scripture do we find divinity urging the business of the light of the world in the very darkest hour of the night? Furthermore, when Horatio charges the ghost to speak "by heaven," "it is offended" (I.i.49–50).

Perhaps most telling of all against the possibility of heavenly origins for the ghost are its purposes. The injunction is revenge. Apart from the widely accepted belief that revenge as a motive for action was totally unacceptable in the sixteenth century,[13] we may observe an unpleasant selfishness prompting the ghost. Revenge

12. All characters refer constantly to the ghost as "it."

13. All the arguments that Prosser gathers to indicate that revenge was unacceptable not only to the church but also to the larger mass of laymen neglect to point out that the ghost, if a spokesman for heaven, is out of character to call for revenge.

me, it says. It argues that Hamlet would prove dull if he would not stir in revenging *him*. Denmark is abused because it has been lied to about "*my* death" (my italics). *I* have lost life, crown, queen; *I* have been denied "houseling"; *my* bed has been sullied. Furthermore the appeal to Hamlet is made on the supposition that he has "nature" in him; it is not made through a commandment from heaven. In fact, the ghost's exhortation to leave Gertrude to heaven may well be read in the sense of leave Gertrude to heaven; we will take care of Claudius between us here on earth (I.v.22–87). If these observations are valid, then the ghost has ineptly conveyed his instructions and inadvertently exposed his aims and his origins. But such carelessness is not unusual in demonic encounters. A good many contracted sinners escape final payment because of flaws the devil has failed to expunge from the indentures. What is more, the just man should have some signs by which he may identify the enemy.

Indeed, Shakespeare causes the ghost elsewhere to err as well. Although the tormented soul means to describe something like purgatory, the picture he draws better fits hell. Dante may bathe his penitents in fire, but the cleansing is joyously undergone. The ghost confesses to "sulph'rous and tormenting flames" (I.v.3). Although he expects Hamlet to have the softer emotions and counts on the youth's love to pry him to revenge, the ghost cares not about such matters himself and tells Hamlet not to pity him (I.v.5). Dante's evil spirits have no interest in pity either and can receive none. Further incautions of the ghost result in his confession that he had no houseling or anelement, that he was "Cut off even in the blossoms of [his] sin," that he went to his account with "all [his] imperfections on [his] head," inadvertent slips indicating that he has indeed been "disappointed" of his hope for heaven (I.v.77–80).

Similar somewhat to a character's giving himself away unconsciously is a device dear to Shakespeare in which a creature in disguise toys with discovery through ambiguities of speech. One of the most familiar of these instances is Viola's words to the Duke, which begin with her description of the person she loves (who is of course that same Duke) as looking a little "by your favor" (*TN*, II.iv.25). The material is perhaps the most extended in all the plays; it continues, on and off, for almost one hundred lines, during which Viola gives her own "history" as though it were her sister's. Iago may be shown to toy often with self-exposure in the same manner, and perhaps the ghost in *Hamlet* goes through similar paces. As the spirit describes Gertrude's "falling-off," it platitudinizes:

> But virtue, as it never will be moved,
> Though lewdness court it in a shape of heaven,
> So lust, though to a radiant angel link'd,
> Will sate itself in a celestial bed,
> And prey on garbage.
>
> (I.v.54–58)

The first two lines are pertinent. The passage is not altogether very different from Iago's "beware, my lord, of jealousy" (III.iii.170), when jealousy is exactly what Iago uses to destroy his man. The ghost, if he is indeed a goblin from hell, hopes to damn Hamlet by assuming a pleasing shape—that of his father, supposed to carry heaven's message. May not the ghost be toying with Hamlet in warning him that though I court you in words from heaven and though virtue will never be moved by such deceptions, I am here to do exactly that?

Let us suppose for the moment that we are dealing with the figure that Hamlet describes at the end of his second soliloquy, a passage that may be fundamental to the fullest understanding of the play:

> The spirit that I have seen
> May be the devil, and the devil hath power
> T' assume a pleasing shape; yea, and perhaps
> Out of my weakness and my melancholy,
> As he is very potent with such spirits,[14]
> Abuses me to damn me.
>
> (II.ii.599–604)

14. The demonologies available to Shakespeare made a point of the melancholic's being a most susceptible target for evil spirits: "if the

The creature then is precisely a devil. This point is quite important. Apparently a ghost may be a shape constructed and assumed by a demonic spirit. The King is manifested as a ghost that is in reality a devil. Devils are much on Shakespeare's mind throughout the four central tragedies. They are everywhere conjured by Edgar in *Lear*, and, if I am correct in my reading of both *Othello* and *Macbeth*, substantive demons are operative in those plays also.[15] I stress the word *substantive*, for in Venice and Scotland these usually incorporeal spirits take upon them bodies in order to move successfully through the upper world and to work their malice. Bodies come to them in different ways. In *Othello* the satanic henchman seems to construct a new body out of something not formerly there and to call it Iago. In *Macbeth* two fiends preempt the souls of Macbeth and his Lady and take their places, in effect commandeering ready-made bodies. The employment of substantive spirits in *Lear* is not indicated, but in *Hamlet* two brief passages may indicate the beginnings in Shakespeare's developing demonological thought of this "bodied" creation that the devil is very cunning in.

Hamlet's first encounter with the ghost, during which startlingly detailed observation is made by the Prince of his father, draws us a strange picture, rarely commented upon:

> . . . tell
> Why thy canoniz'd bones, hearsed in death,
> Have burst their cerements; why the sepulcher
> Wherein we saw thee quietly interr'd
> Hath op'd his ponderous and marble jaws
> To cast thee up again. What may this mean,
> That thou, dead corse, again in complete steel
> Revisits thus the glimpses of the moon . . . ?
> (I.iv.46–53)

Divell doe once perceive that the braine is troubled . . . by . . . melancholy . . . He presently taketh occasion to torment and trouble it the more": *A Treatise of Specters*, p. 132.

15. See chaps. 2 and 4.

Sixteenth-century ghostlore shows that most ghosts were thought by early Englishmen to be solid corpses up out of their graves to walk again.[16] The picture we get is of some body, held still together by its bones (line 47), trailing shreds of its graveclothes (48), and yet solid enough to support an entire panoply (52). The second of these effects comes with Hamlet's second encounter with the ghost, in Gertrude's closet:

> Look you how pale he glares!
> His form and cause conjoin'd, preaching to stones,
> Would make them capable.
>
> .   .   .   .
>
> My father, in his habit as he lived!
> Look, where he goes, even now, out at the portal![17]
>
> (III.iv.129–42)

The ghost's form is stressed again, with all the implication that it exhibits grief and anger over the manner of its death, while the fidelity of the representation shows the dead King as he lived.

King James holds that any spirit that is visible to men has taken to itself a body, most often one from among the dead. Of presences incorporal, James makes distinction of those invisible, which he calls simply spirits, and those visible, which he calls wraiths; but of wraiths he reports the following:

PHI.

> And what meanes then these kindes of
> spirites, when they appeare in the shaddow
> of a person newlie dead . . . to his friendes?

16. "When one from the dead appears it may . . . be a devil who has taken the body of a corpse": *Of Ghostes & Spirites Walking By Nyght* (1572), ed. J. Dover Wilson and May Yardley (Oxford, 1929), p. 234.

17. Shakespeare's stressing of the ghost's exit through a "portal" seems specifically to echo King James: "For if they haue a deade bodie, whereinto they lodge themselues, they can easely inough open without

EPI.
>   When they appeare vpon that occasion, they
>   are called Wraithes in our language.
>   Amongst the *Gentiles* the Deuill vsed that
>   much. . . . And this way hee easelie
>   deceiued the *Gentiles*, because they knew not
>   God . . . . For the [devil] dare not so illude
>   anie that knoweth that, neither can the
>   spirite of the defunct returne to his friend,
>   or yet an Angell vse such formes.
>
>   (*Daemonologie*, I₂ᵛ–I₃ʳ)

Skeptics will note the inability of the sentinels to wound the ghost with their partisans; if solid why do their bills not meet opposition?

>   For it is, as the air, invulnerable,
>   And our vain blows malicious mockery.
>   (I.i.145–46)

But these words, though they make the ghost invulnerable as air, do not make it ethereal. The blows are vain exactly in the way that Othello's thrust at Iago is vain:

>   If that thou be'st a devil, I cannot kill thee.
>   [*Wounds Iago*]
>   .   .   .   .
>   I bleed, sir, but not kill'd.
>   (V.ii.295–96)

Clearly, if King James were called upon to identify the ghost, he would see a devil possessing the dead body of King Hamlet.

Devils may employ the dead bodies of those who have mounted to heaven as well as bodies formerly indwelt by the damned:

---

dinne anie Doore or Window, and enter in thereat" (*Daemonologie*, I₂ʳ). The concept of a solid corpse makes it necessary to provide "portals." Shakespeare's ghosts do not walk through walls.

... the Deuill may vse as well the ministrie of the bodies of the faithfull in these cases, as of the vn-faithfull . . . for his haunting with their bodies after they are deade, can no waies defyle them: In respect of the soules absence.

(*Daemonologie*, I₂ʳ)

Reginald Scot, although no believer in spirits, as well as Pierre le Loyer, a firm believer, shows contemporary opinion at some divergence from King James's. Some allow apparently that the defunct can return to friends and may indeed be angels:

the soules of the dead become spirits, the good to be angels, the bad to be deuils.[18]

... spirits and soules can assume & take unto them bodies at their pleasure, of what shape or substance they list.

(Scot, *A discourse*, Pp₂ᵛ)

As concerning the Divels, God doth permit them both visibly and invisibly to tempt vs, some to their salvation, and some to their damnation.

(*A Treatise*, p. 44)

Presumably the corpse of a reprobate may be used as well as the reprobate himself who would employ, undoubtedly, his own body.

Scot relays from believers the helpful information that "you may know the good soules from the bad very easilie. For a damned soule hath a verie heauie and sowre looke; but a saints soule hath a cheerefull and a merrie countenance" (*A discourse*, Qq₃ᵛ). When Hamlet asks Horatio if the ghost "look'd . . . frowningly?" (I.ii.231), the Prince can only be dismayed to learn that his father's spirit wore a sorrowful countenance (231–32), which though not specifically sour or heavy is nevertheless far from cheerful or merry.

Hamlet's query of the ghost—"What may this mean, / That

18. Scot, *A discourse vpon diuels and spirits* (1584), Nn₆ʳ.

thou, dead corse . . . / Revisits thus the glimpses of the moon"
(I.iv.51–53)—places squarely before us the alternatives of a usurping demon or a damned king; and considerable evidence exists to
suggest that the Prince deals directly with his father. The ghost's
various confessions and/or slips of the tongue indicate that the
King died unprepared and went to punishment. Although he
claims that these omissions have earned him a place in purgatory
rather than in hell, we may suspect that he is lying. Both E. E.
Stoll[19] and John Hankins[20] cite passages from *Pilgrims Wish* (1593)
by Henry Smith and yet ignore or reject his Protestant views on
purgatory:

> Thus the diuel hath many ways to deceiue; and this
> is one & a dangerous one, to draw vs from the word
> of God, to visions & dreames and apparitions, vp-
> on which many of the doctrines of the Papists are
> grounded.
>
> They had neuer heard of Purgatorie, but for
> these spirites which walked in the night, and told them
> that they were the soules of such and such, which suf-
> fered in fire till their masses and almes and pilgrim-
> ages did raunsome them out: So these night spirits
> begate Purgatorie and Purgatorie begate trentalles, as
> one Serpent hatcheth another.
>
> (p. 537)

Unbelievably then Hankins takes the ghost's word: "All . . . doubts
are of course dispelled by the ghost's own statement that it is a
spirit from purgatory."[21]

19. Stoll, *Hamlet: An Historical and Comparative Study* (Minneapolis,
1919), p. 48.
20. Hankins, *The Character of Hamlet and Other Essays* (Chapel Hill,
N.C., 1941), pp. 163–64.
21. Hankins, p. 181. We may go to Shakespeare himself in repudiation of Hankins's conclusion: "oftentimes, to win us to our harm, /
The instruments of Darkness tell us truths, / Win us with honest trifles, to
betray's / In deepest consequence" (*Macbeth*, I.iii.123–26).

Hamlet has heard the ghost's assurances that it will reside in fire only until its "foul" crimes are "burnt and purg'd away," but he is less taken in than the critics, since often subsequently he fears that he may be coping with a "devil" who "abuses [him] to damn [him]" (II.ii.603–4).

In addition to the ghost's own testimony, Hamlet's doubts about his father's "balance sheet" strengthen the case against the dead King:

> 'A took my father grossly, full of bread,
> With all his crimes broad blown, as flush as May;
> And how his audit stands who knows save heaven?
> But in our circumstance and course of thought,
> 'Tis heavy with him.
>
> (III.iii.80–84)

"Full of bread" is an ambiguous phrase that points to gluttony, a sin of which we do not know the King to be guilty; yet Hamlet's overemotional dismay at the "heavy-headed revel" which causes other nations to "clepe" Danes drunkards (I.iv.17–19) reminds us that excessive drinking as well as other kinds of incontinence were gathered under gluttony, the only sin of the traditional seven to apply.[22] In the same speech Hamlet laments for "particular" men who at the "general censure" are condemned for "one defect" (23–38). Little imagination is required to equate "general censure" with judgment day.[23] We note also that when Horatio sums up the dead King's praises, Hamlet can say no more than that "'A was a man, take him for all in all" (I.ii.187).[24]

22. See, for instance, "The Parson's Tale": "This synne [gluttony or *Gula*] hath many speces. The firste is dronkenesse, that is the horrible sepulture of mannes resoun; and therfore, whan a man is dronken, he hath lost his resoun; and this is deedly synne": *The Works of Geoffrey Chaucer*, ed. F. N. Robinson (Cambridge, Mass., 1957), p. 255.
23. In most of the spiritual encyclopedias that I have consulted, doomsday is called the "iugement general," as in the *Art of good lywyng & good deying* (1503), Aa₂^r.
24. If it is difficult to believe that a father, so deeply beloved by a

Not one of these facts is lost on Hamlet; at the conclusion of his confrontation with the ghost, all the Prince's responses are those of a man who fears that he has had to do with infernal forces. Consider his oath, made the moment the ghost leaves:

> O all you host of heaven! O earth! What else?
> And shall I couple hell?
>
> (I.v.93–94)

Although the ghost evokes heaven, asking Hamlet to leave Gertrude to its confines, all other things whisper hell. Hamlet never rids himself of his fear that the ghost may be from hell, a fact echoed in the Prince's second soliloquy:

> Prompted to my revenge by heaven and hell,
>
> . . . .
>
>   The spirit that I have seen
> May be the devil.
>
> (II.ii.585, 599–600)

Hamlet's early concern, after he returns to his friends from his harrowing experience, is to seek guidance: "Look you, I'll go pray" (I.v.133). And though this assertion is followed almost immediately by Hamlet's assurances to his fellows that "this vision here, / . . . is an honest ghost" (138–39), we may see the ambiguity of that claim. One argument holds that later on Hamlet has second thoughts about the ghost's authenticity and employs the mousetrap. An equally valid argument makes this public declaration of the ghost's honesty only a red herring. Hamlet plans, as he has already vowed, to take revenge by killing Claudius. His later pains to include Horatio as an informed aide have perhaps their beginnings here. To justify the death that Hamlet gives to Claudius, the Prince must show a blackened character in the usurper. When,

---

son and counting on that love to bring that son to action, should labor at his offspring's damnation, we should remember that Lucifer himself was once the brightest angel.

30

after Claudius is dead, motives are questioned, Horatio, who has seen the ghost, will testify to the first source of suspicion against Claudius. In another sense, Hamlet's comment on the ghost's honesty might be construed as a dishonesty itself, the first of many that the Prince plans to employ in his antic disposition.

Whatever Hamlet's beliefs and behavior in respect to the ghost as he concludes his first meeting with it, all must be squared with the Prince's convictions after the mousetrap scene: "O good Horatio, I'll take the ghost's word for a thousand pound" (III.ii.284–85). The ghost's truthfulness does not mean necessarily that the spirit is sent from heaven. Shakespeare, elsewhere, is explicit on this point. Iago, who is a devil himself,[25] speaks therefore not in metaphor when he comments on his own demonic nature:

> When devils will the blackest sins put on,
> They do suggest at first with heavenly shows.
> (*Othello*, II.iii.345–46)

But if Iago cannot be certified as speaking himself from the demon world, Banquo at least shows what humans may expect from that world:

> oftentimes, to win us to our harm,
> The instruments of Darkness tell us truths,
> Win us with honest trifles, to betray's
> In deepest consequence.
> (*Macbeth*, I.iii.123–26)

For all this knowledge of the lower world Shakespeare found ready corroboration in his sources:

> The diuel sometimes vttereth the truth, that his words
> may haue the more credit, and that he may the more
> easily beguile them. He that would vtter euil wares,
> doth not only set them foorth in words, but doth also

25. See chap. 2.

so trim and decke them, that they seeme excellent good . . . this Art also the diuel knoweth, for he paint-eth out his stuffe that he may obtrude it vnto other men in the steede of good ware.[26]

But far and away the most significant oddness of the ghost is the direction of his disappearance. We expect an angelic substance to exit upwards. Yet the cries from understage indicate that this ghost has gone another way. He is in the cellarage and works quickly through the earth.[27] Surely no Elizabethan playwright would have an angel below; he might employ the trapdoor to get an angel off the stage surreptitiously, but to have him speak from underground defies probability. Presumably the same geography would apply to spirits from purgatory. To see the ghost as sinister may go far also to explain the often commented upon strangeness of Hamlet's retorts to his dear departed father. The Prince finds himself torn between the great love he has for his father and the scorn his faith has taught him he must have for the damned. We get that special tension here that has been much admired in Dante. Although Virgil constantly instructs Dante to show no pity for the souls in hell—in fact approval is registered for Dante's cruelties to Ciacco and Friar Alberigo—nevertheless, Dante cannot refrain

26. Lewes Lavater, *Of Ghostes and Spirites Walking by Night*, trans. R. H. (1596), p. 173. Prosser has gathered additional proof of the truths that devils employ to deceive their victims; see *Hamlet and Revenge*, pp. 111–13.

27. An interesting parallel to Hamlet's observations and language during the ghost's tunnelings may be found in Reginald Scot: "*Subterranei* and *Lucifugi* enter into the bowels of men, and torment them that they possesse with the phrensie, and the falling euill. They also assault them that are miners or pioners, which use to worke in deepe and darke holes under the earth. Such diuels as are earthie and aierie . . . enter by sub-tiltie into the minds of men, to deceiue them, prouoking men to absurd and unlawfull affections" (Nn7ᵛ). The conjunction of Scot's "*Subterranei*," "phrensie," and "pioners" with Hamlet's references to mole and other workings in the earth as well as his own frenzied behavior and use of the unusual word *pioner* seems telling.

from pity for Francesca da Rimini and a remnant love and admiration for Brunetto Latini.

The terms of Hamlet's addresses to his father are perhaps cruel, irreverent at best—*boy, truepenny, fellow, Hic et ubique?, old mole, pioner*—yet when he has finished extracting the oath from the others, compassion for his father, dead and perhaps damned, overwhelms him: "Rest, rest, perturbed spirit!" (I.v.183).

Many reasons to doubt the good offices of the ghost develop as early as the first act. These reasons never disappear, and we are forced to face the proposition that the ghost may be a demon from hell, assuming a known and beloved shape, to work the usual design of devils: winning souls for hell. Although everything in this play—most of all, the thoughts of its protagonist—remain heaven-oriented, surprisingly little that is good can be perceived in the ghost. But to find the ghost demonic does not mean that Hamlet, when he completes the revenge desired by the ghost, has damned his own soul. Heaven's goal and hell's may be identical. In fact, in terms of results, Elizabethans would argue that they must be identical, for nothing can be counter to God's great design. The difference lies in motives and means. Reestablishment of order and harmony in a corrupt Denmark is called for clearly. The devil simply uses the ready-made murder of King Hamlet to his own ends. He tries to embark Prince Hamlet on private and scourgeful revenge, while heaven demands public and ministerial justice. Only Hamlet's continual practice of prayer (I.v.133) and of holy meditation, which in his weaker moments he equates with cowardice, ultimately thwarts the devil, just as his continual alertness thwarts Claudius. And though, at the end, he loses his life as a result of Claudius's machinations, he does so not because of a failure of alertness. We are told carefully of the ill-feeling about Hamlet's heart. He loses his life to Claudius but has defeated the devil: the readiness is all. He submits to God, becomes a minister, actions which apparently in God's design require the loss of his life; but Denmark is restored to health, and Hamlet goes with flights of angels to a fairer crown than any worn in Denmark.

If then the ghost is evil, it has its own purposes, which are alien to God's ways, but incapable for long of disrupting God's order; and although the ghost walks to pervert Hamlet to evil, it walks also, as God designs, to warn of "some strange eruption to [the] state" (I.i.69). It comes a harbinger, "preceding still the fates," a "prologue to the omen coming on" (I.i.122–23); it means, even to the least of one of those in the play, that "Something is rotten in the state of Denmark" (I.iv.89).

The sign first to show that the Hamlet universe is to be shaken sorely is the preparation for war with Norway. But Horatio, who explains the grim bustle in the land, reports other events of strange and awesome aspect:

> A little ere the mightiest Julius fell,
> The graves stood tenantless and the sheeted dead
> Did squeak and gibber in the Roman streets;
> As stars with trains of fire and dews of blood,
> Disasters in the sun; and the moist star
> Upon whose influence Neptune's empire stands
> Was sick almost to doomsday with eclipse [fig.3].
> And even the like precurse of fear'd events
>
> . . . .
>
> Have heaven and earth together demonstrated
> Unto our climatures and countrymen.
>
> (I.i.114–25)

Unnatural occurrences that accompany the fall or death of kings in Shakespeare's plays are commonly credited to the great theme of correspondences between the microcosm and the macrocosm which the history of ideas traces from pagan culture to the present.[28] Without contradicting all such assertions, we need, however, to illustrate the way in which Shakespeare manipulates the materials to introduce an apocalyptic vision.

Signs such as those enumerated by Horatio are interpreted generally either as God's warnings to men to cast out from their midst the pollution that causes divine displeasure or as a sign of

28. See chap. 7 of E. M. W. Tillyard, *The Elizabethan World Picture* (London, 1943), and chap. 2 of Hardin Craig, *The Enchanted Glass* (New York, 1935).

The sun shall be   *and the starres*
darkned, moon   *shall fall from*
shall lose hir light,   *heauen.*

Fig. 3. Disasters in the sun and moon.
Queen Elizabeth Prayer Book. Press of John
Day, London, 1581.

unavoidable destruction that God means to send a people because
their iniquity is already too great and of too long duration to be
met only with warnings. But Shakespeare limits these portents to
those that foretell the end of the world.[29] Most of these signs he
could find conveniently set forth in any number of the spiritual
encyclopedias of the Middle Ages.[30] Others come directly from
scripture. The war with Norway fulfills Christ's own warnings to
the disciples: "ye shal heare of warres, and rumors of warres"
(Matt. 24.6).[31] Horatio's other "harbingers" may all be found in the

29. For a full history of the development of the fifteen signs in legend, see W. W. Heist, *The Fifteen Signs Before Doomsday* (East Lansing,
Mich., 1952). Heist, however, neglects almost totally the iconographical
tradition, which needs yet to be written. For a brief survey see chap. 3,
pp. 129–32 and chap. 4, pp. 178–90.

30. See Introduction, pp. 3–9.

31. All biblical quotations will come from the Geneva Bible (1560),
by consensus believed the Bible used by Shakespeare.

convention known as the Fifteen Signs of the Last Judgment, which in some treatments total more than fifteen. Readily available to Shakespeare in pictorial form were the doomsday signs in the *Queen Elizabeth Prayer Book* and Wynkyn de Worde's *The craft to liue well and to die well.* For literary variations of the same theme, Shakespeare might have tapped either Lydgate's poem, "The Fifftene Toknys Aforn the Doom," or a passage in the Chester Cycle play, *The Prophets and Antichrist.* Horatio's disasters in the sun and moon (the moist star) are among doomsday signs in the *Queen Elizabeth Prayer Book*[32] and the remaining portentous omens in these verses from Lydgate:

> The fiffte day, herbe, foul and tree
> Shal be bloody dewed to the sight.
>
> .   .   .   .
>
> The tenthe day, from kavernys & ther kavys
> Men shal come out, lyk folk that kan no good,
> And renne abrood lyk drounke men þat Ravys,
> Or as they weren frentyk, outhir wood,
> Dedly pale, and devoyde of blood:
>
> .   .   .   .
>
> The xj[e] signe . . .
> Ded boonys that day shal aryse,
> And grisly stonde on ther sepulture,
> And shewyn outward a dredful foul figure;
> So to stonde al day, with boonys blak and donne,
> Of doom abyde the dredful aventure,
> Tyl goyng doun of the bloody sonne.
>
> The xij[e] day, mor dredful than is werre,
> Ageyns which shal be no Resistence,
> Doun from hevene shal fallen euery sterre,
> With firy levene and ferful violence [fig. 4].[33]

32. Printed by John Day (London, 1581), p. 57[v].
33. *The Minor Poems of John Lydgate,* ed. H. N. MacCracken, EETS, ES 107 (London, 1911), pp. 118–19.

trees and hearbes shall drop blud . . .

They that hid thēselues shall runne forth like mad mē.

The bones of the dead shall appere aboue the Sepulcres.

The powers of heauen shall be shaken.

Fig. 4. Fifth sign (left): "herbe, foul and tree / Shal be bloody dewed"; tenth (center), eleventh (right), and twelfth (bottom) signs: men gone mad, dead bones, and falling stars. *Queen Elizabeth Prayer Book.* Press of John Day, London, 1581.

If Lydgate is Shakespeare's source in this matter, the playwright seems to fuse the Monk of Bury's madmen and rising dead in the image of the shrouded corpses gibbering in the streets. Shakespeare's use of *doomsday* in line 120 appears to show clearly that the poet employs the medieval tradition. The evocation of the apocalyptic vision is so widespread in Shakespeare[34] that it must be seen as an eschatological warning akin to those of the parables in Matthew 24 and 25, all of which are judgment-day parables, carrying the admonition "Watche therefore: for ye knowe nether the day, nor the houre, when the Sonne of man wil come" (Matt. 25.13).

The ghost who prompts Horatio's observations ushers in a topsy-turvy world. Inversions, found everywhere in the play, are another form of the broken chain, the disordered garden, the untuned string, in short the taking away of degree. The earliest disruption in *Hamlet* is the unnatural condition of the country as it prepares for war, the threatened invasion from Norway. Laborers work at night; Sundays are no different from weekdays; night is like day (I.i.72–78). War functions often as God's beadle (*Henry V*, IV.i.168), especially fearsome when internal ulcers in a kingdom are not diagnosed, treated, and healed. The sickly realm is easy prey to an adventurer like Fortinbras.

Through usurpation a false king reigns; one from below has mounted above his proper superior, creating an upside-down relationship in the chain of being. Our first view of Claudius reflects this condition in his bold announcements that he has put by all decorum. He confesses in a series of oxymorons that though propriety demands all "bear [their] hearts in grief," nevertheless has he,

> with a defeated joy—
> With an auspicious and a dropping eye,
> With mirth in funeral and with dirge in marriage,

upended a "whole kingdom" which it "befitted" to "be contracted in one brow of woe" (I.ii.2–12). Newly elevated peers and courtiers have freely gone along; and it would seem a logical concomitant, with evil so successfully in command, that good cannot survive; and so it works out in Denmark.

With the exception of Horatio, all characters of importance

---

34. Reference to doomsday, direct or indirect, occurs in at least twenty-one of Shakespeare's plays. See chap. 3, note 10.

in the play are destroyed. Horatio must have special consideration, for in effect he stands outside the play. He is a potential chorus, a spokesman who must remain to tell the tale aright. Furthermore, he is an informed observer ("I have told thee of my father's death" [III.ii.76]), the only other person in the play besides Hamlet aware of Claudius's true nature; and yet, unlike Hamlet, he is not called upon to act in any critical sense. When Horatio would take part in the final tragedy, Hamlet thrusts him violently back into a world different from the one in which by this time all the principal characters have entered. All have died; none can live in an evil world. All those who remain good and make no special provision to recognize and extirpate evil are destroyed by that evil. In such a category I would place Ophelia and Polonius. Those who would like to remain good but are seduced by evil for various reasons are also destroyed. These are Gertrude and Laertes. And those who create evil or "make love to this employment" (V.ii.57) are obliterated as God rights the perverted order. These are Claudius, Rosencrantz, and Guildenstern. Hamlet is different from all these because he is the armed intelligence. Through the agency of the ghost—be it good or evil—Hamlet is apprised of the serpent "that did sting [his] father's life" and "wears his crown" (I.v.40–41). Although Hamlet, too, is destroyed by the false king, Hamlet's death results primarily from the Prince's submission to the end that God, not Claudius, has charted for him. Hamlet has his premonition and goes, we might say, armed to his death, fully prepared; and the readiness is all.

But until he is ready, Hamlet, in order to survive in the topsy-turvy world, must make adjustments. Among them is Shakespeare's most trusted device: disguise. Hamlet's disguise is of the mind rather than of the body, and through his antic disposition the Prince is successful in staying alive and, in fact, in devising a play to fit Claudius's prologue, wherein he writes *exit Claudius*, wherein he himself is ready to leave the stage, for the readiness is all.

But with the line "this bodes some strange eruption to our state" (I.i.69), and until Fortinbras arrives to inherit a throne strewn about with corpses, the play progresses in a topsy-turvy world, with a false king at its head. An Elizabethan commonplace is the garden metaphor, which in its tare-choked condition reflects the disordered universe:

> How weary, stale, flat, and unprofitable
> Seem to me all the uses of this world!
> Fie on 't, ah fie! 'Tis an unweeded garden
> That grows to seed. Things rank and gross in nature
> Possess it merely.
>
> (I.ii.133–37)

Along with the garden "Corrupting in it[s] own fertility" (*Henry V*, V.ii.40), the "time is out of joint" (I.v.189). Hamlet is instant-old, and "That great baby," Polonius, "is not yet out of his swaddling-clouts" (II.ii.382–83). All goes counter to its natural direction, with a symbol from nature used to show nature itself perverted:

> for yourself, sir, shall grow old as I am, if like a crab
> you could go backward.
>
> (II.ii.203–4)

If Denmark, as seen in the world of nature, is an unweeded garden, in its more civilized aspects it has become merely a prison (II.ii.242–52). Again, its natural conditions are altered:

> this goodly frame, the earth, seems to me a sterile
> promontory; this most excellent canopy, the air, look
> you, this brave o'erhanging firmament, this majesti-
> cal roof fretted with golden fire, why, it appeareth
> nothing to me but a foul and pestilent congregation
> of vapors.
>
> (II.ii.299–304)

Back to the world of sophistication: the tragedians of the city are forced to travel by "means of the late innovation" (II.ii.333), with "no money bid for argument unless the poet and the player went to cuffs in the question" (II.ii.354–56). Apparently the whole world is awry: "Ay . . . Hercules and his load too" (II.ii.361–62). But no cause for the change in the players' world can be charged to professional incompetence: they do not grow rusty; merely they are replaced unnaturally by children, by amateurs. The topsy-turvy condition of the child being father to the man has sent these players to the provinces.

A jump from the general to the particular brings these matters to Hamlet's meditative speculation:

> It is not very strange; for my uncle is King of Denmark, and those that would make mouths at him while my father liv'd, give twenty, forty, fifty, a hundred ducats a-piece for his picture in little. 'Sblood, there is something in this more than natural, if philosophy could find it out.
>
> (II.ii.363–68)

The first two clauses of this speech carry the entire issue in brief: it is not strange, for a usurper is King of Denmark. The displacement is the cause of the world's being upside-down.

The speech that Hamlet requests of the first player enforces the idea clearly; with the death of the true king, the entire realm falls aheap:

> Th' unnerved father [Priam] falls. Then senseless
>   Ilium,
> Seeming to feel this blow, with flaming top
> Stoops to his base.
>
> (II.ii.474–76)

Although he applies it to the wrong sovereign, Rosencrantz utters an identical theory of government:

>   The cess of majesty
> Dies not alone, but like a gulf doth draw
> What's near it with it; or it is a massy wheel
> Fix'd on the summit of the highest mount,
> To whose huge spokes ten thousand lesser things
> Are mortis'd and adjoin'd, which, when it falls,

> Each small annexment, petty consequence,
> Attends the boist'rous ruin. Never alone
> Did the King sigh, but with a general groan.
> (III.iii.15–23)

All these illustrations have been trotted out often to figure forth the great chain of being or as counterparts to Ulysses' speech on order, but they image also the topsy-turvy world.

In such a world, concomitant with nature and government being out of whack, personal judgment inclines to error. Such failure overlaps with the various difficulties in identification already mentioned, but it has an existence of its own. Gertrude misidentifies her man because her senses and emotions have gone haywire:

> Have you eyes?
> Could you on this fair mountain leave to feed,
> And batten on this moor? Ha, have you eyes?
> You cannot call it love, for at your age
> The heyday in the blood is tame, it's humble,
> And waits upon the judgment, and what judgment
> Would step from this to this? Sense, sure, you have,
> Else could you not have motion, but sure that sense
> Is apoplex'd, for madness would not err,
> Nor sense to ecstasy was ne'er so thrall'd
> But it reserv'd some quantity of choice
> To serve in such a difference. What devil was't
> That thus hath cozen'd you at hoodman-blind?
> Eyes without feeling, feeling without sight,
> Ears without hands or eyes, smelling sans all,
> Or but a sickly part of one true sense
> Could not so mope.
> (III.iv.66–82)

All the above is resaid in a brief and telling line, the imagery of which joined with the cozening devil of line 76 above indicates the infernal source of all disorder: "Rebellious hell, / . . . canst mutine in a matron's bones" (III.iv.83–84).

42

The moral order suffers reversal also:

> Forgive me this my virtue;
> For in the fatness of these pursy times
> Virtue itself of vice must pardon beg,
> Yea, curb and woo for leave to do him good.
>   (III.iv.159–62)

Perhaps this passage comes closest to the point I offered originally: in order for good to exist at all in the world of evil, it must accept a subordinate position, at least until such time as things are righted, and even as good works toward that accomplishment.

The social order, of such great concern to the Elizabethan, is emphasized as having been upended:

> the age is grown so pick'd that the toe of the peasant comes so near the heel of the courtier, he galls his kibe.
>
>   (V.i.139–41)

Osric, the waterfly courtier, is an illustration of a similar condition, in which the unworthy becomes important in a court where formerly he would not have been admitted:

> Thus has he [Osric]—and many more of the same breed that I know the drossy age dotes on—only got the tune of the time and, out of an habit of encounter, a kind of yesty collection, which carries them through and through the most fann'd and winnow'd opinions.
>
>   (V.ii.187–91)

Claudius, while he is on top of things, holds this corrupt state in balance; and its incorrect proportions, its inharmony remain hidden to all. But then God sends his warnings, his omens in the usual manner—the graves "tenantless," the dead walking the streets, "stars with trains of fire," etc.—and especially the ghost, who, though he may come for his own purposes, assuredly is one of God's omen-agents. Hamlet is informed, and his trial and ordeal to right the public as well as the private wrong begin. He tells Horatio of the canker-riddled state. Ultimately the inward ulcer bursts, and the chaotic condition of the Danish commonweal can be hid from no one:

> the people muddied,
> Thick and unwholesome in their thoughts and
> whispers
> . . . .
> The rabble call him [Laertes] lord,
> And, as the world were now but to begin,
> Antiquity forgot, custom not known,
> The ratifiers and props of every word,
> They cry, "Choose we! Laertes shall be king!"
> Caps, hands, and tongues applaud it to the clouds,
> "Laertes shall be king, Laertes king!"
> (IV.v.82–83, 105–11)

Things have degenerated so far that the lowest peasant is aware of and becomes part of the disorder, being so mistaken as to try to crown a king who has nothing like a proper claim to the throne.

If Claudius is a false king, there must be a true king. In order for there to be such a thing as a true king, there must be also divine intention. With divine intention, the already much-questioned theory of a ninth-century Danish system of election fades away altogether. As John Dover Wilson demonstrated convincingly, the operative political science in *Hamlet* is sixteenth-century English monarchical succession.[35] Hamlet is the son of the former king. By the law of primogeniture, the prince is heir to the father; but more importantly for an essay that is oriented eschatologically, the moment that King Hamlet dies, his son is anointed in heaven and is the ruler intended divinely to minister to the kingdom. Although Hamlet knows these things, his belief in his kingship has been

35. Wilson, *What Happens in Hamlet*, pp. 26–38.

weakened because another man assumes the throne, his mother collaborates with the new king, and all ministers, lords, and councillors of state have freely gone along. Consider with these conditions the youth of the Prince, who may be confused reasonably that things have not gone in their traditional ways. It becomes one of his chief problems, and perhaps the chief business of the play, to educate the young Prince back to a belief in his first view. As long as he is a man tempted to exact private revenge at honor's dictate, he is on the wrong track. Only when he sees himself as true king, acting as ministerial agent, whose obligation, duty, and service to God require—without fail—that he cleanse the state of its pollution, can he engage in the punishment of Claudius without danger to his own soul. Important then is the developing consciousness in Hamlet of his authenticity as anointed ruler.

All begins with Hamlet's felt but uncertain thought that his uncle has done him wrong:

> A little more than kin, and less than kind.
>   . . . I am too much in the sun.
> (I.ii.65, 67)

The ambiguities of these lines have been worked over much; for my purposes those meanings that identify *sun* with the traditional symbol of kingship are most to the point. Claudius is less than kind in that he has put aside the usual order of succession to mount the throne himself, and Hamlet stands shone upon by the sun, his uncle, when he himself might be that sun shining upon others.

All characters in the play think of him as heir to the throne. Their use of *Prince* carries more than a simple meaning of son to a king. Laertes, in his warnings to Ophelia to be chary of her virtue, argues that

> His greatness weigh'd, his will is not his own.
> For he himself is subject to his *birth*.
> He may not, as unvalued persons do,
> Carve for himself; for on his choice depends
> The safety and health of this whole state,

45

And therefore must his choice be circumscrib'd
Unto the voice and yielding of that body
Whereof he is the head.

(I.iii.17−24, my italics)

What could be more clear? Laertes is not speaking merely of some lesser government official but of a prince who, by birth, will one day be head of an entire state whose welfare depends upon him.

Once the ghost informs Hamlet of the murder and usurpation, the Prince has a much stronger sense of the injustice done him than expressed formerly in the riddling opening speech. John Dover Wilson has isolated the passage in which Hamlet hints at his scant means and lost rule,[36] the force of these hints indicating his belief that he is the rightful king.

Of the passages applicable to this question, most critical is the reference to the royal crown:

a vice of kings,
A cutpurse of the empire and the rule,
That from a shelf the precious diadem stole,
And put it in his pocket!

(III.iv.101−4)

The phrases "cutpurse of the empire," stealing the "precious diadem," putting it "in his pocket" all establish Claudius as a thief but do not clearly distinguish from whom he stole. All these metaphors apply equally to snatching the crown from the elder Hamlet as from the younger. Only the word *shelf* pinpoints clearly a theft from the Prince alone. The diadem does not go to the shelf until a former king is dead, where it awaits the coronation of the next

---

36. Wilson, New Cambridge *Hamlet*, pp. liii–lvi, and *What Happens in Hamlet*, pp. 114−25. Pertinent passages alluded to by Wilson are as follows: I.v.184−86, II.ii.242−77, III.ii.338−45, to which may be added III.ii.323−24, in which Hamlet seems piqued that a chain of command from the King, through his mother to the sponges Rosencrantz and Guildenstern, can govern him.

king. That there can be a theft from the shelf indicates that the
diadem belongs properly to young Hamlet.

Most important of all, before Hamlet may ask of Horatio,

> Does it not, think thee, stand me now upon—
> . . . .
>   is 't not perfect conscience
> To quit him with this arm? And is 't not to be damn'd
> To let this canker of our nature come
> In further evil?
>
>   (V.ii.63–70)

he must understand himself to be the Lord's anointed. *Stand me* is a
strong phrase signifying absolute duty. *Perfect conscience* shows
Hamlet's belief in his ministerial sanction, which frees him from
condemnation in what becomes a deputized punishment. *And is 't
not to be damn'd* indicates further that punishment is due a divinely
appointed ruler who neglects his service to God.

Converse to Hamlet's growing awareness of his own authenticity is the evidence that develops to show Claudius's falseness.
I do not refer to his guilt as a murderer but specifically to the image of him as a false king. His own words condemn him first as a
whited sepulchre:

> The harlot's cheek, beautied with plast'ring art,
> Is not more ugly to the thing that helps it
> Than is my deed to my most painted word.
>
>   (III.i.52–54)

Hamlet's allusion to a "king of shreds and patches" (III.iv.106) is of
the same quality. Claudius is a painted mannequin, a mere image.
Scratch the paint, tear off the gaudies, and beneath is a mere com-
pact of corruption, a vice of kings.

Again, in Claudius's preparation for prayer he asks, "May
one be pardon'd and retain th' offense?" (III.iii.56). Those things
kept back include the crown (line 55). If it is not rightly his, whose
is it? Of course, Hamlet's. Only when awareness of these facts crys-

talizes in Hamlet's mind can he say the words that end his doubts and his delays: "The readiness is all."

And what then constitutes readiness? I have argued that part of readiness is Hamlet's recognition of his authenticity as ruler. But more than that, Hamlet must know also that he acts in accordance with the commandments of God. Other rulers anointed divinely yet have proved scourges. Hamlet's desire to avoid transgression causes his delays and opens up the eschatological matters which I take to be the chief concern of the play. Time and again Hamlet contemplates action which after scrutiny he finds will prove unacceptable to God. Hamlet is Shakespeare's study of a man, good at the outset of a drama, exposed to unusual evil, but intended to prevail. As such he submits all thought and action to this consideration: is it acceptable in God's sight? All the characters of the play take some position in relationship to duty. Hamlet is preeminent among them in his determination to meet all obligations that are due through duty and love to God and country, to father and mother, to beloved, friend, and countrymen. Claudius, in his negative way, shows Hamlet's loving obsequies, done in love as well as duty to the dead king:

> 'Tis sweet and commendable in your nature, Hamlet,
> To give these mourning duties to your father.[37]
>
> (I.ii.87–88)

Such is our first verbal view of Hamlet; physically we see him in his suit of sables, which further accord with "filial obligation." Of course, Claudius charges that Hamlet's extended grief is a "fault to heaven," "most incorrect," and "impious."[38] But we need not worry too greatly over Claudius's assertions; for we learn him to be

37. Claudius has trouble seeing love in Hamlet's grief, and generally has difficulty with the word *love* as *charity* at any time. His few uses of it are self-directed. He remarks Hamlet's "loving and fair reply" (I.ii.121) because it promises for him an unopposed reign. He "loved" Polonius as an unquestioning prop to his schemes, and of course he loved himself (IV.vii.34).

38. Ribner agrees with Claudius's view that Hamlet displays "unnatural grief": *Patterns in Shakespearian Tragedy*, pp. 70–71.

not only a false witness but also self-contradictory. Only a few minutes previously, Claudius has confessed publicly that "it us befitted / To bear our hearts in grief and our whole kingdom / . . . in one brow of woe" (I.ii.2–4).

Thus for love and duty to father. Obedience to God is witnessed in Hamlet's first, sighing soliloquy: "O . . . / . . . that the Everlasting had not fix'd / His canon 'gainst self-slaughter" (I.ii.129–32). Hamlet will not take his own life; he thinks of suicide only to reject it as opposed to divine commandment. Further, he is a virtuous man who "shall in all [his] best obey" all in authority above him: his mother and—at this time—his supposed king: "But break, my heart, for I *must* hold my tongue" (my italics, I.ii.120, 159). Hamlet's love for Ophelia is tendered in "honorable fashion" and accompanied by "almost all the holy vows of heaven" (I.iii.112,115). When informed of the ghost and after speaking to it, Hamlet continues to show his duty, although, of course, some allegiances must change. But that to heaven can be abrogated never, and duty to heaven is despite of hell:

> If it assume my noble father's person,
> I'll speak to it, though hell itself should gape
> And bid me hold my peace.
> (I.ii.243–45)

Furthermore, one may never fail to honor his father, whether that father is living or dead; and although Hamlet does not know the ghost to be that of his father, his father is commemorated when the son says, "Speak. I am bound to hear" (I.v.7). This bond is neither more nor less than filial obligation. When the ghost says immediately thereafter, "So art thou to revenge" (8), Hamlet is placed in the dilemma that holds him until the final act of the play. The ghost, who shows no interest at any time in anything other than revenge, uses the bond between father and son to demand an act that is directly counter to the commandment "thou shalt not kill." Hamlet's initial emotional reaction to the ghost's demand is unthinking: "Haste me to know 't, that I . . . / May sweep to my revenge" (I.v.30–32).

Hamlet has uncomfortable scruple about the ghost's request, for before the ghost has had time to drop through the trap-door, Hamlet wonders if the oath he is about to take engages him in traffic with the underworld: "And shall I couple hell?" His immediate rejection of such affiliation—"O, fie!" (I.v.94)—indicates again, and most strongly, his loathing of a situation that has forced him to contemplate action damnable. When he returns from the ghost to Horatio and the others, to put them off with his wild and whirling words, his desire is to part from them in order that he might pray (I.v.133). Thereafter he characterizes the ghost as honest (I.v.139), but for it to tell the truth and for it to be heaven-sent are not necessarily the same thing.[39] Hamlet follows the label of honesty with the irreverent language of the "cellarage" episode, scene and act ending with the couplet that emphasizes his dilemma:

> The time is out of joint. O cursed spite,
> That ever I was born to set it right!
> (I.v.189–90)

Kittredge observes that "Hamlet is resolved to avenge his father, but he is too highly civilized to welcome the duty that the savage code of his nation and time imposes."[40] Kittredge might have added that Hamlet was also too highly catechized to welcome an injunction that was counter to his faith. That Hamlet feels impelled nevertheless to follow a hell-directed commandment shows the powerful hold that the revenge code had upon the age. Hamlet intends to act; but ever as he comes up against that act, he cannot see it through, for it requires placing his soul into hazard.

Further indication of the terrible agony through which Hamlet goes as a result of the tugs upon him exerted by both heaven and hell is his appearance in Ophelia's closet, disheveled and with a look upon his face "As if he had been loosed out of hell / To speak of horrors" (II.i.80–81). His distraction in this scene has not been treated adequately. His behavior is prime material for those who argue that not all Hamlet's fractious antics are a

39. See pp. 31–32 above.
40. *Hamlet*, ed. G. L. Kittredge, rev. Irving Ribner (Waltham, Mass., 1967), p. 39n.

put-on disposition. Why, for instance, would Hamlet display this extreme melancholic unconcern for the proprieties of behavior and dress for the private audition of Ophelia? No doubt he could count on her to carry the tale, but how widespread a report would he be sure of? Certainly a similar enactment before the entire court would achieve his purpose with less chance of some fine acting going to waste. His severely improper invasion of Ophelia's room is true distraction; and although some part of his dismay results from Ophelia's withdrawal, some part may be understood also to come from the ghost's request, from the horrors of hell he might have to face if he fulfills his oath of revenge. The "look" that goes with hell is too strong a displacement of the natural aspect for a man who has lost his beloved. The horror is appropriate to the conflict in Hamlet's soul: how may he honor his father's appeal yet keep his soul free from reprobation?

Polonius, in words to Claudius, spells out Hamlet's internal struggle:

> I hold my duty, as I hold my soul,
> Both to my God and to my gracious king.
> (II.ii.44−45)

Polonius believes somehow that Claudius is the true king; this "baby [in] swaddling-clouts" (II.ii.382−83) has no difficulty, finds no hazard to his soul in holding his duty to Claudius after God. But for Hamlet things are different, even discounting that Hamlet's king is not Claudius. As Polonius utters these words, he puts God first, king second, of course the proper order. Hamlet also holds his soul in duty to God first, then in the "bond" to his dead father; but comes this ghost—whether that of his father or not—and lays the dread command upon him that separates those duties which should be forced never to pull in opposing directions. Yet one pulls Hamlet toward hell, while that from God pulls always toward heaven. Once again, that pivotal speech, almost at the center of the play, shows that Hamlet, unlike Laertes, will not dare damnation:

> The spirit that I have seen
> May be the devil, and the devil hath power

T' assume a pleasing shape; yea, and perhaps
Out of my weakness and my melancholy,
As he is very potent with such spirits,
Abuses me to damn me.

(II.ii.599–604)

Hamlet requires the additional evidence of the mousetrap because
the ghost may be lying altogether; the Prince will not be damned.
Even if he can prove through some evidence other than the words
of the ghost that Claudius is a murderer and a usurper, he still cannot pursue private revenge. Either something that broods within
him—his fear to lose eternity—or the interference of providence
stays his hand when he might "do it pat." Although the King's response to the players convinces Hamlet of Claudius's guilt, the
Prince hesitates, with false excuses; for he has yet to learn that, in
order for his soul not to be impawned, he must rid the commonwealth of its canker in the proper manner, as true king, as ministerial and anointed protector of the realm.

II

As long as Hamlet heeds the ghost's cry—"Remember me"—
and seeks revenge, he is acting dangerously. He must forget the
ghost, though it be truly the spirit of a father murdered; he must
forget revenge and pursue Claudius as a cutpurse of empire.
Clearly Hamlet is not easily tutored by his own meditations. Equal
to his practice of prayer and thoughtful action is his darker nature.
We know him vengeful. He wishes his "dearest" foes in hell (I.ii.182)
and confesses as much to Ophelia. In the same denunciation, he
accuses himself of pride, ambition, and a host of lesser offenses,
echoing Psalm 51 from the Book of Common Prayer: "it were
better my mother had not borne me" (III.i.123–28).[41]

41. "Behold, I was shapen in wickedness, and in sin hath my
mother conceived me." Anglican Psalm 51 is number 50 in the Roman
psalter: "Ecce enim in iniquitatibus conceptus sum: et in peccatis concepit
me mater mea." Psalm 50/51 is one of the seven penitential psalms and is

Hamlet's deep awareness of the sinfulness of his own nature surfaces immediately after his third soliloquy in which often it has been claimed he contemplates suicide. But suicide is not an act of which Hamlet is capable. He had rejected it in his first soliloquy. He may desire death but not by suicide: "the Everlasting [has] fix'd / His canon 'gainst self-slaughter!" (I.ii.131–32). Death may come in other ways as well: failure in an attempt to overthrow a mighty opposite. The noble mind, in a rebel active against "outrageous fortune," would contemplate military action at the head of a following of loyal resolutes, might indeed take arms against a usurper king. If the adventurer succeeds, he becomes king. By opposing Claudius, Hamlet ends his sea of troubles. To be is to be king through successful palace revolution. Not to be is to die in the attempt, either to fall in the assault or to be executed if apprehended. Death, we know from former statements, as well as from this soliloquy, not only holds no terror for Hamlet, "'Tis a consummation / Devoutly to be wished" (III.i.64–65). But only devoutly.

Again we see Hamlet's unvarying concern for the plight of his soul. He hesitates to die not because of terror of the dissolution of the body but because of fear for the disposition of his eternal self: the dreams to come. His decision not to act, the conscience that makes him a coward, is not his belief that suicide is a certain way to hell, but rather that his pursuit of Claudius's life in a private and vengeful motive is damnable. Surely he does not consider the taking of his own life an enterprise "of great pitch and moment" (III.i.87). He turns aside the current of action because his pale cast of thought reminds him that revenge is a resolution unacceptable in the sight of God.

Having had such sinful thoughts, his immediate cry to Ophelia is that she pray for his sins, soon to be enumerated by him to her and including ambition, pride, and vengefulness, not the usual attributes of the self-destroyer.

In fact, Hamlet's sudden awakening to his own sinfulness in

---

chanted in the Roman Catholic burial procession to the grave just before the antiphon *In paradisum*. See pp. 57, 68 below. *Queen Mary's Psalter* (fourteenth century) provides a graphic illustration of a blessed soul being carried aloft to the accompaniment of angelic music (fig. 5).

these thoughts causes him to initiate a program of redemptive action. Others have observed that Hamlet employs the sacrament of penance.[42] But none has observed the pervasive quality of the theme; none has noticed the exact equivalence to the four ingredients in penance, and none has tied it to the concept that Hamlet as true king would partake also of the nature of true priest. Whether Hamlet functions as priest/king consciously because he knows himself to be true king at the time of his confrontation with Ophelia or whether he acts as priest/king unconsciously since he has not yet understood his divine injunction to purify the state need not be argued. Presently I am showing only Hamlet's constant desire to keep his own soul in grace. Why would he not have also a natural desire to direct those he loves away from the primrose path? Ophelia and Gertrude both are put by Hamlet through the steps of the sacrament of penance before he recognizes that his role as priest/king is obligatory. But unlike Ophelia's "ungracious pastors" he does not show these two women the "steep and thorny way to heaven" while he "recks not his own rede" (I.iii.47–51).

Even as he exhorts Ophelia to confess ("Are you honest?" [III.i.104]), to be contrite ("Why wouldst thou be a breeder of sinners?" [122–23]), and to make satisfaction ("Get thee to a nunn'ry" [122]), he shows the way himself. His method with Ophelia is formally to go through the first two steps—contrition and confession—before her. A commonplace aid to be found in many daily

---

42. Hankins mentions that Hamlet "begs . . . [Gertrude] to continue on the path of true repentance" (p. 51). "Claudius [makes] a futile attempt at repentance" (pp. 87–88), and Hamlet "undergoes an emotional experience something like conversion" (p. 51). Whitaker notes the use of the sacrament of penance in *Hamlet* but only as a means necessary to the Prince's own redemption; see *The Mirror Up to Nature*, pp. 184–99. However, he feels that "Shakespeare makes surprisingly little use in *Hamlet* of the views of kingship that he developed in *Richard II*, *Henry IV*, and *Henry V*": *Shakespeare's Use of Learning* (San Marino, Cal., 1953), p. 272. In these historical English kings, Whitaker finds considerable evidence for a priest/king identity, and I fail to see anything less than that persona in Hamlet.

missals is the matter found under the heading of contrition, which defines the condition as a "ready sorrow for our sins" and suggests that "we may help to stir up this contrition in our hearts by saying . . . especially Psalm 50 (Miserere)."[43] As noted above, Hamlet does indeed stir up sorrow in himself with this very psalm (Anglican 51), employing his own variant phrasing, "I could accuse me of such things that it were better my mother had not borne me."[44] He follows with his own version of the *confiteor*:

> I confess ("I am myself indifferent honest . . . I could accuse me of such things. . . ." [123–24]) that I have sinned exceedingly in thought, word, and deed ("with more offenses at my beck [exceedingly] than I have thoughts [thought] to put them in, imagination to give them shape [words], or time to act them in [deed]" [126–28]), by my fault, by my own fault, by my own most grievous fault ("What should such fellows as I do crawling between earth and heaven? We are arrant knaves, all" [128–30]): here name sins ("I am very proud, revengeful, ambitious" [125–26]).

Ophelia, not guilty, does not succumb to Hamlet's exhortation. He tries once again to get her to confess: "Where's your father?" (131). She says, lying, that Polonius is at home, and she seems to show no contrition. Hamlet, frustrated in his attempts to redeem the girl he takes to be far worse than she is, grows fierce but exhorts her still to go to the nunnery, hoping that there a lively contrition will begin in her.

With his mother, Hamlet's success is greater (for the sinner is more truly guilty). The sacrament is more explicitly administered. As with Ophelia, Hamlet employs first a lengthy and intemperate chiding in order to awaken the sleeping if not obdurate sinner to the nature of her sin. His success is so immediate, so un-

43. See, for example, *St. Andrew Daily Missal*, Dom Gaspar Lefebvre (St. Paul, 1953), p. 1105.
44. See note 41 above.

expected, that when Gertrude pleads he say no more, Hamlet does not or cannot turn off his harangue. Of course he is moved also at that moment by emotions other than the desire to redeem his mother, but Gertrude is contrite and confesses, both in a simple speech:

> Thou turn'st mine eyes into my very soul,
> And there I see such black and grained spots
> As will not leave their tinct.
>
> (III.iv.91−93)

At this point the ghost interrupts; and when Hamlet returns to his priestly cure of his mother, he fears that she has lapsed, that she believes him mad and his exhortation to penance only his ravings. His renewed effort is more temperate, prefaced with an appeal: "Mother, for *love of grace*, / Lay not that flattering unction to your *soul* / That not your *trespass* but my madness speaks" (my italics, III.iv.151−53). He urges again her sin, then uses directly the terms of the sacrament: "Confess yourself to heaven [confession], / Repent what's past [contrition], avoid what is to come [satisfaction]" (III.iv.156−57). Because some additional reason exists for Hamlet's revulsion at Gertrude's sin, the Prince spells out at length a regimen for avoiding further stain in the incestuous relationship. Then a form of absolution is offered. Although Hamlet is hampered by the need to act in what is still a topsy-turvy universe, he need only invert the formula: "when you are desirous to be bless'd, / I'll blessing beg of you" (III.iv.178−79).

Following the ritual with his mother, Hamlet illustrates the pattern, shows her the road to redemption as he initiates his own purification:

> For this same lord,
> I do repent [contrition] . . .
> . . . .
> . . . I must be [heaven's] scourge [confession] . . .
> I will bestow him, and will answer well [satisfaction]
> The death I gave him.
>
> (III.iv.179−84)

Fig. 5. "Flights of angels sing thee to thy rest." *Queen Mary's Psalter*, four-teenth century. By permission of the British Library.

That Hamlet receives absolution ultimately is seen in his epitaph—Horatio's vision of flights of angels singing Hamlet to his rest (fig. 5)—an image borrowed from *In paradisum*, the antiphon sung at Roman Catholic burials while the body is carried in procession to the grave: "In paradisum deducāt te angeli."[45]

Shakespeare uses further the sacrament of penance as a leit-motif or structural element by employment elsewhere, not as a

45. *Processionale ad vsvs . . . Sarum* (1544), Ccvj^v–Ccvij^r. The modern Gradual indicates that a second antiphon was added directly onto the last word of the *In paradisum* and has been a part of the *Rituale Romanum* since at least 1614. J. G. Davies, in *A Dictionary of Liturgy and Worship* (New York, 1972), pp. 98–99, claims that this second antiphon was traditional by the time the 1614 Rite was authorized. The words of the antiphon, if available to Shakespeare, are perhaps closer still to Horatio's words: "Chorus angelorum te suscipiat et. . . . aeternam habeas requiem." *Graduale Romanae Ecclesiae* (Tournai, 1938), Ordinarium Missae, 109. The procession with the corpse at which these antiphons are sung seems to have suggested to Shakespeare the procession which Fortinbras arranges to have Hamlet's body carried "to the stage" (V.ii.397–98).

ministration by Hamlet but as self-examination by Claudius and a form of extreme unction by Laertes.

Claudius's soliloquy serves as a contrast to Hamlet's successful penitence. In the self-examination that is required preparation for the sacrament, Claudius confesses, recites his list of sins, but is unable to awake contrition ("one cannot repent" [III.iii.66]) and unwilling to make satisfaction ("I am still possess'd / Of those effects for which I did the murder" [53–54]). Of course, Claudius fails of absolution. Although following these meditations he reaches toward angels ("Help, angels! Make assay" [69]), at the moment of his death he reaches only for human support: "O, yet defend me, friends; I am but hurt" (V.ii.326).

Laertes, at the verge of death, displays a self-evoked penitence. He confesses to his part in Hamlet's murder, shows contrition, and makes partial satisfaction, all at once, by admitting that he is "justly kill'd with [his] own treachery" (V.ii.310). He makes further satisfaction by offering forgiveness to Hamlet for Polonius's death and his own, and receives a form of absolution as Hamlet picks up for the last time his priestly role and blesses Laertes with the benediction "Heaven make thee free of it" (V.ii.331–34).

The language of the *confiteor*, with its reference to thoughts, words, and deeds, provides a further motif that Shakespeare makes much of in *Lear* but which he uses also in *Hamlet*. Tied in with the love/duty theme as well as with the revenge code is the requirement for action. Hamlet is torn between action and inaction because love for his father and love of heaven pull him in opposite directions. He believes that love for his father requires the action of bloodletting revenge, but he believes that love of heaven forbids him such action. The meditative quality in him ponders this dilemma, and he becomes the melancholy Prince who delays in his oath to "sweep" to his revenge. In his soliloquies, the thoughts of which are always in the direction of implementing his oath, chastising his inaction, whipping himself into fulfillment of his sinful promise to the ghost, he chides himself ultimately with cowardice. But the very "craven scruple" which he identifies as his usual practice of "thinking too precisely on the event"—thought that keeps him from action—proves to be the preservation of his soul.

Shakespeare relies on the rash character that he has created for Laertes to carry the thoughts/deeds motif in the opposite direction. As Claudius primes Laertes to be the instrument of the planned murder of Hamlet, the King discourses on love, duty, revenge, thoughts, words, action:

> love is begun by time,
> . . . .
> Time qualifies the spark and fire of it.
> There lives within the very flame of love
> A kind of wick or snuff that will abate it
> . . . .
> That we would do,
> We should do when we would; for this "would"
>   changes
> And hath abatements and delays as many
> As there are tongues, are hands, are accidents
> . . . .
> What would you undertake
> To show yourself your father's son in deed
> More than in words?
>   (IV.vii.111–26)

Claudius, urging Laertes to thoughtless action, is a false counselor. We learn as much when we hear that Laertes would not blanch to "cut [Hamlet's] throat i' th' church." We recognize further the evil nature of revenge, which Claudius opines "should have no bounds" and "in*deed*" (my italics) may invade the sanctuary itself (IV.vii.126–28). Rather than chide Hamlet as a "tardy son" and join the ghost to whet his revenger's "almost blunted purpose" (III.iv.110–15), we must applaud the scrupulous young man and find him ultimately preserved through his habit of contemplative thought, his path of reasoned action. Contrariwise, and at the instant when he is furious, ripe to impulsive action, Laertes illustrates the willfulness and danger of such rashness in himself:

> To hell, allegiance! Vows, to the blackest devil!
> Conscience and grace, to the profoundest pit!
> I dare damnation. To this point I stand,

That both the worlds I give to negligence,
Let come what comes, only I'll be reveng'd
Most throughly for my father.

(IV.v.133–38)

No accident is the juxtaposition of IV.vii. (Laertes' double-fed rage over his father's murder and his sister's madness) with V.i. (Hamlet's final realization he is king/minister, his escape from the role of revenger/scourge).

The chief purpose of the graveyard episode is to put Hamlet to a *memento-mori* experience.[46] Reminders of the grave—the hideous corruption of the body and the inevitability that all mortals come to the favor of the skull, from Alexander and Caesar to Yorick—warn Hamlet that rash and sinful action, such as revenge comprises, leads only to death. The accident of his passing the graveyard just as the churlish sexton tosses up a skull is a second manifestation of the divinity that shapes Hamlet's end, for from what the Prince tells Horatio in V.ii., we know that he had recognized already heaven's hand in the exposure of the plot to end him in England. Hamlet responds to the *memento mori* as to all occasions and considerations: he determines not to jeopardize his eternal soul. Almost as a period to these matters is the verbal exchange as both Laertes and Hamlet leap into the grave, which should remind each that the pit he stands in is his unavoidable destiny. Laertes rashly looks toward hell: "The devil take thy soul." Hamlet, as he has always done, rejects damnation: "Thou pray'st not well" (V.i.259).

The drama of the time, of course, insisted that the moral order, the topsy-turvy world be righted. Perhaps the earliest indication of reversal is Hamlet's success in wooing the Queen to repentance, gaining her support against the King. Signal is Hamlet's joy in the curtain speech of the third act: "O, 'tis most sweet, / When in one line two crafts directly meet" (III.iv.216–17). Hamlet has taken joy in nothing before this time. Although he is still confused as to his proper role, and although he backslides into a desire for

46. See appendix.

revenge as late as IV.iv.66 ("My thoughts be bloody, or be nothing worth!"), Hamlet has identified himself tentatively as minister as well as scourge. His education has still somewhat to go, for he needs the revelation of heaven's hand in his affairs, not forthcoming until the sea-cabin episode. The audience, however, may see divine providence at work as heaven's mills slowly grind out the ingredients necessary for the restitution of harmony. Initial signs occur in IV.i. where, again in a curtain speech, Claudius exhibits premonitions of disaster to his own designs: "My soul is full of discord and dismay" (45). Hamlet's plans have begun to prosper, even as Claudius's pall. The forces that help Hamlet are uncertainly identified, but noteworthy is the information that the Prince is able to give his mother at the end of the closet scene: "I must to England" (III.iv.207). She had forgot, but Hamlet knows further that "There's letters seal'd" and that Rosencrantz and Guildenstern are chosen to "marshal [him] to knavery" (209–12).

In IV.iii., when the King announces publicly the course for England and Hamlet responds, "Good," the Prince reveals openly that he knows the King's dark plots: "I see a cherub that sees them" (41–52). Apparently those present take Hamlet's "cherub" as a jocular or antic remark, but we must wonder at the source of Hamlet's intelligence. There is cause to suspect that a court faction has always existed that supports the Prince. Horatio has helped at the mousetrap, and we may surmise the continuance of the early decisions of captains and soldiers like Marcellus, Bernardo, and Francisco to risk execution for treason by imparting to Hamlet rather than to the King their knowledge of the ghost and all that phantasm imports to the health of Denmark.[47] The suggestion is that Hamlet has his own palace secret service, but his strange use of "cherub" as his source of information supports further the theme of heaven's interference.

Hamlet grows more candid in his opposition to the King, more open in revealing what he has learned of the King's plans, more public in denunciation of the villain. The seeming riddle of

47. The secrecy with which the guards first bring report of the ghost to Horatio arouses in them great fear (I.ii.207).

Hamlet's words to Rosencrantz and Guildenstern in IV.ii., in one reading, is treasonous: "The body is with the King, but the King is not with the body. The King is a thing—. . . . Of nothing" (28–31). Whatever ambiguities may identify "body" with Polonius, the reference must also be to the body politic, which is with the King insofar as the general populace does not know him to be a murdering usurper, but he is not with the body inasmuch as he is not the true king and subjects that body to the rottenness that pervades the country. Hamlet feels he no longer need "hold his tongue" (I.ii.159), and when he rudely (III.iv.41) wags it against Claudius, he allows himself treble the insolence shown to his mother. He openly to Rosencrantz and Guildenstern—in front of the guard they command—calls Claudius a thing of nothing. Earlier, to his mother, her husband is "A king of shreds and patches" (III.iv.106). To Claudius himself, in IV.iii., prior to confessing that he knows the King's purposes, Hamlet, with negligent innuendo, illustrates how a king may go a progress through the guts of a beggar, with disdain tells the usurper to seek Polonius in hell. Such open challenge arms Claudius, who, with fiery quickness, ships his adversary to England.

Claudius's impotence in dealing with Hamlet is another indication of the King's decay. The ruler fears to move against a foe because "He's lov'd of the distracted multitude" (IV.iii.5); the lover fears to harm an enemy because that enemy's mother "Lives almost by his looks" (IV.vii.12). In fact, IV.iii. opens and closes with confessions in which the King admits that the strong hand with which he first carried all is now weakened, indeed shakes. Along with his cause, the King grows diseased: impostume attacks his rule ("Diseases desperate grown" [9]), fever his body ("like the hectic in my blood he rages" [70]).

The entire fabric that Claudius has woven, in quickening pace, rends in place after place, like cloth utterly threadbare and worn. Ophelia's mad songs and whisperings suggest to "hearers" that "botch the words up fit to their own thoughts" that "There's tricks i' th' world"; her "winks and nods" "strew / Dangerous conjectures in ill-breeding minds" (IV.v.5–15). Polonius's death, with Claudius's ill-considered "hugger-mugger" interment of the body, has made "the people muddied, / Thick and unwholesome in their thoughts" (IV.v.82–85). The Prince exiled, the daughter of the murdered first minister gone mad bring Claudius to bemoan his sorrows, now assaulting him in battalions (80). But the climax of national dissolution is the riot of the populace, which is the ultimate tangle of the chain of being that lies aheap on Danish terrain. The mob's demand that Laertes be king is described by the messenger who brings the news as that condition of chaos which God found upon the deep before he commanded that there be light: "And, as the world were now but to begin, / . . . / They cry, 'Choose we! Laertes shall be king!'" (IV.v.106–9).

Laertes crashes through the palace doors, and Claudius's reign totters on the brink. In one brief glance, one character, unaided by the supernatural agency of the ghost, sees with clarity and makes a correct identification: "vile king" (118). But Claudius is not to be tumbled yet, nor by an instrument with less claim to the throne than he. Claudius's wiliness, his brilliant evil, regains effectiveness momentarily as he is able to redirect Laertes' violence; but he does so with the very bluff which should make himself to tremble: "There's such divinity doth hedge a king / That treason can but peep to what it would" (126–27). Claudius points toward those powers that, even as he speaks, are working to remove the rot of which he is the cankerworm cause. No one knows better how easy it is to penetrate the hedge; yet the growing temblors in his kingdom must awaken fear in the false king that providence has begun to restore the hedge that he breached to reach his brother's life. Of like great bluff with like great temerity is Claudius's bold speech that ends this scene: "And where th' offense is, let the great axe fall" (219).

Important in developing the reversal of Hamlet's fortunes and in furthering his education to awareness that he is the divinely anointed ruler is the brief scene that adds also to audience awareness that the Prince has had good intelligence and a sizable support team. His rescue from the pirate ship could have been accomplished only with considerable help. To fit the world in which they are called upon to act, Hamlet's deliverers take the topsy-turvy form of pirates; but they are "thieves of mercy," and they "knew what they did" (IV.vi.15–21).[48] If the sailors who bring this message to Horatio crewed the ship that rescued Hamlet, clearly they are not pirates. The blessings exchanged between them and Horatio (7–9) lend them a special grace, and Hamlet writes them down as "good fellows" (26). The words that are to strike Horatio dumb when he hears them expose minutely the machinations of Claudius. Hamlet has learned them only by "fingering" Rosencrantz and Guildenstern's packet, the very act that awakes the Prince to the divine providence that guides his ways and, in a sense, hedges him.

After Hamlet escapes destruction in England, he deals with Claudius more openly than ever, while the King, if possible, becomes more devious. The Prince returns to Denmark preceded by a letter announcing his arrival "naked" (IV.vii.44). He promises full disclosure of all that has happened. Claudius reacts with cowardly plans of double poisonings (the foil and chalice), which he expects to succeed for the very reason of Hamlet's openness: "Most generous, and free from all contriving" (135). But success is no longer possible to Claudius, a truth indicated by the failure of his former evil brilliance. He intends that upon Hamlet's death "no wind of blame shall breathe, / But even his mother shall uncharge the practice / And call it accident" (65–67). Yet his stupid plot of

---

48. Debate has centered upon whether Hamlet's rescue by the pirate ship was prearranged by the Prince. Martin Stevens is boldest to date in claiming that "the intervention of the pirates has been carefully prepared for by Shakespeare as part of the subterranean (and off-stage) counterplotting by Hamlet": "Hamlet and the Pirates: A Critical Reconsideration," *SQ* 26 (1975): 276. H. R. Coursen, in "Hamlet and the Pirates Reconsidered," *ELN* 14 (1976): 20, remains unconvinced by Stevens's arguments and concludes, "We cannot answer these questions . . . because to do so is to speculate beyond the limits of the evidence." Obviously I come down on the side of Stevens. Shakespeare's ability to suggest a vast history of offstage activity through a few brief lines is one of his greatest dramatic skills. Hamlet's clear knowledge of the King's plans (even Gertrude had forgot) argues an organized and effective counterespionage group in the service of the Prince, giving him time and means to parry the knavery to which Rosencrantz and Guildenstern will "marshall" him (III.iv.207–12).

the backup poisoned goblet cannot—and does not—escape detection as a heinous treachery.

Upon this conspiring, Gertrude arrives. I have not seen it suggested that she overhears the plotters. Her entrance is given at line 162, as the King says, "But stay, what noise?" and as he concludes proposing the envenomed cup. In light of Dover Wilson's widely accepted hypothesis that Hamlet overhears Polonius's plan to "loose" Ophelia, we might expect some critic to argue that Gertrude is visible to the audience as early as line 156 and overhears at least half the plot:

> When in your motion you are hot and dry—
> As make your bouts more violent to that end—
> And that he calls for drink, I'll have prepar'd him
> A chalice for the nonce, whereon but sipping,
> If he by chance escape your venom'd stuck,
> Our purpose may hold there. But stay, what noise?
>
> (IV.vii.157–62)

If Gertrude drinks the wine—knowing what she does, sacrificing herself to save her beloved son—her appearance in time to hear the King's purposes and her subsequent actions dependent upon that knowledge would be another indication that providence (divine) interferes to reverse Claudius's fortunes.[49]

The graveyard scene follows. Hamlet has his *memento-mori* experience.[50] Knowing that he, as all mortals, must die, he is strengthened in his determination to do so in a state of grace. And although he remembers that some kings have died "young and fair" like Alexander, he is comforted by knowing that any king,

---

49. I do not, however, believe that Gertrude overhears the plot. See discussion on pp. 73–75.

50. Roland Mushat Frye has considered the graveyard skulls in light of the pictorial tradition, supporting conclusions that I had reached in my earlier essay, "*Hamlet* as a *memento-mori* Poem," *PMLA* 85 (1970): 1035–40, and of which the appendix to this book is a greatly expanded version. For Frye's observations, see "Ladies, Gentlemen, and Skulls: *Hamlet* and the Iconographic Traditions," *SQ* 30 (1979): 15–28.

Fig. 6. *The daunce of Machabree.* John Lydgate. Press of Richard Tottel, London, 1554.

even Caesar, can be cut off too. In fact, Claudius appears almost as one in a train with Alexander and Caesar: "Here comes the King" (217). Hamlet's musing with which the *memento-mori* passage begins—"Here's fine revolution, an we had the trick to see 't" (90–91)—when coupled with the lot of Alexander and Caesar may seem further proof to the Prince that "a king may go a progress through the guts of a beggar" (IV.iii.31–32) (fig. 6).

As Hamlet, in V.ii., recounts to Horatio the events aboard ship, we learn that his education has been completed. He knows now how to fulfill his role as heaven's minister. He has noted divine intervention in his own preservation and in providing the means for turning the tables on Rosencrantz and Guildenstern (4–55). He may "quit" Claudius in "perfect conscience," execute him sinlessly because no longer does the son seek private revenge for the death of his father; rather the true king pursues his public obligation to cleanse Denmark. In fact his former fear, causing the fighting in his soul, plaguing him "Worse than the mutines in the bilboes" (4–6), the struggle to reconcile the revenge code with its sinfulness, is replaced by the new fear that *not* to squash this caterpillar of the commonwealth is to merit endless punishment:

> is 't not to be damn'd
> To let this canker of our nature come
> In further evil?
>
> (V.ii.68–70)

Although he suffers that fear of death that attends most mortals, he goes to the match with Laertes recognizing the special providence that attends him (V.ii.217–22).[51] Horatio's response to Hamlet's assertion that God's great design governs all things is in the nature of a choral comment: "That is most certain" (11).

With Hamlet's final step into the knowledge and assurance that gives him the complete steel he needs to challenge Claudius and to right the upside-down realm, Claudius reaches the nadir of his declining powers. His former grasp of all the reins of government and subtle threads of Machiavellian cunning becomes a nervous twitching that will undo him whether Hamlet serves as agent or not. The doctored chalice cannot escape detection. Furthermore, the villain goes so to pieces when Laertes loses the very first bout that he urges Hamlet to drink the poisoned cup at once. When Gertrude drinks, she knows immediately what she has ingested and cries aloud to the court, "The drink, the drink! I am pois'ned" (V.ii.313). Quite clearly the King, who has tampered with the vessel ("in the cup an union shall [I] throw" [270]) and offered it to Hamlet, would be recognized as the poisoner.

Hamlet realizes finally that divine providence may work through him, without his own damnation. He is able to kill Claudius sinlessly. The man, good at the outset of an onslaught upon his soul and body by forces supernatural as well as natural, has prevailed and concludes his earthly passage within the limits of grace.

51. As it attends the sparrow. In citing Matt. 10.29, John Dover Wilson warns that we must read the verse in context: "And feare ye not them which kil the bodie, but are not able to kil the soule: but rather feare him, which is able to destroye bothe soule and bodie in hel" (verse 28).

The language cited to come from the Catholic burial anthem, *In paradisum*, is one of Shakespeare's not unusual directed epitaphs. Hamlet goes with flights of angels, having removed the pollution in his state. Only one man has he sinned against: Polonius. Absolved from the grievous deed by his sacramental act of penance, symbolically completed when, as Gertrude tells us, "'a weeps for what is done" (IV.i.27), Hamlet reaps the further forgiveness of Laertes, who also absolves Hamlet from any guilt in Laertes' own death.

Some have argued that an ineradicable blot stains Hamlet for the death he arranges for Rosencrantz and Guildenstern, "Not shriving-time allow'd" (V.ii.47). Although no mercy can be seen in the Prince's sentence, neither can injustice. In fact, when Horatio asks how the order for their death was sealed, Hamlet cites the sanction of heaven: "Why, even in that was heaven ordinant" (48).

Rosencrantz and Guildenstern are not the hapless bumblers that some have labeled them, caught between "two mighty opposites"; nor are they victims of a remorseless fate that swallows ultimately all humans, the stamp given them by Tom Stoppard.[52] Shakespeare puts them carefully to a stern test, which they fail grievously. Hamlet receives them initially as his "excellent good friends" (II.ii.224). Merely as such and no more, under terms of Renaissance masculine love, their obligations to him are great. But also as beneath him in the chain of being, were he no more than prince, their love is all the more required. And since he is the true king, they have no obligation higher. Only doubtfully can it be argued that Rosencrantz and Guildenstern have reason to believe they serve the true king in Claudius. Other "excellent good friends" like Horatio, Marcellus, and Bernardo know to whom love and duty belong. Moreover, Rosencrantz and Guildenstern's none-too-subtle testing of Hamlet's "ambition" (II.ii.252–61) shows they guess cannily the King's interest in the Prince's behavior. But Hamlet's demand upon them is severe and explicit:

52. Stoppard, *Rosencrantz and Guildenstern Are Dead* (New York, 1967).

in the beaten way of friendship, what
make you at Elsinore? (270–71)

dear friends. . . . Come, come, deal
justly with me. (274–77)

let me conjure you, by the rights of
our fellowship, by the consonancy of
our youth, by the *obligation of our
ever-preserv'd love.* . . . (284–87, my italics)

If you love me, hold not off. (291–92)

    With such repeated, solemnly charged appeal and adjuration, the consequent failure of Rosencrantz and Guildenstern to give the love required to their friend and prince labels them especially heinous. Precisely with this term *love* does Hamlet condemn them: "Why, man, they did make love to this employment" (V.ii.57). Since they so callously pervert their love away from God's surrogate on earth, and in that sense from God himself, "They are not near [Hamlet's] conscience" (58). Neither is their execution an act of private revenge (since they are executed publicly by a state government on a mandate from a neighboring prince, on authority of a valid document, validly sealed by a true king with the authentic signet of the precedent true king); for "even in that was heaven ordinant" (48–50).

    In a study the chief purpose of which is to examine eschatological matters, it cannot be amiss to check Shakespeare's concern with the final disposition of his lesser characters. Herein we see Shakespeare's gentle nature at work. Although Claudius, Rosencrantz, and Guildenstern go to it (almost as they must in order for the play to illustrate that some shall be punished as well as some pardoned), evidence exists to the effect that Ophelia, Polonius, Gertrude, and Laertes, as well as Hamlet, are to be saved. Beginning with *Romeo and Juliet*, Shakespeare exhibits great dismay that otherwise good men should inherit everlasting damnation for a momentary lapse. The best reading of *Romeo and Juliet* is one in which the piacular guilt of the young lovers is an important consideration. In the words of the Prince, at play's end, Shakespeare intends that "Some shall be pardon'd, and some punished" (V.iii.308). Many readers are appalled at the thought that the handsome young lovers are damned if considered in the light of Christian judgment, and they refuse to regard the play as morally oriented. Of course, Shakespeare was appalled also, and he probes deeply the same issue in *Hamlet*. The great exposition of the idea is in Hamlet's lecture to Horatio. While peering down upon the King, who takes his "rouse," the Prince discourses on drunkenness as a single flaw in the Danish national character and in individual men:

> So, oft it chances in particular men,
> That for some vicious mole of nature in them,
> As in their birth—wherein they are not guilty,
> Since nature cannot choose his origin—
> By the o'ergrowth of some complexion,
> Oft breaking down the pales and forts of reason,
> Or by some habit that too much o'er-leavens
> The form of plausive manners, that these men,
> Carrying, I say, the stamp of one defect,
> Being nature's livery, or fortune's star,
> Their virtues else, be they as pure as grace,
> As infinite as man may undergo,
> Shall in the general censure take corruption
> From that particular fault.
>
> (I.iv.23–36)

"General censure" seems an obvious figure for judgment day, so that condemnation is not merely a diminishment of worldly reputation but also an eternal doom. Shakespeare laments that one sin alone disappoints a man of heaven if he die unhouseled and unaneled, his "virtues else, be they as pure as grace." Othello, an otherwise good man, is betrayed even to damnation out of an uncharacteristic and falsely developed jealousy. Escalus, in *Measure for Measure*, anguishes over those who are "condemned for a fault alone" (II.i.40).

In recourse to *Hamlet*, I have argued that the ghost is probably the spirit of dead King Hamlet, and therefore I must accept
that this "goodly king" (I.ii.186) is damned for his seeming only
flaw of gluttony.[53] Nevertheless, the gentle Shakespeare lets off
from damnation several other figures whose lapses spring not
from malice or ingrained evil but from blindness, stupidity, or
weakness. Ophelia, for instance, whom the gravediggers would
deny Christian burial, is by no means to be cast away so readily. She
fits the category of the one-fault-alone sinner, if even that. She was
an obedient daughter, who entertained the love-suit of Hamlet "in
honorable fashion." She goes mad over the loss of a father and a
man whom she deeply loved.[54] If she sinned at all, it was in the act
of suicide. But did she commit suicide? Shakespeare is at pains to
have the branch on which she climbs break under her. And although we wonder how Gertrude is able to give us so detailed an
eyewitness report, we note nevertheless that Ophelia is also "incapable of her own distress" (IV.vii.178). The malice of the gravediggers is that common pettiness that the small sometimes bend
upon the great: "Will you ha' the truth on 't? If this had not been a
gentlewoman, she should have been buried out o' Christian burial"
(V.i.23–25). If we are less biased, we should note that the coroner
has found it "Christian burial" (5). And although the uncharitable
priest who officiates at her burial does so with pursed lips and grit-
ted teeth as well as with repetition of the opinion of the gravediggers, he may say only that "her death was doubtful" (226–34).
To my mind, Laertes speaks her epitaph, delivering the line that is,
like Horatio's for Hamlet, Shakespeare's gentle assurance that this
weak creature does not suffer the fate of King Hamlet:

53. See pp. 23–29 above.
54. Ophelia's mad songs merge pathetically her father and Hamlet, so that in the unbalanced girl's troubled mind Hamlet has died as well
as her father. The depth of her feeling for the Prince is eloquently at-
tested at the conclusion of the "nunnery" scene: "And I, of ladies most
deject and wretched, / That suck'd the honey of his music vows, / . . . . /
O, woe is me!" (III.i.158–63). See also Harry Morris, "Ophelia's 'Bonny
Sweet Robin,'" *PMLA* 73 (1958): 601–3.

from her fair and unpolluted flesh
May violets spring! I tell thee, churlish priest,
A minist'ring angel shall my sister be
When thou liest howling.

(V.i.239—42)

Laertes has essentially been dealt with. Hamlet calls him "a very noble youth" (V.i.224), is sorry that with Laertes he "forgot [him]self," and excuses the young man's passion as "the image of [his own] cause" (V.ii.76—77). Laertes goes through a self-imposed penitential act, with contrition beginning as he assures Claudius that he will get to Hamlet in the third bout: "And yet it is almost against my conscience" (V.ii.299). He confesses, "I am justly kill'd with mine own treachery" (310) and, with the admission of a just death, apparently makes satisfaction through forfeit of his own life. Hamlet grants him forgiveness, as he Hamlet (331—34). Hamlet's language—"Heaven make thee free of it"—is epitaphic and, like the lines that accompany both Ophelia's and Hamlet's deaths, evokes heaven or heavenly creatures.

The father of these two, Polonius, is a more difficult case. If men such as Marcellus, Bernardo, and Francisco know where their loyalties lie, one would expect this man "of wisdom and of reach," with his "windlasses and with assays of bias" to "find directions out" (II.i.61—63). But Polonius is always wrong. He diagnoses incorrectly Hamlet's distraction as lovesickness. Apparently he cannot find out "Where truth is hid" (II.ii.157—58) though circumstances lead him by the nose. He is at least the brother of if not the model for Prufrock: full of high sentence, obtuse, ridiculous, indeed a fool.[55] If he wins salvation at all, it must be granted either because of his naivety or because as Hamlet says, "That great baby . . . is not yet out of his swaddling-clouts" (II.ii.382—83). As other little children, he may be suffered to come into the kingdom. If he has an epitaph at all, Gertrude provides it: "The unseen good old man" (IV.i.12).

55. T. S. Eliot, "The Love Song of J. Alfred Prufrock," in *The Complete Poems and Plays: 1909—1950* (New York, 1962), p. 7.

We are left with Gertrude herself. I have offered the possibility that Gertrude overhears Claudius's conversation with Laertes, the plot upon Hamlet's life. Claudius seems surprised by the noise that the Queen makes just as he refers both to the poisoned "stuck" and the "chalice" (IV.vii.159–61). Some critics have taken the position that at V.ii.285 ff. either the Queen or Hamlet, and possibly both, knows what the cup contains:[56]

QUEEN
    The Queen carouses to thy fortune, Hamlet.
HAMLET
    Good madam!
KING
    Gertrude, do not drink.
QUEEN
    I will, my lord; I pray you pardon me. [*Drinks.*]
KING
    [*Aside*] It is the pois'ned cup. It is too late.
HAMLET
    I dare not drink yet, madam; by and by.
                             (291–96)

If the Queen knows of the plot before the present moment, she hides her knowledge well. Immediately after her coming upon the conspiring twosome, she is full of the death of Ophelia and dissembles convincingly if she has overheard. As to where Hamlet

56. The earliest writer to argue that the Queen knowingly drinks from the poisoned cup is Amanda L. Bartholomew, "Queen Gertrude," *Shakespeariana* 3 (1886): 451–54, who attributes the act to a desire to protect her son and to atone for her sins of the past. A reasonably diligent search has failed to turn up any critic to suggest that Hamlet believes the cup deadly; yet I cannot think the idea is my own. Any writer who argues that the "To be or not to be" soliloquy represents Hamlet's serious consideration of suicide would be quick to find in the promise to drink "by and by" the implication that once the Prince achieves the revenge he set out to obtain he is more than ready to leave the life he finds so flat and stale. He does not "dare" drink, of course, if he hopes still to get at the King.

would get the information remains unclear. His "cherub" spy system would not have access to this oral information. Only Gertrude could have informed him. Hamlet mentions nothing to Horatio although an uneasiness about the fencing match is expressed. If Gertrude heard about the cup, she heard about the foil also, since it is referred to after the chalice. But her fears for Hamlet in the bout do not include fears of treachery, only that "He's fat, and scant of breath" (V.ii.289).

Perhaps, it may be suggested, either or both guess at the contents of the cup or, perhaps, merely consider, what with the King's passes over the chalice, that poison is a possibility. If so, one or both then intend clearly to commit suicide. In the case of Hamlet, suicide is a course of action many times rejected by the Prince in his meditative moments and unlikely to be entertained after he has professed himself "ready" to shape himself to divinity's ends. With Gertrude, we must decide whether Hamlet's priestly ministration, his evocation in her of penitential vows, has had ongoing efficaciousness. She may, indeed, once free of Hamlet's accusations and his presence, have lapsed. Yet all things indicate that Gertrude is truly repentant, and nothing happens after her promises to Hamlet to suggest that she has reneged on her oath to her son or fallen away from her determination to reform. Noteworthy is her support of Hamlet against her consort. She has been warned not to "ravel . . . out" that Hamlet is "crafty" mad. To this request she responds with gusto, telling Claudius that her son is "Mad as the sea" (IV.i.7). Between that moment and the swordplay, the only evidence to be adduced is the Queen's protection of her husband when Laertes breaks past the Switzers, into the palace. Gertrude protects her own rule when she protects Claudius's; she works for order in the state, which would deteriorate beyond its Claudian rottenness if mob rule were to take over. She may even be protecting the crown for Hamlet. If, however, we must admit that she has again inclined toward her former sins, her last act carries her toward redemption. Thus, letting "the end try the man," this ultimate repudiation of Claudius is the satisfaction necessary to her full penance. If any doubt about the welfare of Gertrude's soul is raised by Hamlet's words as he forces the remnant poison down Claudius's throat—"damned Dane, / .... / Follow my mother" (V.ii.327–29)—we may remember Romeo's hope to send Tybalt after Mercutio. Romeo could hardly wish that both go to the same rest.

With Gertrude we have followed to the grave all who in *Hamlet* are cut off. Claudius, Rosencrantz, and Guildenstern, who choose to accept the evil of the universe that murder and usurpation created, may be presumed damned. King Hamlet, unhappily dispatched at an unguarded moment and with perhaps only one particular fault freshly indulged, may be seen pouring poison eternally into Claudius's ear.[57] Laertes and Gertrude, who succumbed to evil under grave weaknesses in their own makeups and who pursued further malefactions under Claudius's malign genius, repent in time, and we hope are saved. Ophelia and Polonius, essentially good persons who are unaware of the evil that enmeshes them, though destroyed by it in the body, may be presumed saved also. Hamlet, a man good at the outset of his drama, his soul the object of an onslaught by forces supernatural as well as natural, has prevailed and concluded his passage on earth within the limits sanctioned. He has restored order to his realm, an obligation thrust upon him as true king. By eschewing private revenge yet achieving ministerial execution of the polluter of his kingdom, he has held above his own welfare the "safety and health of [the] whole state, / ... / Whereof he is the head" (I.iii.21–24). Sinless for his restraint and blessed for his ultimate fulfillment of a heavenly deputizement, he goes, in a flight of angels (see fig. 5), to his reward, the celestial coronation of the man in grace at his death.

57. In the same manner that Ugolino gnaws eternally on the head of Archbishop Ruggieri. For this view of the horribly altered "goodly king," see pp. 23–29 above, and especially footnote 24.

2. *Othello:*
No Amount of Prayer
Can Possibly Matter

hakespeare criticism has for some time been embroiled in a controversy over the validity of a Christian interpretation of the plays. The number of writers who have asserted the Christian implications of *Othello* is now considerable.[1] Perhaps, more recently, the rejections and denunciations of religious interpretations have seemed to turn the tide.[2] But the trouble in the case of *Othello* is not that a Christian reading is mistaken; rather, those we have been given to date have

---

1. See G. Wilson Knight, *The Wheel of Fire* (London, 1930); G. R. Elliott, *Flaming Minister* (Durham, N.C., 1953); Paul Siegel, *Shakespearean Tragedy and the Elizabethan Compromise* (New York, 1957); Bernard Spivack, *Shakespeare and the Allegory of Evil* (New York, 1958); Irving Ribner, *Patterns in Shakespearian Tragedy* (New York, 1960); Joseph A. Bryant, Jr., *Hippolyta's View* (Lexington, Ky., 1961); Kenneth Myrick, "The Theme of Damnation in Shakespearean Tragedy," *SP* 38 (1941): 221–45; S. L. Bethell, "Shakespeare's Imagery: The Diabolic Images in *Othello*," *Shakespeare Survey* 5 (1952): 62–80.

2. Clifford Leech, *Shakespeare's Tragedies and Other Studies in Seven-*

not gone far enough. The benefit of still another attempt is, as I see it, twofold. We may be able to develop a coherent view of the play that will be rid of the objections thus far made against the various Christian interpretations we now have. And, perhaps more important, we may be able to add a dimension to the larger issue that has sometime attached to these matters: Is Christian tragedy possible?[3]

In the tetralogy which I am hypothesizing, *Othello* provides us with a man who as his drama begins is as much in a state of grace as a mortal may claim. His pilgrimage will issue in one of two destinations: along the way he will reject all evil, keep in grace, receive God's mercy at judgment, and rest in beatitude; or he will lapse into reprobation, die in that state, be cast out at judgment, and, in his own words, "wash . . . in . . . liquid fire."

As much as anything else, it is because Othello calls for devils and asks for torment that he gives up his part in salvation; and *Othello*, like *Macbeth*, is a play about damnation. If about damnation, therefore about the four last things.

------

teenth-Century Drama* (London, 1950); Geoffrey Bush, *Shakespeare and the Natural Condition* (Cambridge, Mass., 1956); R. M. Frye, *Shakespeare and Christian Doctrine* (Princeton, 1963); Sylvan Barnet, "Some Limitations of a Christian Approach to Shakespeare," *ELH* 22 (1955): 81–92; Edward Hubler, "The Damnation of Othello: Some Limitations of the Christian View of the Play," *SQ* 9 (1958): 295–300; Robert H. West, "The Christianness of *Othello*," *SQ* 15 (1964): 333–43, expanded in his *Shakespeare & the Outer Mystery* (Lexington, Ky., 1968), pp. 96–148.

Reuben A. Brower, *Hero & Saint: Shakespeare and the Graeco-Roman Heroic Tradition* (Oxford, 1971), pp. 1–28, confesses a Christian overlay to the character of Othello but argues that the "heroic" pagan struggles to emerge. H. R. Coursen, Jr., *Christian Ritual and the World of Shakespeare's Tragedies* (Lewisburg, Pa., 1976), supports and expands Brower's view, seeing in Othello's final speeches a "pagan cast" that "presses" the Moor to an "indictment of himself as Turk" (p. 230).

3. This issue has been discussed by Leech, *Shakespeare's Tragedies*, p. 18; I. A. Richards, *Principles of Literary Criticism* (London, 1925), p. 246; William F. Lynch, *Christ and Apollo* (New York, 1960), passim; and Laurence Michel, "Possibility of Christian Tragedy," *Thought* 31 (1956): 403–28, among others.

Othello, the Moor, is to die. But since Shakespeare, unlike Dante, does not want to take his drama beyond the mortal world, the usual eschatological order is reversed: judgment, heaven, and hell all precede death. The reversal is accomplished symbolically, for any other method would stretch our credulity. The reversal also makes it unnecessary for us to go beyond the final curtain. Bradleyans were much attacked for speculating about characters before they came on stage or after they left. The salvation/damnation critics are swinged soundly not only for following certain characters beyond this mortality but also for presuming to have an insight into God's judgments.[4] But can we not answer these objections by showing that Shakespeare has reversed the order of judgment and death? He has brought into his play either hellfires or flights of angels, and we are told the final disposition of the souls of some of his protagonists in order that we will *not* speculate about their final abode. Shakespeare is able to take this judgment out of God's hands, and we are able to write about judgment, because these are Shakespeare's characters and not God's. Shakespeare knows well, as do the rest of us, exactly what actions are damnable; these are the sinful acts that specifically he wishes to explore. He does not want the very terror or joy, the intensity of which strengthens the *agon* requisite to all great drama, to be vitiated by an ambiguity as to whether his hero wins or loses at the end.

The precedent drama of which Shakespeare was the inheritor was either altogether the drama of the morality plays,[5] or it was a drama inescapably influenced by them. What is strange about a play that asserts damnation? *Dr. Faustus* is a play that insists we be made aware what has happened after the final curtain. So were all the morality plays. So was all Christian allegory. But to suggest that Shakespeare would write allegory will set many teeth on edge.

4. Harold S. Wilson's refusal to comment on the disposition of Othello's soul is rendered in gospel warning: "Judge not, that ye be not judged": *On the Design of Shakespearian Tragedy* (Toronto, 1957), p. 67.

5. This point has been presented at length by Willard Farnham, *The Medieval Heritage of Elizabethan Tragedy* (London, 1936), and Spivack, *Shakespeare and the Allegory of Evil.*

Even the boldest of the religious interpreters will not go that far.[6]
S. L. Bethell writes, "I would not have it thought that, in proposing
three levels of interpretation for *Othello* and in crediting Shakespeare with a considerable consciousness of what he was about, I
intend to countenance any allegorizing of the incidents. The three
levels coalesce into one; the deeper meanings, social and metaphysical, are directly applicable to the human story."[7] Yet, what is
Bethell doing but reading *Othello* allegorically? How does any
claim of coalescence rid us of the word *allegory*? Has not the anagogical coalesced with the moral in Dante? Are not Bethell's social
and metaphysical Dante's moral and anagogical? What are all the
Christian interpreters doing but explicating allegory? M. D. H.
Parker puts it this way: "'To hold a mirror up to nature' was
Hamlet's dramatic recipe, and, he might have added had he lived
to the later plays, 'to grace.'"[8] What is this concern with grace
other than allegory and anagogy? I am struck more and more with
the necessity to read some of Shakespeare's plays after some manner similar to the old fourfold interpretation of scripture, a method
Dante insisted upon for the *Divine Comedy* in his letter to Can
Grande. I can escape less and less the awareness that an anagogical
statement is made in many of the plays—comedies as well as tragedies—while no violence is wrought upon the playwright's care to
keep his characters in this world—in a Renaissance world more
than in a medieval world—and to keep them consistent within a
framework of plausibility.

Why have some critics been so reluctant to grant Shakespeare
the genius that clearly he had, the ability to pile meaning upon
meaning without doing damage to any one of them? All would
grant such skill to Dante as well as to a good many writers of talent
less than Dante's. The age had not outgrown pure allegory. Spenser
would have been working still upon the *Faerie Queene* at the time
Shakespeare was finishing *Othello*, had Spenser lived. Neither had

6. Bryant's *Hippolyta's View* is an exception, interpreting several
plays as allegories of Christian belief.
7. Bethell, "Shakespeare's Imagery," p. 79.
8. Parker, *The Slave of Life* (London, 1955), p. 10.

the age given up that kind of intellect that we associate with the anagogical correspondence of things:

> Is the Pacifique Sea my home? Or are
>   The Easterne riches? Is *Ierusalem*?
> *Anyan*, and *Magellan*, and *Gibraltare*,
>   All streights, and none but streights, are wayes to
>   them,
>   Whether where *Iaphet* dwelt, or *Cham*, or *Sem*.
>
> We thinke that *Paradise* and *Calvarie*,
>   *Christs* Crosse, and *Adams* tree, stood in one place;
> Looke Lord, and finde both *Adams* met in me;
>   As the first *Adams* sweat surrounds my face,
>   May the last *Adams* blood my soule embrace.[9]

If it is argued that Spenser looked backward when he wrote the *Faerie Queene*, it cannot be denied that Donne looked forward. If Shakespeare is a true product of the Renaissance, then too is Donne. And if Donne may be concerned about his own part in Adam and in Christ, so also may Shakespeare be concerned about Othello's part.

I have already paired *Othello* with *Macbeth* as two plays concluding with damnation. In the Scottish play, the protagonist succumbs at once to evil. His progress in iniquity is so rapid, his degeneracy so complete, that he may be said to be a demon on earth. He is not the good man damned for a single flaw; he is a catalogue of evil. Macbeth shows the growth of satanism in a fertile field. Othello is practically flawless; if he has any shortcoming, it is his overabundance of goodness.[10] He has been charged with pride by

9. John Donne, "Hymne to God my God, in my sicknesse," in *The Poems*, ed. H. J. C. Grierson, 2 vols. (London, 1912), 1:368.

10. A. C. Bradley coupled Othello with Hamlet to say that "each is a man exceptionally noble and trustful": *Shakespearean Tragedy*, 2d ed. (London, 1905), p. 175. Alice Walker's iteration of Bradley's terms includes an additional idea that I find close to my own: "The Othello story

several writers. If they mean pride of strength, of victories, of travel, of achievement, they are straining at gnats. These rehearsals of his exploits are conveyed either in intimate, personal, and friendly recountings, impliedly at the request of the auditors, or in the final summation of the good he has done for the state. The first are to be ignored; the second may be held a small enough claim at life's end: the killing of a turbaned Turk who traduced the state while beating a Venetian. But if this summary speech must still be considered pride, it comes after Othello has fallen, after his murder of Desdemona, and before his intended suicide. I would not argue the goodness of Othello after the devil has triumphed over him.

The only charge of pride that can be brought against Othello is the pride glossed by the theologians as despair—his suicide—the pride that makes a man believe himself so evil that not even God's grace will redeem him. But again, this lapse comes after Othello's initial fall, his first submission to the devil. I assuredly do not intend to claim that Othello is damned in a state of innocence but rather that he is led to sin—to jealousy, to murder, and to suicide—to pride, because he was not strong enough to stand.

But before his seduction to evil, Othello is among the purest of heroes in Shakespeare. Like Hamlet,

> The Moor is of a free and open nature,
> That thinks men honest that but seem to be so,
> And will as tenderly be led by th' nose
> As asses are.
>
> (I.iii.400–403)

Unlike Hamlet, he does not require that completeness of revenge,

---

. . . [is] a particular example of . . . [a] 'process of poisoning' at work upon a character of *exceptional nobility*, corrupting *his very soul* and dragging him down from the height of human happiness *to the gates of Hell itself*": "Introduction," New Cambridge *Othello* (Cambridge, Eng., 1957), p. xiii (my italics).

which in the case of Claudius, Rosencrantz, and Guildenstern prompts Hamlet to kill the soul as well as the body:

OTHELLO
> I would not kill thy unprepared spirit.
> No, heaven forfend! I would not kill thy soul.
> (V.ii.33–34)

Othello, then, is the good man who does not have the defenses to defeat the devil. He is Shakespeare's denial to the then still unstated Miltonic assertion that God made man "Sufficient to have stood" (*Paradise Lost*, III.99).[11] The theme pervades Shakespeare that a good man cannot cope with a villain who may "smile, and smile" (*Hamlet*, I.v.109), for "nature with a beauteous wall / Doth oft close in pollution" (*Twelfth Night*, I.ii.48–49). Duncan, having been taken in by the first Thane of Cawdor, says,

> No more than Thane of Cawdor shall deceive
> Our bosom interest.
> (*Macbeth*, I.ii.67–68)

But he confesses in a speech that might be held central to all Shakespeare's assertions about the nature of evil and might be found operative in all his plays,

> There's no art
> To find the mind's construction in the face.
> (I.iv.11–12)

Therefore, even with knowledge gained through the treasons of the first, the King is deceived easily by the second Thane of Cawdor, Macbeth.

In the same way that Desdemona comes to an undeserved death, Othello comes to what we might call an undeserved damna-

11. Milton, *The Complete Poetical Works*, ed. Douglas Bush (Boston, 1965), p. 259.

tion, undeserved not because he committed no sins but because he was incapable, insufficient to perceive villainy. We must turn his own words to commentary upon himself: "But yet the pity of it. . . . the pity of it!" (IV.i.194–95).

Writers like Roland Frye might claim that such a view creates a heretical Shakespeare,[12] but if so the heresy is one of which every man has been guilty in his heart, in hope to outgrow, but at its inception a searing question. Sometimes subdued with that most paradoxical of prayers, "Lord, I believe; help thou mine unbelief" (Mark 9.24), othertimes it erupts in all its heretical rebellion as a serious question along with Job and Jeremiah, the holy; along with Gerard Manley Hopkins and Graham Greene, the rebels, "Thou art indeed just, Lord, if I contend / With thee; but, sir, so what I plead is just."[13]

Is Christian tragedy possible? The naysayers are best represented, perhaps, by I. A. Richards: "Tragedy is only possible to a mind which is for the moment agnostic or Manichean. The least touch of any theology which has a compensatory Heaven to offer the tragic hero is fatal."[14] But such a view ignores or denies the mystical element in the doctrine of the atonement; it denies the passion of Christ and the sacrificial quality of his act, all of which are possible only when we believe that "for our salvation He came down from Heaven and was incarnate by the holy ghost of the virgin Mary, and was made man." With the incarnation came all the attendant mortal conditions, such as fear of death and doubt in salvation. For though the God in Christ said to the good thief that he would that day be in heaven (Luke 23.43), the man in Christ cried out, "My God, my God, why hast thou forsaken me?" (Mark 15.34). Such, I should think, is the answer to be made to the repudiators of Christian tragedy. But let us hypothesize still another answer. If the doctrine of the atonement will not serve, then possibly Shakespeare, in *Othello*, has written the only Christian tragedy.

12. Much in the way that Frye deals with Siegel and Ribner, *Shakespeare and Christian Doctrine*, pp. 26–28.

13. Hopkins's rendering of the Vulgate Jeremiah, 12.1.

14. Richards, *Principles of Literary Criticism*, p. 246.

Since the play is about damnation, the forces of good and the rewards of heaven are underplayed. The forces of evil and the pangs of hell dominate. Desdemona, who symbolically or allegorically (if we are permitted) is Othello's good angel and who stands for grace, fights a losing battle. As all angels are surrogates for Christ, Desdemona functions not only as angel but also as Christ. She has been thrust into Othello's life as the white lamb ("ewe," I.i.90). Her father calls her perfection (I.iii.102), and Cassio calls her divine (II.i.74) and apostrophizes her as the Christ enthroned and triumphant, which indeed she is in Cassio's case:

> Hail to thee, lady! And the grace of heaven,
> Before, behind thee, and on every hand,
> Enwheel thee round!
>
> (II.i.86–88)

Othello would stake his "life upon her faith" (I.iii.297), as he must and does; he calls her his "soul's joy" (II.i.182), which she is until he falls from grace. Even Roderigo perceives that "she's full of most bless'd condition" (II.i.249–50). The adjectives that describe her invariably, other than when she is denounced falsely by Othello and Iago, are *virtuous, good, innocent, heavenly, true*, and the nouns that name her are *angel, goodness, perfection*, etc. The only serious charge ever made by the critics against Desdemona's perfection is voiced best by Brabantio: "She has deceiv'd her father" (I.iii.296). Desdemona is not disobedient, as sometimes she has been called; hers is not the direct defiance of Juliet or of Hermia. Brabantio looks about him one evening, and she is no longer there. She has simply disappeared, and he is put to the labor of seeking her out. Such is her deceit. Here is Christ's:

> Sonne, why hast thou thus dealt with vs? beholde, thy father and I haue soght thee with heauie hearts.
>
> Then said he vnto them, How is it that ye soght me? knewe ye not that I must go about my fathers busines?
>
> (Luke 2.48–49)

Let us reverse the sexes for the allegory, a switch made commonly in literature. Since all mortals are the body of the church, Christ the bridegroom (Desdemona) is wedded to the church (Everyman-Othello), and He (Desdemona) goes about his Father's business, which is the salvation of men (Othello). But the devil triumphs in the tug of war for Othello's soul, and Desdemona returns to heaven from whence she came.

The victory belongs in this play to Satan; his emissary fills the stage, dominates the play, and crowds all other actors off the boards, with the exception of his victim. Symbolically, in the same way that Desdemona is Othello's good angel, Iago is his bad one that "fires the good angel out." But to establish Iago as a demonic principle is not new. Many writers have suggested the idea,[15] and A. C. Bradley, in a note to *Othello*, makes a tentative jest: Iago says, "You see [Othello] is right; I *am* a devil" (his italics).[16] S. L. Bethell comes to the verge of asserting the truth of Bradley's humor but finds finally that Iago is only a "demi-devil"; he "has not quite the stature of a devil."[17] I shall pursue the notion that Iago is literally a full-fledged fiend, but if I cannot persuade my readers, then at least I should like to suggest to them an anagogical reading of the play in which, allegorically, Iago stands for a devil.

Bethell finds sixty-four "diabolic images" in *Othello* and partly on the strength of their numbers asserts that the play has a "profoundly theological structure."[18] His findings can be employed also to contend that *Othello* is a morality drama in which a

15. Robert Heilman sees him as a viper and demidevil, reminding us of Dante's fiends in the seventh bowge of the eighth circle (Canto 24). See *Magic in the Web* (Lexington, Ky., 1956), pp. 94–96. See also John Lawlor, *The Tragic Sense in Shakespeare* (New York, 1960), p. 99, and Ribner, *Patterns in Shakespearian Tragedy*, p. 111, not to mention Bradley and Bethell.

16. Bradley, *Shakespearean Tragedy*, p. 438.

17. Bethell, "Shakespeare's Imagery," p. 78.

18. Bethell, "Shakespeare's Imagery," p. 68. He finds only thirty-seven in *Macbeth*. Kenneth Myrick claims that such words as *damned, devil, hell, soul*, etc. occur in *Othello* more than in any other play of Shakespeare. See "The Theme of Damnation," p. 238.

devil from hell is an active participant, that Iago represents the Elizabethan concept of demonic temptation through direct abuse by one of hell's denizens. We know from *Hamlet* that "the devil hath power / T' assume a pleasing shape," which he employs in order to "abuse" and "damn" (II.ii.600–604) an unwary mortal. That this demonic appearance to earthly eyes must be in the form of a ghost is not maintained. Pierre le Loyer, in fourteen refutations to arguments otherwise, asserts that "God doth permit [spirits] both visibly and invisibly to tempt vs, some to their salvation, and some to their damnation."[19] Reginald Scot of course denies corporeal manifestation but in his rejection states the received beliefs: "Some hold opinion, that Spirits and Souls can assume and take unto them bodies at their pleasure, of what shape or substance they list."[20]

As can be seen, I am making of Bradley's jest a serious proposal. I want to go beyond Bethell to suggest that Shakespeare intended Iago as a visitor from hell, a devil who assumed a human shape in order to abuse the souls of men and tempt them to their damnation. If we accept this view, *Othello* becomes Shakespeare's most profound, most pessimistic tragedy. Whereas in *Hamlet* the good man's inability to pierce the disguises of evil leads to his mortal destruction, in *Othello* the completely flawless man's blindness to the demonic substance itself leads to eternal damnation. *Othello*, then, is perhaps Shakespeare's only play that unequivocally proves Christian tragedy to be possible. I. A. Richards's argument that salvation kills tragedy cannot be applied to *Othello* as it can to *Hamlet*. The Moor plays the tragedy through to eternity. The objections of those who maintain that we cannot follow a character after the final curtain are put aside. By bringing a vision of torment and punishment into the play in the terrifying imagery of Othello's last speeches, Shakespeare demands that we consider Othello's immortal destination. Judgment and damnation are the chief concerns of the play:

19. *A Treatise of Specters or Straunge Sights, Visions and Apparitions appearing Sensibly vnto men*, trans. L. Jones (London, 1605), Sig. M₄ʳ.
20. Scot, *Discouerie of Witchcraft* (London, 1584), Sig. Bbb₃ᵛ.

> When we shall meet at compt,
> This look of thine will hurl my soul from heaven,
> And fiends will snatch at it. . . .
>
> . . . .
>
> Whip me, ye devils,
> From the possession of this heavenly sight!
> Blow me about in winds! Roast me in sulphur!
> Wash me in steep-down gulfs of liquid fire!
>
> (V.ii.282–89)

Surely we were meant to consider judgment in the other great tragedies as well, but only Othello is the good man betrayed by a devil whom he cannot see, lured into an act of evil which he takes to be a sacrificial and ministerial execution, yet which "hurls [his] soul from heaven." The candle Othello brings to his task, the "flaming minister" (V.ii.8), symbolizes for him his deputizement. Her "balmy breath . . . dost almost persuade / Justice to break her sword" (V.ii.16–17)! The decision to kill Desdemona is made with an oath to God:

> Now, by yond marble heaven,
> [*Kneels.*] In the due reverence of a sacred vow
> I here engage my words.
>
> (III.iii.464–66)

Othello had thought her death a "sacrifice" (V.ii.68).

Othello is mistaken, and he does commit foul murder. But Shakespeare is trying to tell us that Othello's only flaw is blindness, a darkness that in no way could he pierce. What defense does he have? Iago's tales cannot be questioned, for the devil has established himself as honest Iago, and not a person in the play doubts him.[21] Furthermore, Desdemona has "deceived" her father, and

21. Iago's reputation for honesty with Othello, Desdemona, and Cassio, as well as Emilia's ignorance of her husband's true nature, have never received the attention they deserve. Iago's demonism does not spring full-blown into being at the moment of his disappointment over

even though we know this desertion of her parent to be her proper role as a Christ-figure, Brabantio does not understand her action (Christ's also was misunderstood); and Iago does not let Othello forget Brabantio's words: "She did deceive her father, marrying you" (III.iii.212). Thus in choice between their honesties, Othello has less cause to question Iago than he has to question Desdemona. Finally, Iago gives Othello what is almost the "ocular proof" the ensign declares it is too tedious to attempt. Too little is made of the visions Iago puts before the imaginative Othello's mind:

> naked with her friend in bed
> An hour or more, not meaning any harm?
> (IV.i.3–4)

IAGO
> Lie—

OTHELLO
> With her?

IAGO
> With her, on her; what you will.
> (IV.i.34)

> I lay with Cassio lately;
>
> . . . .
>
> In sleep I heard him say, "Sweet Desdemona,
> Let us be wary, let us hide our loves!"
> And then, sir, would he gripe and wring my hand,
> Cry, "O sweet creature!" and kiss me hard,
> As if he pluck'd up kisses by the roots
> That grew upon my lips; then laid his leg
> Over my thigh, and sigh'd and kiss'd.
> (III.iii.418–29)

Cassio's preferment. Lines 42–66 of I.i., concluding, "I am not what I am," suggest that Iago has dealt always in evil. If we ask how he has so successfully and for so long deceived these and others, Shakespeare might fetch the answer from *Hamlet*: "the devil hath power / T' assume a pleasing shape" (II.ii.600–601).

And too little is made of the scene in which Othello does indeed "grossly gape on" (IV.i.94–160) and imagine Cassio to be telling Iago "how she pluck'd him to my chamber" (140–41). Hamlet, for all his delays, required far less proof: the word of a ghost (who might have been as much a creature from hell as Iago) and the behavior of the King at a play, who may as much have blenched because the Gonzago episode employed the incest theme as because it showed a murder.

Othello, then, is a good man destroyed even to damnation, the tragic victim in a morality play in which the contestants for his soul are an angelic wife and an actual demon.

As all students of Shakespeare know, the single most pervasive theme, running throughout almost the entire canon, is that of false appearances. Deception is intricately tied in with the problem that is the crux of this play: the inability of the good man to perceive evil. In *Othello*, the audience, as in most Shakespeare plays, is immediately apprised of what no person in the play knows—except Roderigo, who is told by Iago himself: Iago is not the honest man which everyone takes him to be. As the play opens, the audience is thrust into a topsy-turvy world: the good seems evil, the evil good. Ultimately, Iago will be proved a devil, but to everyone he appears honest. Othello (at the beginning of the play) is a completely good man; but until trial of him is made, he appears to be a devil. Desdemona, also good, at first looks evil. These reversals are what happens in the world of unarmed perceptions. With slight effort one may know the good man. It would seem then an inescapable corollary that immediately thereafter he would know the bad; but such is not the case simply because evil, with comparative ease, disguises itself successfully. It gets the help even of the good man who employs no deception himself and seldom looks for any.

As Iago tells Roderigo his true nature, indicating the lengths to which he will go to mask his inner hate, he turns the world upside down:

> In following him, I follow but myself—
> Heaven is my judge, not I for love and duty,

But seeming so, for my peculiar end.
For when my outward action doth demonstrate
The native act and figure of my heart
In compliment extern, 'tis not long after
But I will wear my heart upon my sleeve
For daws to peck at. I am not what I am.

(I.i.59–66)

Honest men are knaves (I.i.50), and only villains have souls (55). But chiefly the good man must be made to appear the very devil himself. The Elizabethan demon was black, not the red of modern color-cartoonists. Iago stresses Othello's color, "an old black ram" (I.i.89) who is about the business of all devils, the taking of souls to hell: "you have lost half your soul" (I.i.88). And if nobody gets the point about Othello's color, Iago drops subtlety and cries out, "Arise . . . / Or else the devil will make a grandsire of you" (I.i.90–92). Apparently he has convinced Brabantio, who calls Othello either a devil or practicer of demonic art at least eight times. It should be remembered that *foul* meant *devilish* in a strict denotative sense and that *foul thief* was specifically *the devil*.[22] Brabantio, in I.ii, berates Othello as "foul thief" (63), "Damn'd as thou art" (64), "abuser of the world" (79).[23] He charges that Othello has "practic'd on her with foul charms" (74), "abus'd her" (75), practiced "arts inhibited" (80), "abus'd" (again, I.iii.62), and employed "witchcraft" (I.iii.66) and "practices of cunning hell" (I.iii.104).

Desdemona is made to seem bad only insofar as she has deceived her father.

Iago, except for his confession to Roderigo, is already known, as the play opens, as a good man. He helps his pretense along in these beginning scenes with understatement of his virtue, a reticence the good man is supposed naturally to have: "I hold it

22. See *OED* entry 7 under *foul* and entry 2 under *fiend*.
23. *Abuse* seems to carry the sense of causing a person to fall to reprobation. See *OED* citation of Lyndesay, *Mon.* I.1004, "Rychtso the woman hir excusit, / And said: 'the serpent me abusit.'" Hamlet also employs the word in such a sense: The devil, perhaps, "Abuses me to damn me" (II.ii.600–604).

the very stuff o' th' conscience / To do no contriv'd murder. I lack
iniquity" (I.ii.2–3); "with the little godliness I have, / I did full
hard forbear him" (I.ii.9–10). We learn first of Iago's success in
disguising his true nature when Othello puts Desdemona into his
keeping with the proclamation that "A man he is of honesty and
trust" (I.iii.287).

However, by I.iii, much of the wrong has been righted. The
Moor's symbolic blackness is washed away. First there are his own
claims: "my perfect soul" (I.ii.31) and "as truly as to heaven / I do
confess the vices of my blood" (I.iii.124–25). Since there proves
none, Othello is observed to be a practicing Christian of immacu-
late human virtue. In his long speech (I.iii.130–72), Othello employs such terms as *redemption*, *heaven* (twice), and *prayer*, which
emphasize his good standing in the religion of his conversion. The
whole of the pre-Cypriot scenes ends with Othello established as
"far more fair than black" (I.iii.293), with Desdemona as undeceit-
ful (at least in Othello's eyes), "My life upon her faith!" (I.iii.297),
but with Iago still "honest Iago" (I.iii.297). The good people have
been exonerated easily from false charges that have arisen from
false appearances. But the evil fiend has kept his mask entire.

I have shown so far only that Iago is not what he appears to
be: "I am not what I am" (I.i.66). But in the pre-Cypriot scenes,
which comprise all three of the first act, Iago gives the first clue to
his true identity by indicating that the only emotion of which he is
capable is hate (I.i.7–9). A devil's purpose is to win souls from potential bliss and send them to hell. Is not that Iago's purpose?

> Call up her father.
> Rouse him, make after him, poison his delight,
> Proclaim him in the streets; incense her kinsmen,
> And, though he in a fertile climate dwell,
> Plague him with flies.
>
> (I.i.68–72)

While Othello is with the angel/Christ (Desdemona), he is, in a
sense, in paradise ("fertile climate"); Iago, who knows what punishments are to be found in hell, means to send him there ("Plague

him with flies"). Iago need not be specifically identified with Beelzebub, the lord of flies; only as one of his agents, who plans to send a soul to his master's domain.

Similarly, as Iago goes forward with his plan, he must pervert Roderigo to his designs. The seduction is cast in a garden (and we remember again the "fertile climate"):

> Our bodies are our gardens, to the which our wills are
> gardeners; so that if we will plant nettles or sow lettuce,
> set hyssop and weed up thyme, supply it with one gen-
> der of herbs or distract it with many, either to have it
> sterile with idleness or manur'd with industry—
>
> (I.iii.323–28)

the management of Eden is within our own strength, rule, and election—

> why, the power and corrigible authority of this lies in
> our wills.
>
> (I.iii.328–29)

Love is only "a sect or scion" of lust (334–35).

Othello must also be seduced. The delicacies of the garden in which he at the moment resides with Desdemona will, if Iago succeeds, lose the Moor paradise:

> The food that to him now is as luscious as locusts shall
> be to him shortly as bitter as coloquintida.
>
> (I.iii.350–52)

Coloquintida is known commonly as bitter apple.

Iago likes to flirt with discovery by masking true statements behind phrases he expects no one to believe. As he cries up to Brabantio at the senator's window, he warns, "you are one of those that will not serve God if the devil bid you" (I.i.109–10). Who but the devil bids him? In this light, the phrase "with the little godliness I have" (I.ii.9) can be taken literally. He has none. Brabantio, with unknown truth, a device Shakespeare uses often, calls him "profane" (I.i.115), etymologically, "outside the temple," and thus outside the grace of God.

As a devil, Iago is something of an artist of damnation. When Roderigo threatens to drown himself, first Iago says, "If thou dost, I shall never love thee after" (I.iii.309). Roderigo as a suicide would be damned and devils in hell spend only hate upon each other. But suicide would allow Iago no finesse; he will have a hand in the action. Besides, if Roderigo is kept alive, perhaps he can be used to draw other souls down with him, as Iago indeed tries to use him:

> If thou wilt needs damn thyself, do it a more delicate
> way than drowning. . . . A pox of drowning thyself! It
> is clean out of the way. Seek thou rather to be hang'd
> in compassing thy joy than to be drown'd and go with-
> out her.
>
> (I.iii.355–63)

Who knows! if Desdemona succumbs, Iago might throw her soul into his bag; and if Othello seeks revenge, Iago gets his too, not merely this puny, practically-forfeited-already soul of Roderigo's.

Iago apparently can call on the help of other hell-denizens: "If sanctimony and a frail vow . . . be not too hard for my wits and *all the tribe of hell*, thou shalt enjoy her" (I.iii.357–60, my italics). In fact, he will need help: "Hell and night / Must bring this monstrous birth to the world's light" (I.iii.404–5). As Iago sneaks away from under Brabantio's window so as not to be exposed, he reassures Roderigo, "I do hate [Othello] as I do hell-pains" (I.i.156). We might query: how does he know hell's pains unless he has felt them? All these arguments will be attacked perhaps on the grounds that they are based on figures of speech which all persons use in moments of duress, and I should have to admit the truth of such an observation. But the weight of evidence, already somewhat impressive in its plenitude, is only a small fraction of its sort. Similar materials can be gathered from all parts of the play, and although

I shall cite more of it, I trust the reader will believe that much more shall remain uncited.

However, of more significance than this linguistic evidence of Act I are two special matters that further support the idea of Iago as a devil. The first begins at line 82 of I.i. Shakespeare brings Brabantio onto the Globe balcony to set up a physical relationship between the senator and Iago in which the older man peers down as though into a black pit. Various speeches imply that little light is anywhere, but especially is it dark below. Brabantio cannot see at all. He learns that one of two men below is Roderigo only because he is so informed. Iago does not reveal himself, ostensibly so that he can be on both sides at once. Symbolically the scene establishes the impossibility of the good man to see a villain. Exactly at this moment, as Brabantio peers down toward the sound of Iago's voice, crying up to him *de profundus*, Brabantio gives Iago unknowingly his proper epithet, "profane," outside the temple, outside of grace, outside of heaven, a denizen, in fact, of hell, the pit of darkness. Shakespeare follows through with the belief that evil cannot bear light. As Brabantio cries out to strike tinder, bring tapers, Iago whispers ambiguously to Roderigo that to be discovered is not "wholesome to my place" (I.i.144).

The second matter concerns the ancient's ability to have certain information which it seems impossible for him to possess. As Iago departs from Roderigo in the scene just outlined, he says,

> he's embark'd
> With such loud reason to the Cyprus wars,
> Which even now stands in act, that, for their souls,[24]
> Another of his fathom they have none.
> (I.i.151–54)

We might ask how Iago has obtained this information. Only an ensign, he is better briefed than his general, Othello. Iago utters more than mere rumor. The information is specific, and it seems knowledge that not even the council yet has. The words *Which even now stands in act* indicate the very moment the council debates; and

24. Note that Iago has his mind always upon business: souls.

when we get to the council scene in I.iii., we find that neither the Duke nor any senator is as informed as Iago. A messenger arrives to say Rhodes will be the site of action, but a second, with later news, clears the council's confusion, reporting that the Turkish fleet heads for Cyprus. Iago, not present and, we may assume, never privy to council debates, was sure it would be Cyprus. The implication of this knowledge is that Iago has supernatural powers. Either he is prescient or he has runners from hell to supply him with dispatches. The latter is a strong possibility, since he plans to use "all the tribe of hell" (I.iii.359–60) in his campaign to destroy Othello. Later in the play occurs a second instance of actual support for Iago from demonic cohelpers.

Along these same lines we may explain the arrival of the ships at Cyprus. We know that Othello leaves Venice the night the council calls him (I.iii.281) and that Iago, bringing Desdemona, cannot leave until after nine o'clock the following morning (I.iii.282). But despite tempests raging on the seas which impede and delay Othello, Iago arrives first. Cassio explains how: not because Iago, with demonic powers, has control of the elements, but rather because Desdemona, at this very moment termed "divine" (II.i.74), has powers like those of Christ when he calmed the waters at Gennesaret:

> And there arose a great storme of winde, & the waues
> dashed into the ship, so that it was now ful . . . . And
> he rose vp, and rebuked the winde, and said vnto the
> sea, Peace, and be stil.
>
> (Mark 4.37–39)

Cassio describes Desdemona's passage:

> Tempests themselves, high seas, and howling winds,
> The gutter'd rocks and congregated sands—
> Traitors ensteep'd to clog the guiltless keel—
> As having sense of beauty, do omit
> Their mortal natures, letting go safely by
> The divine Desdemona.
>
> (II.i.69–74)

95

The words *traitors* and *guiltless* seem to have pointed application to a Christ figure.

We have reached the point in the play where the battle over Othello's soul must begin. All the principals have gathered at Cyprus. The forces for good and evil have been identified, and their purposes to go about their heaven- and hell-directed designs have been stated. Othello is to be seen at this point consonant with flawless goodness,[25] standing in a state of grace. On his ship's docking, he approaches Desdemona not with terms we expect of lovers separated by duty and still to consummate their marriage night (II.iii.10) but rather with a sense of spiritual serenity:

> It gives me wonder great as my content
> To see you here before me. O my soul's joy!
> If after every tempest come such calms
> May the winds blow till they have waken'd death!
> And let the laboring bark climb hills of seas
> Olympus-high, and duck again as low
> As hell's from heaven! If it were now to die,
> 'Twere now to be most happy; for, I fear,
> My soul hath her content so absolute
> That not another comfort like to this
> Succeeds in unknown fate.
>
> (II.i.181–91)

I have commented already on the miraculous nature of Desdemona's arrival in Cyprus before Othello's, but its importance is stressed, enforced upon us, by Othello's wonder at the miracle and his contentment with its covenant. The contentment is of the soul. Desdemona, as Christ, is of course his "soul's joy." If Christ awaits after the storms of life, let death come soon. If life is a constant ship-journey, filled with near disasters, destruction coming when a person is in danger of hell or when he is close to heaven (Olympus), these vagaries of fortune are unimportant, just so calm of the soul comes after. Othello knows that at his arrival in Cyprus he is guilt-

25. "My perfect soul / Shall manifest me rightly" (I.ii.31–32).

less of any sins. His faith in Desdemona symbolizes his acceptance of his savior and that "If it were now to die, / 'Twere now to be most happy." The most complete state of happiness is beatitude. If Othello dies sinless and with faith, salvation is his reward.

Othello makes one mistake, common enough, thinking that the idea a mortal has of heavenly bliss is consummate, but Desdemona, the proper spokesman on all matters of faith, corrects him in phrases that take the form of a collect: "The heavens forbid / But that our loves and comforts should increase, / Even as our days do grow!" (II.i.191–93). Desdemona puts no limit to their days, and love does not end with mortality. If Othello forgot his catechism for the moment, he comes quickly under his heavenly tutor's instruction and responds with the very amen with which all collects conclude.[26] Scene i of Act II then is all Desdemona's; but lest we forget her demonic adversary, the scene ends with a soliloquy by Iago.

The rest of the second act is employed by Iago to accomplish Cassio's disgrace. Scene ii provides a prayerful hope, dramatically to be defeated, that "Heaven bless the isle of Cyprus and our noble general Othello!" (II.ii.10–11). Scene iii places Cassio in charge and contains Othello's ironic reminder that "Iago is most honest" (II.iii.6) just prior to the point where Iago's "honesty" comes close to destroying Cassio utterly. Iago, as devil, will take what souls he can get. Cassio becomes a potential victim, and Iago does his best; but it becomes clear in this scene, at the very moment that Cassio sinks to his lowest, that redemption is a lively possibility for him. He has the requisite faith; he needs only Christ's intercession for him. Desdemona will plead his cause, and we know that his later repentance saves him.[27] Shakespeare, as is typical, prognosticates a little on these matters:

26. I have in mind the collect of the Anglican burial service: "grant that increasing in knowledge and love of thee [we] may go from strength to strength . . . in the heavenly kingdom."

27. For a view allotting to Cassio a much more important role in the eschatological concerns of the play, see Bryant, *Hippolyta's View*, p. 140: "Othello . . . reflects, if anything, the office of God and . . . Cassio, not Othello, stands as Shakespeare's figure of Adam."

CASSIO

> Well, God's above all; and there be souls must
> be sav'd, and there be souls must not be
> sav'd.

IAGO

> It's true, good lieutenant.

CASSIO

> For mine own part—no offense to the general,
> nor any man of quality—I hope to be sav'd.

IAGO

> And so do I too, lieutenant.

CASSIO

> Ay, but, by your leave, not before me; the
> lieutenant is to be sav'd before the
> ancient. . . . God forgive us our sins!

$$(\text{II.iii.97}-107)$$

Cassio believes that God is above all; he asks for pardon. He hopes to be saved. Iago's answers are ironic; he misleads Cassio throughout the scene. Yet, I would understand him to say, "true, good lieutenant" with a special gleam in his eye for that part of Cassio's speech that mentions the souls to be "not sav'd." Prophetically, Cassio will be saved before both Othello and Iago, since they are not to be saved at all.

As he has implied at least twice before, Iago needs the help of his fellow devils in hell to accomplish some acts beyond his individual powers. To create a mutiny in Cyprus, Iago and Roderigo are not enough. As Iago both eggs on and seems to part Montano and Cassio, Roderigo is sent through the streets to cry mutiny; but it is some third creature who rouses the entire town (II.iii.156) by tolling the alarum bell. Even Iago is surprised momentarily. He knows where Roderigo is employed. "Who's that which rings the bell" (II.iii.155) so helpful to his enterprise? Immediately thereafter he realizes his aid has come from those forces invoked at I.iii.404–5; and he cries out his helper's name, "Diablo, ho!" (II.iii.155).

A considerable number of what we might call morality-play terms then follow the appearance of Othello, wakened from his nuptial bed and taken freshly from the "divine" Desdemona: *heaven, Christian shame, holds his soul light, self-charity, sin, foul, love, God forbid,* etc. But there is a very special bit in which Shakespeare associates Cassio's fall directly with the devil. Although wine has been the agent, wine is apostrophized as the devil himself: "O thou invisible spirit of wine, if thou hast no name to be known by, let us call thee devil!" (II.iii.275–77). "It hath pleas'd the devil drunkenness to give place to the devil wrath" (II.iii.290–91). "Every inordinate cup is unbless'd, and the ingredient is a devil" (II.iii.301–2). As the scene comes to its end and to Iago's third soliloquy, we are reminded again of the tug of war: Desdemona is full of "graces" (312), "holds it a vice in her goodness not to do more than she is requested" (314–16),[28] and is "virtuous" (324).

Iago, who is "honest" right up to the moment of his soliloquy (329), and who plays with great delight upon his "reputation," identifies himself unmistakably after all auditors are cleared from the stage:

> And what's he then that says I play the villain?
> When this advice is free I give and honest,
>
> . . . .
>
>   For 'tis most easy
> Th' inclining Desdemona to subdue
> In any honest suit; she's fram'd as fruitful
> As the free elements.
>
> . . . .
>
>   Divinity of hell!
> When devils will the blackest sins put on,
> They do suggest at first with heavenly shows,
> As I do now. . . .
> So will I turn her virtue into pitch,

28. "And whosoeuer wil compell thee to go a mile, go with him twaine" (Matt. 5.41).

And out of her own goodness make the net
That shall enmesh them all.
(II.iii.330–56)

Iago's method is clear. He had employed it with Othello in the opening scenes. As he had called Othello black in order to identify him with the devil, so must he establish Desdemona's blackness ("turn her virtue into pitch") while he continues to emphasize his heavenly purposes ("honest" advice and "heavenly shows"). But these are the ways of hell—false appearances that cannot be penetrated by the virtuous man, neither by Othello nor by Cassio. (Desdemona herself—in the helpless condition of her incarnation—will be "subdued" easily by what she cannot perceive is other than an "honest suit.") That Iago is a demon from hell he confesses in soliloquy: "Divinity of hell!" "Heavenly shows" are employed by "devils" when they "will the blackest sins put on."[29] Here we have Shakespeare's most complete statement of the central theme of his play. God expects man to exercise his free will in right choice, but, the poet laments in this alone of all his plays, man does not have the tools required to do the job. If this is heresy, it is not the critic who invents it in an otherwise orthodox Christian play; it is a heresy to which Shakespeare fell subject. It is a heresy of deep despair, a heresy that makes possible, even if paradoxically only, a Christian tragedy.

Acts III and IV continue the campaigns of Iago in his demonic work; in these acts his iniquity reaches high-water mark when he has turned successfully the entire world of Othello topsy-turvy. The honest Cassio is made to appear dishonest; the white Desdemona is made to appear black; the "fair" Othello is actually turned black; and the evil Iago continues to appear honest.

First, the honesty of Iago is spread and reasserted. In III.i. Cassio calls the fiend "A Florentine . . . kind and honest" (43). In III.iii. Desdemona adds her testimony: "O, that's an honest fellow" (5). Iago, very modestly, announces himself to be honest in four separate speeches: III.iii.158, III.iii.380–85, III.iii.417,

29. See discussion on pp. 31–32.

and IV.i.278. Othello, chief victim, despite one outburst of raging doubt, seals his officer blameless also: III.iii.123, III.iii.249,
III.iii.264, and III.iii.390.

Cassio, already soiled in the drinking bout, must be made to
appear dishonest in the usual Elizabethan sense of unchaste. True,
Desdemona remains undeceived as to Cassio's virtue and employs
her special powers for his redemption:

> If I have any grace or power to move you,
> His present reconciliation take;
> For if he be not one that truly loves you,
> That errs in ignorance and not in cunning,
> I have no judgment in an honest face.
>   (III.iii.46–50) [30]

But Othello succumbs to evil's deception: "Ha! I like not that"
(III.iii.35). Iago's reluctant exposure of his friend is well known,
"Honest, my lord? . . . / My lord, for aught I know" (III.iii.106–8).
With incredible irony Iago speaks the words that describe himself but which are meant to destroy Cassio: "Men should be what
they seem; / Or those that be not, would they might seem none!"
(III.iii.131–32). With the warning put before him, out of the mouth
of the enemy himself, Othello is unable to penetrate the disguises
of evil or the veils of darkness that evil can cast over the visage of
goodness. So successful is Iago's misrepresentation of Cassio that
Othello calls for his lieutenant's death by the end of the same scene
in which Iago began his machinations: "Within these three days let
me hear thee say / That Cassio's not alive" (III.iii.476–77).

Such a triumph of malignity is awesome. But it pales compared to Iago's achievement in blackening Desdemona. As III.iii.
opens, Desdemona, as she should be, is the darling of Othello's
soul. I select the word *soul* with careful choice, for Shakespeare has

---

30. Notice in lines 62–64 immediately following, Desdemona
uses such terms as *faith, penitent,* and *trespass,* and urges that Cassio's rein-
statement—his resurrection, so to speak—not be put off longer than
"three days."

enforced it on us. All other meaning that Othello's love for Desdemona might include has been thrust carefully into the background. The physical side of their love is constantly downplayed.
At III.iii.68, Othello wonders in his "soul" what his beloved might
ask and he deny. At this point also Othello's grace, his union with
his Christ/angel is asserted:

> Perdition catch my soul
> But I do love thee! And when I love thee not,
> Chaos is come again.
> (III.iii.92–94)

But then Iago begins his poison, and significantly, *foul* is one
of the first words he chooses to describe Desdemona (III.iii.240).[31]
Since *foul* means *demonic* or *fiendlike*, in Othello's mind clearly
Desdemona has assumed that pitchlike hue to which Iago vowed
he would alter her:

> Her name, that was as fresh
> As Dian's visage, is now begrim'd and black
> As mine own face.
> (III.iii.391–93)

Changed to a devil, she now deserves damnation in Othello's eyes;
terms and titles of his new view of her illustrate Iago's success:
"Damn her, lewd minx! O, damn her, damn her" (III.iii.479), "fair
devil" (III.iii.482), "here's a young and sweating devil" (III.iv.42),
"It is hypocrisy against the devil" (IV.i.6), "be damn'd tonight"
(IV.i.180–81), "Devil" (IV.i.241), "O devil, devil" (IV.i.245), "damn
thyself" (IV.ii.35), "be double damn'd" (IV.ii.37), "thou art false as
hell" (IV.ii.39). All these vituperations lead to Othello's identification of Emilia as the guardian of Desdemona's new and foul
abode:

> You, mistress,
> That have the office opposite to Saint Peter,

31. He uses it again at IV.i.200 and 202.

And keep the gate of hell!
                    (IV.ii.90–92)

These same acts, III and IV, are, of course, also the acts of Othello's real destruction. Although Desdemona's reputation with Othello is destroyed and her body is sacrificed in the ensuing fifth act, and although Cassio's position worsens and worsens, Desdemona's soul goes off to heaven and Cassio's redemption is obtained and his honor and rank restored. But Othello's downfall bears it out even to the edge of doom. From the beginning of Act III, where Othello's soul is in a state of grace, a change takes place which is signaled first by Othello himself reminding us of the color of his skin (III.iii.269). Reestablished, this time properly, as one doomed to be a denizen of hell, Othello gives up his part in salvation:

All my fond love thus do I blow to heaven.
'Tis gone.
Arise, black vengeance, from the hollow hell!
Yield up, O love, thy crown and hearted throne
To tyrannous hate! Swell, bosom, with thy fraught,
For 'tis of aspics' tongues!
                    (III.iii.449–54)

Much doubt has arisen about the point exactly at which Othello succumbs to Iago's devices, the point at which he is convinced of Desdemona's adultery; but no doubt can exist in terms of the demonic imagery of the play. Iago who has desired promotion gets it: "Now art thou my lieutenant" (III.iii.482). With what we know of Iago now, this lieutenancy is a subalternate of evil. Iago has become a Mephistopheles to Othello's Faustus. The true demon will help the reprobate accomplish any iniquity, but, of course, the price is the bargainer's eternal jewel. When Iago says subsequently, "I am your own for ever" (III.iii.483), "for ever" has a special ring. These two will keep eternal watch among infernal legions. Additional imagery to suggest the change in Othello can be found in Desdemona's fear that something "Hath puddled his clear spirit"

(III.iv.144). But we must wait until Act V to complete the portrait of the damned Othello.

In Acts III and IV, then, Shakespeare has allowed his demonic villain successfully to turn the world topsy-turvy, making all things good seem bad and the one thing bad continue to seem good. Yet the playwright must keep going his subtle control, indicating the true state of things. Thus, he continues to expose Iago to the audience as the actual demon we have learned him to be in earlier scenes. We are reminded that Iago is an expert on souls, "Good name in man and woman, dear my lord, / Is the immediate jewel of their souls" (III.iii.160–61). He goes quickly about to destroy the "good names" of Cassio, Desdemona, and Othello. Othello, on the rack, cries out, "By heaven, I'll know thy thoughts," but, as Iago informs him, "You cannot" (III.iii.167–68). Not in heaven are the kind of thoughts found which Iago harbors. Iago, as a sometime citizen of hell, knows that hints of infidelity in the beloved of a jealous man "Burn like the mines of sulphur" (III.iii.334). And, as Othello takes his new oath by hell, Iago becoming his true lieutenant in evil, the real demon performs a ritualistic heaven-defying companion oath, establishing him most pointedly as a Mephistophelian agent:

> Do not rise yet.
> [*Kneels.*] Witness, you ever-burning lights above,
> You elements that clip us round about,
> Witness that here Iago doth give up
> The execution of his wit, hands, heart,
> To wrong'd Othello's service! Let him command,
> And to obey shall be in me remorse,
> What bloody business ever.
> (III.iii.466–73)

Several of Iago's own statements are of the sort that toy with self-exposure: "I mock you not, by heaven" (IV.i.60) and "I am a very villain else" (IV.i.126) are two of them. Not by heaven does Iago mock Othello, but by hell; and assuredly he is the villain he says he is when the tone in which he says it implies he is none. Unwitting identification of Iago as devil is also prominent. Othello, just prior to his epileptic trance, and, perhaps, in his unnatural state given direct vision for one brief moment, cries out as he swoons, "O devil" (IV.i.43). Previously, he nicked truth in near recognition of Iago's exact nature:

> If thou dost slander her and torture me,
> Never pray more; abandon all remorse;
> On horror's head horrors accumulate;
> Do deeds to make heaven weep, all earth amaz'd;
> For nothing canst thou to damnation add
> Greater than that.
>
> (III.iii.373–78)

Othello describes a second rebellion in heaven and a second fall of angels. The slander of Desdemona is an attack upon the Godhead, after which the damnation reaped by the offending devil is rendered in secondary imagery anticipating Milton's "dungeon horrible" (*Paradise Lost*, I.61).

Even Bianca hits upon the truth when, nettled over the handkerchief Cassio has asked her to copy, she shouts at him, "Let the devil and his dam haunt you" (IV.i.147), as indeed the devilish Iago has haunted him in the likeness of a man. But the most profound, though unwitting, identification comes from Emilia, the fiend's mortal wife, incapable herself of perceiving Iago's demonic nature after some period of marriage. What name to give her visionary monster she does not know, but she can portray his dimensions (I have italicized the terms of Iago's eschatological identification):

> If any wretch have put this in your head,
> Let heaven requite it with the *serpent's curse*!
>
> (IV.ii.15–16)

> I will be hang'd if some *eternal* villain
>
> . . . .
>
> Have not devis'd this slander.
>
> (IV.ii.132–35)

A halter pardon him! And *hell gnaw his bones!*

.   .   .   .

The Moor's *abus'd* by some most villainous knave.

                (IV.ii.138–41)

Iago himself comments on one of his wife's outbursts, laughing in-wardly to himself: "Fie, there is no such man" (IV.ii.136). He is both wrong and right: wrong in the sense that there is such a crea-ture; he himself is it; right in the sense that there is no such man; for man he is none, only evil spirit.[32]

As I have indicated, some readers find it difficult to deter-mine exactly at what point Othello succumbs to Iago's vilifications. Desdemona seems also not to know precisely when or even how she, as guardian angel/Christ savior, has lost Othello's soul to the enemy: "by this light of heaven, / I know not how I lost him" (IV.ii.152–53). She functions in this speech both as supernatural creature and as mortal wife, who like the other ordinary mortals of the play cannot see through the masks of evil.

Emilia prays that heaven uncover the abusers of man, for man cannot do it by himself:

O heaven, that such companions thou'dst unfold,
And put in every honest hand a whip
To lash the rascals naked through the world
Even from the east to th' west!

                (IV.ii.143–46)

32. Shakespeare enjoys this sort of flummoxing. Cf. the clown in *Hamlet*:

HAMLET
    What man dost thou dig [the grave] for?
FIRST CLOWN
    For no man, sir.
HAMLET
    What woman, then?
FIRST CLOWN
    For none, neither.

The central theme again is evoked. Unless evil is paraded naked through the world to its verges for all men to see, no man may help himself, no man stand up against evil as an unreasonable God requires. Surely this is extreme boldness, a despairing utterance, but such, I believe, was Shakespeare's mood at the writing of *Othello*. Meanwhile, Iago gloats triumphantly; Othello seems lost; Desdemona is disgraced. The devil has new victims in his continuing program of damnation. He has had such successes before, and he or his demonic fellows will have others after:

> Work on,
> My medicine, work! Thus credulous fools are
>   caught;
> And many worthy and chaste dames even thus,
> All guiltless, meet reproach.
>   (IV.i.44–47)

This speech is an extremely important one, always overlooked, even in the motiveless malignity discussions. What point can Shakespeare hope to make about chaste women, "All guiltless," being branded faithless? Who goes about destroying the name of chastity? What creature adds name on name to a list he keeps of those who have been unjustly maligned? The answer to all these questions is the same: only an obdurate demon.

The play comes in Act V to the fruition of Iago's labors. He has won the Moor to evil, and only the deeds that grow out of that

---

HAMLET
> Who is to be buried in 't?

FIRST CLOWN
> One that was a woman, sir, but, rest her soul, she's
>   dead.
>   (V.i.130–36)

Also cf. *Macbeth* (in light of my discussion on p. 173):

> I dare do all that may become a man;
> Who dares do more is none.
>   (I.vii.47–48)

evil need be perpetrated. But, of the other persons Iago has jug-gled with, Cassio has escaped Iago's snares for his soul: "He hath a daily beauty in his life / That makes me ugly" (V.i.19–20). If the soul cannot be won to hell, Iago will spread as much pain and tor-ment as he can. Like Milton's Satan, "To do aught good never will be [his] task" (*Paradise Lost*, I.159). Cassio then will simply be killed. Roderigo's soul may be presumed forfeit so far as Iago is con-cerned. He has only to kill this "young quat" to reap the bounty for hell. Significant at this point is Roderigo's dying cry: "O damn'd Iago! O inhuman dog!" (V.i.63). Is this that momentary vision of fading mortality in which a person has a flashing glimpse of the angels or demons that will carry him to heaven or to hell? Roderigo calls him damned as all devils are, and he calls him inhuman as is any satanic creature. Doglike is reminiscent of the dog-faced de-mons of pictorial representation, and possibly an outgrowth of the juvenile atheism of the day, such as that of the so-called School of Night, which took, we are told, delight "to spell God backwarde." [33]

For Desdemona it is time to leave. The soul under her guid-ance, she "know[s] not how [she] lost" (IV.ii.153). But she must re-turn to heaven. Her departure is worked out in the action of the play in terms of her murder by Othello, an economical device for the playwright, who must engage Othello in some damnable act. Desdemona is still the blackened wife of Iago's plot. Othello, who purposes only a sacrificial execution, exhorts his victim to prayer, confession, and repentance (V.ii.26–34). The language of the first sixty lines of V.ii. is replete with terms that, though they falsely rep-resent the condition of the souls of both Desdemona and Othello, remind us that the play's chief concern is eschatological: *soul* (4 times), *heaven[ly]* (five times), *pray'd*, *crime* (in the sense of sin), *grace*, *unprepared spirit*, *amen* (twice), *sin[s]* (twice), and *justice* (in the sense of heavenly justice). And thus, like Christ, Desdemona goes to a death of opprobrium unjustly. [34]

33. Robert Parson's well-known claim against Ralegh and others in his *Responsio ad Elizabethae edictum*. Quoted in F. S. Boas, *Marlowe and His Circle* (London, 1931), p. 71.

34. Siegel, *Shakespearean Tragedy*, pp. 132–34, points out the con-siderable amount of Christ symbolism that attaches to Desdemona. Fur-

After her death Shakespeare must right the upside-down world that Iago has created. God's agent put forward to tear the veil from the eyes of Iago's wretched victim is Emilia. As Othello tries to justify the murder, Emilia unmasks the true victim, the deluded sinner:

OTHELLO
> She's like a liar gone to burning hell!

EMILIA
> O, the more angel she,
> And you the blacker devil!

. . . .

EMILIA
> thou art a devil.

. . . .

EMILIA
> O, she was heavenly true!

. . . .

OTHELLO
> O, I were damn'd beneath all depth in hell
> But that I did proceed upon just grounds.
>
> (V.ii.134–43)

Following these exchanges, Iago must be brought upon the scene to be proved no longer "honest." Anticipating his arrival, Emilia, who will be his interrogator, describes what may perhaps be the increased torments God will heap upon him for his new iniquities: "may his pernicious soul / Rot half a grain a day!" (V.ii.162–63). During her questions to Iago she leagues herself with heaven, her husband with hell: "You told a . . . damned lie! / Upon my soul" (V.ii.187–88). When Iago tries to put the lie upon her, she retorts, "By heaven, I do not [lie]" (V.ii.239), and, again, "So come my soul

---

ther typology might be seen in "When I have pluck'd the rose" (V.ii.13) and "I'll smell thee on the tree" (V.ii.15). Although, in tradition, the rose is more frequently a symbol for Mary, occasionally the metaphor stands for Christ. See p. 138 below and the appertaining footnote, number 19.

to bliss, as I speak true" (V.ii.259).[35] With these words she dies and her testimony is completed. But she has unhooded Othello, who at last sees clearly but too late. He wonders, as perhaps does Shakespeare in this play, why the forces of good have not smashed flat this demon: "Are there no stones in heaven?" (V.ii.242). Montano identifies Iago as a soul chained in hell, "a damned slave" (V.ii.251).

With these same words, Desdemona is recognizable again by all who had mistaken her; she is now "the sweetest innocent" (V.ii.206) who, like the Christ she stands for, may say, "A guiltless death I die" (V.ii.127). Thus Cassio is exonerated, although he remains forgotten, is unmentioned in the rectification of these misrepresentations. Only in the whirlwind final catastrophe, there too almost as an afterthought, is Cassio explicitly recognized. He gently informs his general he gave no cause for mistrust, and Othello believes him and asks his pardon. Cassio replaces Othello as ruler in Cyprus, where it remains for him to torment the usurped body of Iago and ultimately put an end to its upper-earth existence until, perhaps, commissioned by his infernal master, he invests another mortal body to do immeasurable harm to unnumbered Othellos, the counterparts to the fallen Moor, themselves unable to cope with the deceptions of evil.

As for Othello, complete self-recognition comes as he looks upon his bloody deed with eyes unsealed for the first time. He knows finally that Iago is a "precious villain" (V.ii.243) and that therefore Desdemona and Cassio were completely virtuous. What then must he be? He had been valiant, courageous, honest, unblemished, a pure soul, put in the ward of a guardian angel. But he could not see his angel for what she was and could not distinguish his devil. Though he was all that was good, he is none of these things now:

> I am not valiant neither,
> But every puny whipster gets my sword.

35. If I were directing a performance, I would have Emilia glare directly at Iago when she cries, "Let . . . devils, let them all, / All, all, cry shame against me, yet I'll speak" (V.ii.228–29). Iago is the one who bids her hold her tongue.

But why should honor outlive honesty?
Let it go all.

> (V.ii.252−55)

The critics who believe Othello to win through to salvation after all do not make enough of his attitude, begun in this speech: "Let it go all." He repents clearly for the murder of Desdemona, but he repudiates God, and with God he rejects salvation. He wants no part of it. Whatever theology we read by—Catholic, Calvinist, Anglican—personal acceptance of the savior is requisite. Yet Othello has wished it "go all." He does not reach toward heaven; he does not embrace God; rather he yearns toward hell; he calls for demons:

> O ill-starr'd wench!
> . . . When we shall meet at compt,
> This look of thine will hurl my soul from heaven,
> And fiends will snatch at it.
>
> . . . .
>
> Whip me, ye devils,
> From the possession of this heavenly sight!
> Blow me about in winds! Roast me in sulphur!
> Wash me in steep-down gulfs of liquid fire!
>
> (V.ii.281−89)

Othello's plea is an antimask of penitence. He has deemed himself beyond God's grace; he has determined already to take his own life. The great penitential psalm—used also at the Catholic burial service—gives Othello a pattern for his renunciation of God. Desdemona at "compt" will be both victim and judge. Whereas the penitent of Psalm 51 begs that God "Hide thy face from my sinnes, and put awaie all mine iniquities," Othello knows that the Christ/Desdemona's "look . . . will hurl [his] soul from heaven." The penitent pleads,

> Wash me throughly from mine iniquitie, and clense
> me from my sinne.
>
> . . . .

Purge me with hyssope, and I shal be cleane: wash
me, & I shalbe whiter then snowe.

Othello asks that his lavings be in "liquid fire," his purgings in "sulphur." "Cast me not awaie from thy presence, and take not thine
holie Spirit from me," cries the penitent. Othello, already hurled
away, wants further to be whipped "From possession," blown "about
in winds."

Here is Shakespeare's means for disposition of the protagonist's soul within the framework of the play and not after its
final curtain. It seems sheer perversity for the critic to stretch his
ingenuity in order to save Othello from this hell.[36] The very suicide
that for some critics is proof of Othello's damnation is not the first
cause. Rejection of God and heaven is the first cause; the sequent
suicide is merely the action of a man in total despair. The cause of
that despair is the theme of the play. Like another tragic hero—
Romeo—who loved not wisely but too well, Othello blames his destruction on fate:

> O vain boast!
> Who can control his fate?
> (V.ii.273–74)

Othello understands Desdemona's death also as misfortune: "O ill-
starr'd wench" (V.ii.281). But fate or fortune, stars or planets, are
only God's agents. These outbursts are Othello's way of saying that
the good man cannot perceive evil, and, not being able to penetrate its disguise, he goes to destruction and damnation.

In the final scene all characters are identified as good or evil.
Iago is clearly the villain he is now regularly called, but *villain* does

36. Ribner, *Patterns in Shakesperian Tragedy*, p. 114, sees Othello ul-
timately saved. So also do Parker, *The Slave of Life*, p. 129, and Elliott,
Flaming Minister, p. 239. Critics agreeing that Othello is damned include
Siegel, *Shakespearean Tragedy*, pp. 130–31; Bethell, "Shakespeare's Imag-
ery," p. 78; Honor Matthews, *Character & Symbol in Shakespeare's Plays*
(London, 1962), p. 138; and Bettie Doebler, "Othello's Angels: The Ars
Moriendi," *ELH* 34 (1967): 158.

not describe fully his otherworld existence. At the curtain, Shakespeare wants once again to brand accurately this evil force. We are back to Bradley's jesting proposal:

OTHELLO
>   I look down towards his feet; but that's a fable.
>   If that thou be'st a devil, I cannot kill thee.
>   [*Wounds Iago*]
>
> . . . .
>
IAGO
>   I bleed, sir, but not kill'd.[37]
>
>   (V.ii.294—96)

Bradley's comment is provocatively accurate but offered in the wrong sense. Bradley, as he assumes Iago to be, is tongue in cheek: "he is meant to be alluding to Othello's words, and saying, with a cold contemptuous smile, 'You see he is right; I *am* a devil'" (Bradley's italics).[38] But Iago is not smiling; his next speech is ill tempered, and it is his last. The very fact that it is his last pronouncement concludes his role in the play on the strongest possible note of identification. Othello nears the truth with the epithet he employs:

> Will you, I pray, demand that demi-devil
> Why he hath thus ensnar'd my soul and body?
>   (V.ii.309—10)

The question itself shows just how much Othello errs in "demi-devil." The creature has ensnared *soul* as well as body, and, incidently, we might note that in Othello's mind his soul is already forfeit. None but angel or demon may carry off the soul. Still, Iago's words tell the story:

37. Spivack, *Shakespeare and the Allegory of Evil*, p. 434, comes very near my point: can we "be sure of [Iago's] death?" His gaiety at the end "glints with the impervious immortality of his abstract forbears."

38. Bradley, *Shakespearean Tragedy*, p. 438.

Demand me nothing. What you know, you know.
From this time forth I never will speak word.

(V.ii.311–12)

Ludovico puts a crucial question: "What, not to pray?" (V.ii.313).
Iago does not answer this awestruck query. Why does he not answer? Why will he not pray? Because it is pointless to pray: he is a
soul already judged, a soul eternally damned; and no amount of
prayer can possibly matter.

3. *King Lear:*
The Great
Doom's Image, I

he third play in my hypothetical tetralogy is *King Lear*, which in the scheme is that play whose central figure is a man bad at the outset. The possibilities for Lear are two-fold: he will remain evil, reaping at his death a doom that sends him to hell, or he will reform, winning at his death the re-demption that carries him to heaven. Since Lear is clearly repentant for his rejection of Cordelia, since he con-fesses the evil he has done her, since he makes satisfaction with his suffering and his renewed love for his daughter, and since she ab-solves him clearly of any harm done her, we may believe that, on the score of breaking the sacred bond between parent and child, Lear is redeemed. However, Lear is guilty also at play's beginning of severing the chain of state, of which he is the top link, and which he breaks by abdicating. This act may be seen as parallel in the sec-ular realm to that of Celestine V in the spiritual domain. Dante calls Celestine's resignation of the papal crown "lo gran rifiuto,"

the great refusal, and assigns him, if not to hell proper, to the antechamber, where the punishments are at least hell-like and the hope to see God extinguished permanently. Lear makes the great refusal.[1]

Almost lost in the emotional upheaval of Lear's putting away of his youngest daughter is the greater sin of repudiation of God. God had set Lear upon the throne and only God might remove him. As the Earl of Kent remonstrates with Lear, pawning his life in defense of Cordelia's love, the King loses his temper, inaugurating a mighty oath, which, however, Kent concludes:

LEAR
   Now, by Apollo—

KENT
    Now, by Apollo, King,
   Thou swear'st thy gods in vain.
      (I.i.161–62)

The evil that Lear has done in disowning his daughter is momentarily buried under the awesome attempt of a divinely anointed

1. Few critics adopt the position wholeheartedly that *King Lear* is a Christian play, and none, to my knowledge, goes so far as I do in this essay. William R. Elton, *King Lear and the Gods* (San Marino, Cal., 1966) is the most forceful and expansive proponent of those who see Lear merely as a pagan. He confesses that Christian elements may be found in the play but asserts that "the devastating fifth act shatters . . . the foundations of faith itself" (p. 337). Elton, in his first chapter, gives a comprehensive survey of the debate between critics of pro- and anti-Christian readings and may be consulted. H. R. Coursen gives also a good, concise summary of the opposing views in footnotes 1, 2, and 4 of his chapter on *King Lear* in his *Christian Ritual and the World of Shakespeare's Tragedies* (Lewisburg, Pa., 1976), pp. 307–8. He echoes several critics in taking a middle view: *Lear* becomes a dynamic play when the King is seen progressing from some dark paganism to "Christian" awakening to the values represented by Cordelia (p. 238). Maynard Mack, *King Lear in Our Time* (Berkeley, 1965), comes closest to the view presented here concerning Edgar but stops far short of equating him with the Christ triumphant.

king to remove the chrism of coronation. What Lear has given away to his two elder daughters and their spouses he can no more divest himself of without penalty than could Celestine the papal mantle. Kent, threatened with death by a nearly apoplectic king, shows clearly that the protagonist of this play is a man evil in great degree, even as his drama begins:

> Kill thy physician, and thy fee bestow
> Upon the foul disease. Revoke thy gift,
> Or, whilst I can vent clamor from my throat,
> I'll tell thee thou dost evil.
>
> (I.i.164–67)

The chance that this point might be lost is enhanced by the return, immediately following, to the sin against Cordelia. Nevertheless, Kent has his final words in which we see that a topsy-turvy world has resulted from Lear's removal of himself as top link in the chain of being. Instead of an orderly transition taking place, with God grasping willingly the new surmounting double or quadruple link of the daughters and/or their consorts, an upside-down condition ensues as the chain drops to some mystical ground and all things reflect the chaos by appearing opposite to what things ought to be:

> Fare thee well, King. Sith thus thou wilt appear,
> Freedom lives hence, and banishment is here.[2]
>
> (I.i.181–82)

2. Robert Ornstein has argued that Lear is not guilty of any serious breach of order, that his purpose is sound when he divides the kingdom in order "that future strife / May be prevented" (I.i.44–45), and that disorder ensues chiefly because two of the daughters happen to be evil: *The Moral Vision of Jacobean Tragedy* (Madison, Wis., 1960), p. 264. But such reasoning rejects the Christian framework I argue here, admittedly a framework that too few critics allow. I persevere in my view, however, as the rest of this essay manifests, and answer Ornstein and the others at this point by repeating Kent's demand that Lear "revoke" his gift of the king-

The often observed "negatives"[3] of the play are further illustrations of the quality of the divided kingdom that Lear offers
his daughters. Not only does Lear threaten to withhold "something" from Cordelia if she does not please him better but also he
gives her "nothing" even if she receives a third of chaos, which is
certain to follow the parting of the coronet. The divided crown
is itself a symbol of the perfect circle broken, a symbol of the link
of kingship cut, a parable of the verses in Matthew 12.25: "Euerie
kingdome deuided against it self, shalbe broght to naught: &
euerie citie or house, deuided against it self, shal not stand."[4]

The texture of the entire Lear universe is raveled; where all
has become nothing, nothing is as it should be, nothing functions
properly. The kingdom becomes an illustration of the need for
revelation, since the ordinary modes of perception fail. Despite the
constant warning of the medieval church, which placed the senses
below reason and reason below faith and made faith dependent
upon revealed religion, the Lear universe is the *exemplum* of that
evil world where the senses, inevitably defective, lead to woe on
woe. Shakespeare makes this important thematic statement a motif
pervasive throughout the play. Introduced by the fifteenth line of
the first scene, it becomes, in one development, the double blind-

---

dom to his daughters. Kent believes clearly that Lear rules by divine ap-
pointment ("by Apollo, King"), and that to remove his crown is the symp-
tom of a "foul disease" (I.i.161, 165) and an act of cosmic "evil" (167).
In further refutation of Ornstein and others who accept Lear's self-
divestiture, one might cite the contemporary *Homilie agaynst disobedience
and wylful rebellion* (1570), itself quoting Romans 13.1–2: "the powers that
be are ordayned of God. Whosoeuer therefore resisteth the power, resisteth the ordinance of God: & they that resist, shal receaue to them
selues damnatiō" (A$_{iii}$^{r}).

3. See, for instance, *King Lear*, The Arden Shakespeare, ed.
Kenneth Muir (New York, 1952), p. 9n.

4. The pertinence of these verses to the condition of the realm has
been noted by John Dover Wilson, *King Lear*, The New Cambridge Shakespeare (Cambridge, Eng., 1960), p. 146.

ness of Lear and Gloucester, and, in another development, the impaired senses of all the inhabitants of the play.

Gloucester, in fact, initiates the theme of faulty senses in what is almost so farfetched a metaphor that one feels Shakespeare drew his image with awkwardness expressly to awaken attention:

> Sir, this young fellow's mother . . . had . . . a son for
> her cradle ere she had a husband for her bed. Do you
> *smell* a fault?
>
> (I.i.13−16, my italics)

Not only is the ordinarily otherwise perceptive Kent unable to smell the fault but also the perpetrator of the sin himself puts aside the testimony of his nose, and the continually darkening Lear universe reduces his vision until he is literally blinded; nevertheless, he "stumbled" when he "saw" (IV.i.19).

Kent's inability to "smell" Gloucester's fault shows that not only the errant are misled by their senses. All creatures must beware at all times of the pitfalls of perception. Most of all must the man who purposes not to err gauge narrowly the testimony of his senses in a universe turned topsy-turvy. Nevertheless, that person inclined to evil will go farthest astray, since he remains, willfully, farthest from the correctives to the faulty senses: revelation and faith. Lear is deceived easily by the first daughter who feeds his hearing with the words of love he seems so desperately to require. As she does so, she emphasizes that eyesight which she deludes as well as Lear's hearing (I.i.56). When Regan follows with lies of her own, she too evokes the senses (I.i.74). Therefore, when Lear repudiates Cordelia for her inability to "heave / [Her] heart into [her] mouth," he drives her wrathfully from his "sight" (I.i.124). So does he also with Kent (I.i.158). Kent, recognizing the failure of the aged King's perceptions, warns him to "See better" (159).

With the kingdom moving into darkness farther and farther, Kent himself, already deficient in smell, has trouble also with hearing. Only with difficulty can Lear open the ears of the aroused Earl: "Hear me, recreant, on thine allegiance, hear me!" (I.i.168).

Kent, his banishment pronounced along with Cordelia's, reiterates to the girl his vision of the now upside-down kingdom, the ambiance that further defeats the frail senses: "Thou losest here, a better where to find" (I.i.263).

As I.ii. opens with Edmund's soliloquy, we see the inevitable spread of chaos, rendered again in imagery of the topsy-turvy:

> Edmund the base
> Shall top th' legitimate.
> (I.ii.20–21)

Up and down are reversed; a link lower in the chain shall replace one higher. The growing chaos is underlined by the arrival of Gloucester, who, in terms more familiar to the tragedies of Shakespeare, outlines an entire state, indeed an entire universe, off its sure base: eclipses of both sun and moon; love, friendship, and brotherhood declining; countries at war; the nation in civil turmoil; the cities in riot—all nature ruinous (I.ii.106–17).

Edmund takes full advantage of this dysfunction of the senses. He pours into an ear easily deceived what he himself has "seen and heard" (I.ii.178), even as Edgar submits to the deception ("Shall I *hear* from you anon?" [my italics, line 181]), not yet aware of what has happened to his world.

Edgar's world is now a dark and evil universe, much like the universe that results in *Hamlet* and *Macbeth*, other plays in which kings are replaced by usurpers, usurpers of brilliant villainy who dominate the befogged realms they have created, who move more surely in the darkness while men of good will cannot penetrate the murk. This situation exists also in *Othello*, despite the fact that no ruler is displaced, unless we allow that Othello malfunctions as Governor of Cyprus. But Othello is replaced in rule only in the sense that Iago manipulates him, and in the hoodwinking creates in Cyprus the mutiny that weakens perceptions. Shakespeare sees all four central tragedies as enveloped in a miasma that fogs the senses, especially of the good man, while the villain moves somewhat more surefooted in the bog. Such conditions are made clear through a series of speeches from these plays that for the most part paraphrase each other. Hamlet is "remiss, / Most generous, and free from all contriving" (IV.vii.134–35); Othello is "of a free and open nature, / That thinks men honest that but seem to be so" (I.iii.400–401); Edgar, whom we here follow, is "a brother noble, / Whose nature is so far from doing harms / That he suspects none" (I.ii.183–85). On Edgar's "foolish honesty," Edmund's "practices ride easy"; Othello will "as tenderly be led by the nose / As asses are"; and Hamlet "will not peruse the foils, so that, with ease, [Laertes] . . . / may . . . / in a pass of practice" destroy Claudius's dangerous enemy. Duncan's destruction is handled similarly, although similar language is absent. A genial host and hostess lead him lamblike to slaughter, and we know from Duncan's own words that his perceptions cannot cope with the evil that hides behind the smiling greeting: "There's no art / To find the mind's construction in the face" (I.iv.11–12).

In Shakespeare's pursuit of this theme of the senses perverted, Goneril is thrust forward to represent the false ruler in an overturned world. She utilizes unnatural conditions to further her own evil purposes and also sows the seeds of the ultimate destruction of her own estate. Again Shakespeare reaches for one of the senses, going far in his metaphor chiefly to emphasize the theme. Goneril, unwilling to endure further the outrages of her father, determines to check him: "If he distaste it, let him to my sister" (I.iii.15). Lear's sense of taste is of course disoriented in the chaotic kingdom created by his abdication. Instead of seeking harmony with his disturbed child—probably impossible since God scourges the disobedient King and his realm—Lear finds his medicine bitter and intensifies the disorder. Goneril shows the kind of ruler she is and would be as long as she continues in power: "What grows of it, no matter . . . / I would breed from hence occasions, and I shall" (I.iii.25–26). When Goneril comes fully into the open, putting restraints upon her father in most unloving manner, Lear questions his senses. Referring to himself in the third person, he wonders first who he is, then what has happened to his perceptions: "Where are his eyes? / Either his notion weakens, his discernings / Are lethargied—Ha! Waking? 'Tis not so. / Who is it that can tell me who I am?" (I.iv.223–26). Later in the same scene,

Albany questions also the sight of Goneril: "How far your eyes may pierce I cannot tell" (343). Judging from the outcome of her plans, we may conclude that she was as blind as her father.[5]

To the evil, conversely, when senses operate correctly, evil is dismantled. Cornwall, Goneril, and Regan, for example, do not want Lear to hear reason. In their combined views, that would be "To have his ear abus'd" (II.iv.307).

Nowhere so obvious is this theme of perverted senses manifested as in the Gloucester story. The Earl is worked upon by his illegitimate son who crams his father's eyes and ears with deceivable report concerning Edgar. A manufactured letter, a seeming reluctance to betray a brother, an apparent guilty behavior culminating in flight all delude Gloucester's eyes; clever phrases, promised eavesdroppings, easy lies abuse the Earl's ears. When Edgar commits himself to the rescue of his father from despair, the true son is well aware that part of the cure includes a lesson on the senses. Gloucester himself learns part of the truth through his blinding. Immediately after his second eye is put out by Cornwall, Gloucester "sees" that he was practiced upon by Edmund, and Edgar "was abus'd" (III.vii.92). But Gloucester puts the blame for his own deficient senses, or rather the blame for his reliance on the faulty testimony of eyes and ears upon the gods, who "kill us for their sport" (IV.i.37). Deep in the way toward despair, Gloucester determines on suicide, after uttering paraphrases of Job and Matthew that point up his condition.[6]

Edgar, who has heard these expressions of despair, is asked to lead his father to the edge of a cliff, from which place he "shall

5. Elton argues the entire theme of eyes/sight/blindness in terms of his view of the play as pagan, seeing in both the real and the figurative blindness of most of the principals some working out of what he calls the *lex talionis*. See *King Lear and the Gods*, pp. 107–12.

6. "I such a fellow saw, / Which made me think a man a worm" (IV.i.32–33) echoes Job 25.6: "man . . . is but a worme." "'Tis the time's plague, when madmen lead the blinde" (IV.i.46) echoes Matthew 15.14: "if the blinde leade the blinde, bothe shal fall into the ditche." Although these admonitions from scripture are meant to guide man to humility and faith, they drive Gloucester only to impatience and despair.

no leading need" (IV.i.78). The son commits his own endangered life totally to the redemption of his father: "Poor Tom shall lead thee" (IV.i.79). This commitment brings him to the cliffs of Dover and to a scene that has been condemned sometimes for its incredibility. But perhaps the most significant thing about the scene is the way in which Edgar uses the situation to prove to Gloucester that the senses can be deceived. Son tells father they labor upward, though apparently they are in a level meadow. Gloucester, by his senses, thinks "the ground is even" (IV.vi.3). He is told to "hear the sea," which, not being there, of course, he cannot. His ears tell him that Poor Tom's speech is less eccentric than previously. To all his observations he is told that his other senses must be imperfect like his eyes and that he is "much deceiv'd" by what those senses tell him (5, 9).

At this point Edgar goes about to deceive Gloucester's senses so dramatically that surely the lesson never can be forgotten. Through his father's ears the son pours a mind's-eye vision of fearful heights, and adorns his tale with a moral: "I'll look no more, / Lest my brain turn, and the deficient sight / Topple down headlong" (22–24). Gloucester, brought to the verge, utters a farewell speech which shows how much he is deluded in his reason. The very act of suicide he calls *patience* (36), which three lines before, Edgar has properly labeled *despair*. These are terms from the old medieval psychomachia in which *patientia* and *desperatio* are often combatants (fig. 7).[7] Edgar, himself knowing well how greatly

---

7. The combat of vices and virtues is found in other of Shakespeare's plays as well as elsewhere in *Lear*: see I.iv.248–59; II.iv.229, 271; III.ii.37, 74–77 (the fool's song, the theme of which is to "make content with his fortunes fit"); III.vi.4–5; V.ii.8–11; and V.iii.164, 195. Shakespeare's use of the *Psychomachia* may have been suggested by John Day's *A Booke of Christian Praiers* (London, 1581). A first edition appeared in 1569, but the 1581 edition is the earliest to include a fine series of woodblock illustrations that crowd every page and bring together a complex of eschatological themes, several of which are found in *Lear*. In addition to the battle between the vices and virtues, the prayer book contains the fifteen signs before doomsday, a last judgment, and, rather interestingly in light of their treatment in *Lear*, a sequence of the five senses personified.

Patience ouercõmeth all thinges. Wrath deuoureth it selfe.

Fig. 7. Patience. *Queen Elizabeth Prayer Book.* Press of John Day, London, 1581.

the senses may delude the reason, fears that his cure has killed the patient:

> And yet I know not how conceit may rob
> The treasury of life, when life itself
> Yields to the theft. Had he been where he thought,
> By this, had thought been past. Alive or dead?
>
> (IV.vi.42–45)

Thought in these lines seems the substitute for reason, and *conceit* for that which comes to the man through his senses. If life welcomes readily the substitute, life itself, yielding to the theft, pays with life itself. *Life* serves both for that of the body and that of the spirit, and the entire passage is eschatological. The question has been one of identity, a theme prominent in the plays discussed thus far, a theme prominent in many of the plays in the Shakespeare canon insofar as it overlaps inevitably with false appearances, and prominent additionally in these plays where it overlaps also with the idea of the imperfectness of sense perception.

Edgar's first words to his stirring father, in the form of a question, attempt to establish the old man's spiritual condition: "What are you, sir?" (48). Gloucester wants only to die; his despair is so deep, he no longer cares about his soul. Edgar then draws an image of fall from such great height that it suggests the original fall of the angels. Urging strongly that the gods hold out still for Gloucester's redemption the offer of grace, Edgar indicates that nothing less than miracle has taken place (55), "that the clearest gods, who make them honors / Of men's impossibilities, have preserv'd" Gloucester (73–74). Faith or revelation, appealing to reason, must supersede the witness of the senses. Gloucester, slowly waking, not yet restored spiritually but already doubting his senses, asks, with secondary eschatological significance, "But have I fall'n, or no?" (56). When Edgar reasserts the tremendous drop a second time and directs his father to "Look up a-height. . . . / Do but look up" (58–59), we cannot doubt that the command sets the goal of sight much higher than the cliff top. Gloucester complains that without eyes he cannot look up, but Edgar raises him gently, tells him he stands (65), and attributes his former waywardness to an unholy guide who led him to the edge of the abyss: "It was some fiend" (72). But the gods have preserved him (73–74), and Gloucester recovers his faith, promising to bear affliction. He agrees it was "The fiend, the fiend" who "led me to that place" (75–79).

The lesson on the senses is not yet over, however. Tacked on immediately to the illustration of Gloucester's deficiencies in these matters is the appearance of the unbalanced Lear, whom Edgar describes forthwith as one not under conduct of "The safer sense" (81), i.e., senses under control of the reason. After several exchanges in which Lear responds with "matter and impertinency mix'd" (174), the unstable King demands that Gloucester read an imaginary challenge penned to call a blind Cupid to the field. Gloucester mentions his own blindness, and Lear continues the instruction begun by Edgar:

> A man may see how this world goes with
> no eyes. Look with thine ears. . . .
> Robes and furr'd gowns hide all. Plate sin with gold,
> And the strong lance of justice hurtless breaks;
>   . . . . Get thee glass eyes,
> And, like a scurvy politician, seem
> To see the things thou dost not.
> (IV.vi.150–72)

Not only may a man know the truth of things without the sensible avowal of his eyes but also the evil man who pretends to know things knows only the evil world, his eyes little better than glass since he is blinded to righteousness. One might say the lesson is laid on with a trowel, but Gloucester has been a slow student and his sense perceptions are stronger than in other people. At scene's end he has learned to refer to "vile sense" (280), but his senses "stand up" (281), and he continues with great difficulty to suffer his afflictions, his "huge sorrows" (282), because he is so "sensitive." If he had given way to distraction, a condition he ascribes to the mad Lear of this scene, he had been better able to bear his griefs. Perhaps because of his continued sufferings he relapses once more (V.ii.8) but is quickly restored by his savior/son Edgar.

The theme of the senses is brought to a proper end in respect to Lear also. As he emerges from the world of his darkened mind, he resorts to his senses first to inform him where he is and what is his state. Appealing to sight and touch, he cries, "Let's see; / I feel this pin prick" (IV.vii.56–57), but remains unassured of his condition. Ultimately, Cordelia selflessly restores him as king: "Is he array'd?" (IV.vii.21); and Kent humbly establishes him as head of state: "In your own kingdom, sir" (78). These acts and words that have involved sacrificial love redeem him and teach him who he is.

The evil creatures who remain at play's end find that the senses that led them to triumph for the while that evil was briefly successful become in the upright world as untrustworthy for them as for anyone else: "The eye that told you so look'd but a-squint" (V.iii.74).

Although the senses are never to be trusted wholly but their testimony subjected always to the corroboration of reason and faith, especially are they untrustworthy in a topsy-turvy world. Some indication of the universal upheaval in Lear's kingdom has been shown. The moment that Lear relinquishes his crown, Kent observes that freedom is elsewhere and banishment in Britain (I.i.182), that for Cordelia to lose "here" releases her to find a "better where" (263). The same upside-down condition scourges the entire realm, and Shakespeare is quick to show the displacement in the Gloucester plot. Edmund's soliloquy that opens the second scene of the play culminates in the determination that "the base / Shall top th' legitimate" (I.ii.20–21). Gloucester intrudes on Edmund's musings with a news report: Kent is banished, France has departed angry, a limited king has left his palace. When Edmund concludes the first phase of the deception that will bring about the triumph of bastardy, Gloucester recites his panoramic description of universal upheaval. All is awry, from the heavenly orbs to national and international broils, from civic mutinies to in-camera treasons, from broken families to cooled friendships: "all ruinous disorders follow us disquietly to our graves" (I.ii.106–17). Shakespeare's most complete picture of widespread disorder has brought critics to refer justly to a Lear "universe"[8] whose very foundations crack. One might go further to suggest that in Gloucester's view are hints of Apocalypse. Other critics, notably Frank Kermode and Mary Lascelles,[9] have observed doomsday imagery and significance in *King Lear*, but to my knowledge no one has suggested that the theme begins as early as Gloucester's description of "portentous" happenings in I.ii.106 ff.[10] Compare Gloucester's eclipses of sun and moon with Matthew 24.29: "And immediatly after the tribulatiõs of those dayes, shal the sunne be darkened, & the moone shal not giue her light, and the starres shal fall from heauen, & the powers of heauen shalbe shaken." Although Gloucester mentions only sun and moon, Edmund, com-

8. Perhaps the first to refer to the Lear universe was G. Wilson Knight, "Chapter X, The Lear Universe," in *The Wheel of Fire* (London, 1930), pp. 194–226. In the third edition of *The Shakespearian Tempest* (London, 1953), Knight prepared a chart of what he called "Shakespeare's Dramatic Universe," probably the impetus to the now common practice of referring to the "Hamlet universe," the "Macbeth universe," etc.

9. Frank Kermode, *The Sense of an Ending* (Oxford, 1966), p. 38, discusses what he calls the "consciously false apocalypse of *King Lear*," ties it only to the last scene of the play, and finds no religious significance in it at all, especially since it is a "Broken apocalypse . . . a false ending, a human period . . . in an eternal world" (p. 88). Mary Lascelles, "'King Lear' and Doomsday," *Shakespeare Survey* 26 (1973): 69–79, sees the appearance of a naked Edgar (reflecting pictorial imagery from the judgment scenes on chancel arches) and Lear's heath scene with its "dreadful summoners" as two early evocations of a doomsday theme that culminates in V.iii.267–68.

10. No critic has yet indicated the full extent of judgment-day imagery throughout the Shakespeare canon. Indirect or specific reference to doomsday may be found in at least twenty-one plays as well as in *Lucrece* and sonnets 55, 107, and 116. Furthermore, I would argue that all tragedies which, like *Richard II*, encompass "the death or fall of kings" (II.iv.15), borrow their omens, signs, portents, or harbingers from those associated traditionally with judgment day.

menting upon his father's dismay, gives to the stars considerable influence in men's disasters (123–36; see fig. 3).

Matthew 24 and 25 give visions and parables of Apocalypse, answers to the request by the disciples that Jesus tell them the "signe" of his coming "and of the end of the worlde" (24.3). Christ's first word of warning, "Take hede that no man deceiue you" (4), would serve Gloucester well in this exchange with his second son. But, sadly, Gloucester remains asleep to the signs, the more so since he echoes other early warnings of Christ. Gloucester's report of "in cities, mutinies; in countries, discord; in palaces, treason" is a paraphrase of Christ's prediction that "ye shal heare of warres, and rumors of warres . . . . For nacion shal rise against nacion, and realme against realme" (6–7). Gloucester's observation that "Love cools, friendship falls off, brothers divide" is a paraphrase of Christ's warning that "then shal manie . . . betray one another . . . . And because iniquitie shal be increased, the loue of manie shalbe colde" (10, 12).

These same chapters of the gospel of Matthew provide one of the chief sources for the apocalyptic signs developed in the spiritual encyclopedias of the Middle Ages.[11] Clearly they are the source for the following passage from *The craft to liue well and to die well*. I produce this somewhat extended passage for its extreme relevance to Gloucester's portentous omens as well as to the rest of *Lear* and also for its importance to all judgment-day materials in the other plays considered in this book.

> The iiii. token of ye nombre of .iiii. precededes of
> ye Jugement generall and ye ende of the worlde in
> token y^t the tyme shall approche in ye whiche god y^e
> creatoure wyll Juge his people after theyr demery-
> tes shall be whan comocyons/warres/debates & mer-
> uaylous comocyons shall be made in dyuers partyes of
> ye worlde. And amonge all ye creatures lyuynge in it.
> For fyrst after ye worde of our redemptoure Jhesu
> cryst reherceth in saint Mathewe in y^e .xxiiii. chapytre

11. See Introduction, pp. 3–9 and chap. 1, pp. 35–38.

Batayles & warres shall be made amonge men ennemyes & aduersaryes yᵉ one wᵗ the other ouer all yᵉ
worlde. The one people shall moeue ayēst the other/&
yᵉ one realme ayenst another. Falsnesse begylynges &
treasons shall be made in townes & in cytees bytwene
yᵉ cytezyns & enhabitaūtes. Peas shall be out of yᵉ
lande The grete men shall aryse ayenst the lytell &
ayenst themselfe. The lytel ayenst yᵉ grete & ayenst
themself/yᵉ one cyte ayenst tother. Euery housholde
& house shal be deuyded in itself. One persone shal
arme hȳ ayēst yᵉ other.yᵉ yonge ayēst yᵉ olde yᵉ pore
ayēst yᵉ ryche/yᵉ prȳce ayēst yᵉ subget: & yᵉ subget
ayēst his prȳce. One relygyon ayēst yᵉ other/there ne
shal be monestary ne colege but there shall be stryfe
& debate & yᵗ shal be fulfylled yᵗ is wryten in Jheremye
in yᵉ xi. chapytre. Unusquisqs a proximo suo se
custodiat & cetera que sequūt.[12] That is to say. Euery
man & woman shall kepe hym from his neyghbour
& shal not haue trust in his broder. for euery man
spekȳge vnto his frende shal walke frawdelently: & yᵉ
one brother shall mocke yᵉ other & shall not speke of
trouthe wᵗ hym / he shall speke peasybly & under
[cowleur of pays wyth ys freynd bot he shal falsly
dyssayf hym and secretly put hym to dyshonnowr yf
he may.

Selfwayes than shalbe fulfyllit ewvrych thyng
be this that ys said be the prophet Mycheas. Et keyp
the of thy propyr wyf the qwyche sleppyd betwys thy
armes][13] for she shal than betray her husbande. yᵉ
sone shall do iniury and falsehode vnto his fader/&
the doughter vnto yᵉ moder. The seruaūtes men &

---

12. The verses come from Jeremiah 9 (not xi). 4–5 and differ
slightly from those given.

13. Material between brackets comes from *Art of good lywyng &
good deying* (Paris, 1503), Cc₁ʳ-Cc₁ᵛ because my copy text is imperfect at
this point.

women & of a mannes owne housholde shall be his
ennemyes/ & there shall be more/for yᵉ one broder
shall delyuer the other vnto yᵉ dethe. The fader shall
forsake his son & delyuer hym to yᵉ dethe/The chyldren shall aryse ayenst theyr faders & thē pursue to yᵉ
dethe/& truely the aboue sayd cōmotion shall be in
the body of the thynge publysshed/yᵗ shal be tokē euy-
dent of yᵉ ende & extremyte of yᵉ worlde. Other
cōmocyons shal there be in the elementes:for before
yᵉ ende of yᵉ worlde shal be general famynes not in
one region or prouynce al onely but ouer al the
worlde generally/ for there shal be scarcenes in yᵉ erth
yᵗ shall bere no fruyte ne other thynge necessary &
couenable for yᵉ lyf.so grete moeuynges of the erth
shal be made ayenst yᵉ comune cours of nature &
maner accustumed yᵗ many cytees/toures & castelles
shal be distroyed & beten downe/in yᵉ oce & in the waters shall be greter tēpestes & cōmocyons than in
tymes past/yᵉ ayre shall be replynysshed wᵗ pestylēces
& wᵗ infeccions wherof shal come pestylences/mor-
talytees & corrupcyōs innumerables as well in men as
in bestes/thondres/lyghtenynges/tēpestes wyndes &
stormes shal be impyteous more thā euer they were in
suche wyse yᵗ yᵉ men shall be brought & put in meruayllous fere & drede/& therfore as it is sayd saȳt
Jherome reherceth yᵗ he hath founde .xv. specyall
tokēs comȳge before yᵉ grete iugement general of god
wherof we shal speke here by ordre. But it is to un-
d[er]stāde also yᵉ sayd tokēs shall be continualles
wᵗout ony interrupcōn But whyder there shall be ony
inter[v]alle amonge yᵉ sayd tokens the gloryous saynt
Jherome expresseth not ne declareth ne yᵉ other doctours ne affermeth nothȳge certayne but it leueth &
putteth in yᵉ wyl of god yᵉ creature.[14]

14. *The craft to liue well and to die well* (1505), folio lxxxxviiiʳ–
lxxxxviiiᵛ.

Apart from the general appropriateness of those signs that foretell of brother against brother, son against father, father against son, children against father, tempests and earthquakes beyond the usual experience of men, and the toppling of towers, etc., special notice should be taken of the sentence that warns that "seruaūtes . . . of a mannes owne housholde shall be his ennemyes." So may we understand the "servant that he bred" (IV.ii.74) who opposes Cornwall and is the instrument of the Duke's death.[15]

Other signs of a world awry less drastic than doomsday omens abound throughout the play. Goneril's description of domestic and palace turmoil opens I.iii. She complains that father (household disruption) and knights (palace or state disorder) have set all at odds, making the "grac'd palace" more like a "riotous inn" as well as a "tavern or a brothel" (I.iii.5–6; I.iv.237–42). Beyond her power to restore to order, the kingdom in fact suffers through her own waywardness, showing incidentally how unfit she is to rule. She urges neglect of Lear upon her servants and outright scorn for the King's entourage. She desires inharmony: "I would breed from hence occasions, and I shall" (I.iii.26). An im-

---

15. Indirectly, it might be noted here also that "corrupcyōs innumerables . . . in bestes" explains in a way never suggested before the horses of King Duncan:

ROSS

> And Duncan's horses—a thing most strange and
>   certain—
>
> . . . .
> Turn'd wild in nature, broke their stalls, flung out,
> Contending 'gainst obedience, as they would
> Make war with mankind.

OLD MAN

> 'Tis said they eat each other.

ROSS

> They did so, to th' amazement of mine eyes
> That look'd upon 't.
>
>   (*Macbeth*, II.iv.14–20)

The phrase accounts as well for the "mousing owl" that "hawk'd at and kill'd" the falcon (II.iv.12–13).

age of the retrogression of the entire kingdom is caught in her description of her father's presumed senility: "Old fools are babes again" (20).

When Lear walks into the household chaos that Goneril has ordered, the respect due him in the even-tenored world has been removed at all degrees, from servant to duchess/daughter, so that in Lear's view "the world's asleep" (I.iv.47–48). His conclusions are supported by one of his hundred knights who, perhaps in some measure attempting to shift blame for some of his own boisterous behavior, argues a "great abatement of kindness . . . as well in the general dependents as in the Duke himself also and your daughter" (56–61). That this knight includes Albany in his general censure, a man who condemns his wife's niggardly treatment of her father and whom we know to be ignorant of her reprehensible orders, taints the complainant's testimony. We should believe that real disorder exists on both sides; for this upheaval is the inevitable result of the great refusal, the bitter harvest of Lear's abdication.

No one knows better than the fool that Lear more than any other is to blame for conditions, and the fool perceives readily the topsy-turvy state of things. In his first appearance of the play, he echoes Kent's statement of reversed conditions: "Why, this fellow has banish'd two on 's daughters, and did the third a blessing" (99–101). Kent is advised to put on a coxcomb and change estates from high to low (something he has actually done already by disguising himself—an earl—as a common servant). Further than this, the fool learns that truth must be whipped out of doors while the bitch falsehood lies comfortable by the fire (109–11). Lords, great men, and ladies want to be fools (150–53), while Lear himself has changed places with a beast of burden, bearing his "ass on [his] back" (159), and all because the King has broken his crown in two and has given away both parts (157–59). The fool continues to draw images of reversals in nature until we get a picture of universal upending: daughters have been made Lear's mothers (169–70), fools are better than kings (190–91), young birds bite off the heads of the mature (212–13), and carts draw horses (220–21).[16]

16. These images of inversion may be found throughout the play. In Lear's mock trial of his daughters (III.vi.), see especially lines 12–14,

As the rumors of war grow (II.i.10−11), we see the astounding triumph of Edmund's new allegiance to the goddess Nature. Elizabethans, less susceptible than later generations to a romantic idealization of nature, felt that nature, though capable of great good, beauty, and bounty, was filled, nevertheless, with equally great capacity for cruelty, violence, and destruction. In the realm of this goddess as well, then, the Lear universe exhibits an overturning of order. Edmund, through his carefully prepared deceptions and with the help of his father's dimmed vision, first calls his brother unnatural, charges him with "unnatural purpose" (50), then succeeds so well that the victim/father in return calls the disguised villain "Loyal and natural boy" (85). Base tops legitimate in terms of unnatural topping natural and, in the eyes of all, until later revelation, assumes the epithet of loving and natural, while the good and true becomes labeled with the unnatural vileness of desiring the death of his father.

Regan and Cornwall are dressed in this sort of imagery when at first they refuse to see Lear who overtakes them at Gloucester's castle. Initially they assume a posture above that of the true king by denying to speak with him (II.iv.86), and Lear immediately translates their behavior into terms of disorder: "The images of revolt and flying off" (88). When the undutiful girl comes finally before her father, only to maintain the reversed roles of authority, Lear puts into graphic and dramatic display the fool's assertion that he has made his daughters his mothers:

Do you but mark how this becomes the house:
"Dear daughter, I confess that I am old;   [*Kneels.*]

---

where son overtops father; 21−22, where madman and fool become judge and wise man; 37−38, where Kent also is made a judge (he is only a servant in Lear's eyes). In Lear's mad scene on the fields of Dover, the entire passage from line 146 to line 165 is especially rich: senses are reversed (146−51) and roles are reversed: thief/justice, 150−54; farmer/dog, 154−59; and evil/good, 160−65.

Age is unnecessary. On my knees I beg
That you'll vouchsafe me raiment, bed, and food."

(II.iv.151–54)

The very maintenance, support, and sustenance that the parent provides the child is begged of the child by that parent.

In following the thread of the Cornwall story, we see the first acts of retributive justice, brought about by the very upside-down conditions that the false rulers have wrought. As Cornwall attempts to put out Gloucester's remaining eye, a lifelong servant opposes him. In the human, social, and political hierarchy, Cornwall tops a ladder near the bottom of which is his servant; for he comes of peasant stock. These very archtraitors, who saw little wrong with their own upending of the order of things, scarce believe what is happening. Regan exclaims, "How now, you dog?" lowering the servant below even human status, and with incredulity wonders that "A peasant stand up thus?" (III.vii.76, 81). The immense gulf between duke and peasant is emphasized in the retelling, as one of Albany's courtiers announces the death of Cornwall by "A servant that he bred . . . / . . . bending his sword / To his great master" (IV.ii.74–76). Cornwall seems almost a father to his servant and parallels Gloucester who has sons opposed also. Cornwall's death begins a process in which, as the moral order rights itself, the upside-down condition is reversed and the evil world finds its former prerogatives overturned.[17]

The inner man is not exempt from these external disorders. The clearest sign of mental inversion is madness, to which, clearly, Lear succumbs. His initial breakdown is rendered in imagery of rotation, such as anything must undergo for the lower to take over from the higher. Lear is not so far gone that his rational mind is unaware of what is happening, and he supplies the metaphor: "My wits begin to turn" (III.ii.67). In this light, the fool's

17. See, for example, IV.ii.3–11, 17–18, 39–40, and V.i.3–5, where all passages exhibit a language of return to "upside-up" and "downside-down."

song (sung right after Lear's pronouncement of failing sanity) comments as much upon Lear and the point involved as it does upon the fool and all like him whom we identify as the less fortunate of the world:

> "He that has and a little tiny wit—
>> With heigh-ho, the wind and the rain—
> Must make content with his fortunes fit,
>> Though the rain it raineth every day."
>>> (III.ii.74–77)

The Lear universe, as constituted under Goneril and Regan, is a squall-darkened domain. The weakened wit, as well as the man weak in fortune, had best remain content; for his resources, mental and economic, are insufficient to cope with a hostile environment. Contentedly accepting his role as madman/creature-on-the-dole—in other words, not making waves—he is suffered to survive. The fool has twice before tied inclement weather to the condition of the topsy-turvy state and suggested that survival is possible only through submission:

> Nay, an thou canst not smile as the wind sits, thou'lt catch cold shortly.
>> (I.iv.98–99)

> Winter's not gone yet, if the wild-geese fly that way.
>> (II.iv.45–46)

Both these observations, directed at Kent, are comments on the disguised Earl's foolishness in braving the new world. Yet we are sure that the professional fool approves this other fool:

> But I will tarry; the fool will stay,
>> And let the wise man fly.
> The knave turns fool that runs away;
>> The fool no knave, perdy.
>>> (II.iv.80–83)

If the topsy-turvy world is a place that makes some sane and lawful men insane, in which condition they are essentially ignored, it follows then that one of the ways for sane and lawful men to survive in an evil place is to counterfeit the madness that the place engenders. Such was Hamlet's recipe to escape detection and destruction. Such is Edgar's. Having heard himself outlawed, Edgar determines to survive as well as to remain in the evil world determined equally to destroy him. His device is to counterfeit beggarliness and near bestiality (II.iii.7–9). As Edgar, son of Gloucester, he would be hunted to the death and thus as Edgar he is "nothing." But as a madman, as "Poor Turlygod! Poor Tom!" he is "something yet" (20–21), since he remains alive. His antic disposition preserves him in a world dominated totally by evil. A picture of this world awry, given by Edgar as he makes his decision for disguise, presents conditions pervasive throughout the Lear universe. This picture, by its secondary imagery, makes of Edgar and all his counterparts figures crucified by the world, outlawed, so that, like the Son of Man, they have not where to lay their heads (Luke 9.58):

> No port is free, no place
> That guard and most unusual vigilance
> Does not attend my taking. . . .
>
> . . . .
>
> . . . My face I'll grime with filth,
> Blanket my loins . . .
> And with presented nakedness outface
> The winds and persecutions of the sky.
> The country gives me proof and precedent
> Of Bedlam beggars, who, with roaring voices,
> Strike in their numb'd and mortified arms
> Pins, wooden pricks, nails, sprigs of rosemary;
> And with this horrible object, from low farms,
> Poor pelting villages, sheep-cotes, and mills,
> Sometimes with lunatic bans, sometime with prayers,
> Enforce their charity.
>
> (II.iii.3–20)

The Christ symbolism, sometimes seen in Cordelia,[18] may be perceived also in Edgar, beginning with this passage and evoked by the wooden pricks (thorns), nails (of the crucifixion), and perhaps also by the herb rosemary.[19] Certainly like Jesus of Matthew 4.1, Edgar is "led aside of the Spirit into the wildernes, to be tēpted of the deuil," for so he sees and presents himself when first turned

18. See S. L. Bethell, *Shakespeare and the Popular Dramatic Tradition* (Durham, N.C., 1944), pp. 66–68. Other writers make Edgar so mirror-like a reflection of Christ that one wonders why they do not take the final step. See Derek Traversi, "King Lear," *Stratford Papers on Shakespeare*, 1964, ed. B. W. Jackson (Toronto, 1965), and R. A. Foakes, "Shakespeare's Later Tragedies," *Shakespeare: 1564–1964*, ed. Edward Bloom (Providence, R.I., 1964). The idea that two characters in the same play may both be Christ figures seems not so farfetched if we remember that the play has two plots and that Christ has two roles: the sacrificial lamb and the victor over the beast of the Apocalypse.

19. Although the etymology of *rosemary* is *ros marinus* and means simply *sea-dew*, the *OED* states, "In English . . . the first element has been assimilated to Rose *sb.*, and the second may have been taken as the name of the Virgin." The rose is, of course, preeminently a symbol for the Virgin Mary and appears as such in many Middle English lyrics and carols. A sprig of that plant accords with the idea that Christ is a branch of the rose:

> Of a rose, a louely rose,
>   Of a rose is al myn song.
>
> .   .   .   .
>
> The flour sprong in heye Bedlem,
> That is bothe bryght and schen;
> The rose is Mary, heuene qwyn;
>   Out of here bosum the blosme sprong.
>
> The ferst braunche is ful of myght,
> That sprong on Crystemesse nyght;
> The sterre schon ouer Bedlem bryght,
>   That is bothe brod and long.
>
> The second braunche sprong to helle,
> The fendys power doun to felle;
> Therin myght non sowle dwelle;
>   Blyssid be the tyme the rose sprong.

out of his hovel by the terrified fool: "Away! The foul fiend follows me!" (III.iv.45).[20]

If Lear is a man driven truly mad by his world gone awry, Gloucester illustrates the process whereby grief and anger over loss of all the coherencies of life may lead a man to a state that mirrors the conditions about him: "Thou sayest the King grows mad . . . / I am almost mad myself. . . . / The grief hath craz'd my wits" (III.iv.163–68). Gloucester's determination to commit suicide is a form of madness, and when, with Edgar's help, the old Earl throws off his temporary insanity, he complains that he is unable to go truly mad, for madness is clearly a way to survive in a desolate place:

> The King is mad. How stiff is my vile sense,
> That I stand up, and have ingenious feeling
> Of my huge sorrows! Better I were distract;
> · So should my thoughts be sever'd from my griefs,

> The thredde braunche is good and swote;
> It sprang to heuene, crop and rote,
> Therin to dwellyn and ben our bote;
>   Euery day it schewit in prystes hond.
>
> Pray we to here with gret honour,
> Che that bar the blyssid flowr,
> Che be our help and our socour
>   And schyld vs fro the fyndes bond.

Furthermore, Rose Sunday, the fourth Sunday in Lent, has been commemorated since the twelfth century by the gift of the Golden Rose, bestowed by the Pope upon that person most deserving such recognition. Popes Julius II and Leo X both gave a Golden Rose to Henry VIII. Pope Alexander III in *Ex antiqua* (1163) explained to Louis VII that "the flower is the symbol of Christ the King" (*New Catholic Encyclopedia* [New York, 1967], 6:599). For still further identification of the rose with Christ, see appendix, pp. 318–19 and the footnote dependent, number 7.

20. Other lines in which Edgar sees himself as "vexed" by the devil yet determined to put the fiend behind him include III.iv.59–61, 79–82, 95–97, 139, and at least an equal number of passages in III.vi.

And woes by wrong imaginations lose
The knowledge of themselves.

(IV.vi.280–85)

The Gloucester-story disorders reach highest degree of displacement when Cornwall elevates the evil son to the rank of his father: "True or false, it hath made thee Earl of Gloucester" (III.v.18–19). Hoping at first only to climb over his brother and "top th' legitimate," Edmund has succeeded so well as to supplant his father. He casts beyond even the earldom when, in his later plans, he sees a royal crown within reach through marriage with one or the other of the reigning duchesses, but his overtopping his father completes the reversals of the Gloucester subplot.

In a topsy-turvy world, where all things take on values opposite to those in a harmonious and moral order and where the senses fail seriously, problems of identification may be expected as well. Shakespeare explored the theme of identity in *Hamlet* more than he does in *Lear*; yet since human delineation is inescapably blurred in a darkened world, the theme has significant proportions in the Lear universe, in fact in the somber world of all the tragedies. Shakespeare, characteristically early, announces his intention to weave the identification motif into *Lear*. When Gloucester introduces Edmund to Kent, the younger man says to the older, "My services to your lordship," and Kent's response is, "I must love you, and sue to know you better" (I.i.29–30). The Earl knows what is required of him; he must love his neighbor as himself (note that Edmund fails to use the word *love*, but offers service instead); yet, being taught caution by the forty-eight years on his back, Kent wants also to know his new acquaintance better, something not accomplished easily, as we have said, in the growing gloom of a kingdom about to be abandoned by its anointed head.

At the very core of the play is, of course, the identity of Lear himself. Two of his daughters, with all their entourage (especially Cornwall), are only too eager to forget who he is. They are helped by the old man himself who attempts the "great refusal," attempts to divest himself of crown and scepter. This feat he cannot accomplish, since these outward symbols of an invisible election, bestowed by God, can be removed by God alone. Goneril is foremost among the kingdom who would forget her father's ineradicable anointment: "I would you would . . . / . . . put away / These dispositions which of late transport you / From what you rightly are" (I.iv.216–19). The fool refines Goneril's distinction finer than she desires: "May not an ass know when the cart draws the horse?" (220–21). Not only an image of the inverted kingdom, the fool's response to Goneril's words shows also that daughters come behind fathers and duchesses behind kings; it is the daughter who refuses rightly to know who her father is. But Goneril is representative of a general condition. When Lear acts out his little interlude—

> Does any here know me? This is not Lear.
> Does Lear walk thus? Speak thus? . . .
> Who is it that can tell me who I am?—

no one answers, except the fool, who tells Lear he is reduced to a shadow. Lear continues his playlet when he demands of Goneril, "Your name, fair gentlewoman?" (I.iv.222–32). Not only King and daughter have identity alterations; followers on both sides must look again in their mirrors. Lear is to be allowed in his train only men "Which know themselves and you" (248); clearly they have misidentified Goneril's people: "your disorder'd rabble / Make servants of their betters" (252–53). When Regan goes through much the same quarrel with her father in front of Gloucester's castle, Kent, in the stocks, is used, among other things, to continue the identification theme: "What's he that hath so much thy place mistook / To set thee here?" (II.iv.11–12). In all these passages, those of the Goneril/Regan persuasion refer constantly to Lear in ways that avoid his title—"this man," "old man," "sir," etc.—while all the spokesmen for good are made by Shakespeare to refer very carefully to Lear as "King," "majesty," "royal," etc.

Act III, scene ii, opens with the same words that open I.ii. in *Hamlet*. As does the soldier Bernardo, Kent cries out, "Who's there?" The significance of this question is much the same in both plays. The new world, established at the overturning of the harmonious old order, is a world of darkness, cold, and storm ("foul weather"). The cry "Who's there?" carries the metaphysical and mystical fears of all men at all times: who are you? what are you? whom and what do you represent: foe or friend, evil or good? Implicitly it contains also the troubling concern of who am I?—in short, the importance of identification and identity.[21] Kent's first cry turns up an anonymous gentleman, like-minded with the foul weather. When searching for Lear on the heath, Kent calls out a second time: "Who's there?" (III.ii.39). He is answered first by the fool—"Marry, here's grace and a codpiece"—then, rather indirectly, by Lear. The disturbed King comments on man's difficulty in identifying his enemies; it takes the omnipotent to do that: "Let the great gods, / That keep this dreadful pudder o'er our heads, / Find out their enemies now" (49–51). Of course, enemies to God are our enemies also. The ambiance of the drifting Lear universe is foulness; the inhabitants, chiefly, enemies and fools born out of lechery (codpiece). But the ineradicable grace of kingship is discernible still. Lear, who has asked one enemy already, "Are you our daughter?" (I.iv.215), is identified by the self-proclaimed lecherous fool[22] as a creature of "grace." Nevertheless, Lear's grace is stained. Although he urges others to "cry / These dreadful summoners grace," with the implication that he is not so much in need as they—"I am a man / More sinn'd against than sinning" (III.ii.58–60)—he is just beginning to fulfill the role of true king. Perhaps for the first time in his life he shows care and love for one beneath him in the chain of being—and all are beneath him in that chain. For king above, the irreducible obligations owed downwards are care and love. Lear, who says these things to the fool, one who has been close to him always, does not restrict his new concern to close friends. Apart from urging the sinners in his kingdom to seek for

21. For additional observations on the implications of "Who's there?" and the identity theme, see chap. 1, pp. 16–19.
22. See I.v.49–51.

grace (III.ii.51–59), he acknowledges his own earlier failures to provide for the sinless wretched of his realm:

> Poor naked wretches, wheresoe'er you are,
> That bide the pelting of this pitiless storm,
> How shall your houseless heads and unfed sides,
> Your loop'd and window'd raggedness, defend you
> From seasons such as these? O, I have ta'en
> Too little care of this! Take physic, pomp;
> Expose thyself to feel what wretches feel,
> That thou mayst shake the superflux to them.
>
> (III.iv.28–35)

In these two utterances, Lear shows a new identity, one he has learned painfully, but one that all proper kings must have. Lear has begun to know himself as king. He mistook to think that he could play the role in any manner he chose as well as to think that he could throw off the robes of responsibility—of rule—that cast the kingdom initially into the darkness and turbulence he finds there.

These awarenesses in the King are but new and fresh when the fool creeps into the hovel where Edgar as Poor Tom hides from this same storm and all that it represents. As the fool comes flying out in terror, crying for help, for protection from some unidentified spirit, presumably evil, Kent illustrates the proper role—love and protection—for one below him: "Give me thy hand" (III.iv.41). At the same time the disguised Earl demands (the third time for this crucial question), "Who's there?" (41). The person who emerges is Edgar, in his previous appearance in the play adorned with Christ-iconography. He asserts that he is surrounded and vexed by fiends. Among the various answers, then, to the question "Who's there?" is the clear statement that we are all in the midst of a world of working evil, whose inhabitants we must identify so as to be able—as Edgar instructs—to "defy the foul fiend" (III.iv.96–97).

Part of Lear's continuing self-knowledge includes not only

the growing sense of his responsibilities as king but also his identification first as mere mortal—"They told me I was everything. 'Tis
a lie, I am not ague-proof" (IV.vi.104–5)—and second as mortal
common with the rest of mankind:

> Is man no more than this? . . . unaccommodated man
> is no more but such a poor, bare, forked animal. . . .
> Off, off, you lendings! Come, unbutton here.
>
> (III.iv.101–8)

But Lear's belief in his kingship—which he never doubted and
never relinquished (only its responsibilities)—is so strong that even
in his worst bouts of madness he remains clear on that point: "they
cannot touch me for coining; I am the King himself" (IV.vi.83–84);
"Ay, every inch a king" (107); "Come, come, I am a king, / Masters,
know you that?" (199–200). In answer to this last assertion and
following question, the gentleman addressed, as all those loyal to
Lear, emphasizes not only the King's persona but also the obligations of a subject: "You are a royal one, and we obey you" (201).

When Lear is restored to Cordelia both in person and in
mind, she is concerned to restore also his trappings and his rever-
ence: "Is he array'd?" (IV.vii.21); "How does my royal lord? How
fares your Majesty?" (45). To restore him as father (and just as importantly, herself as daughter) is still another need: "O, look upon
me, sir, / And hold your hand in benediction o'er me. / You must
not kneel" (58–60). Truly, Lear comes out of his stupor slowly,
with much confusion and doubt as to his identity, his whereabouts,
and the identities of those around him; but the language in which
these matters are cleared up, the stage-time spent upon them,
serve to emphasize the importance of this theme. From the moment of Lear's awakening under the doctor's hands to the later
point at which the doctor pronounces that "The great rage / . . . is
kill'd in him" (80–81)—almost forty lines of the final scene of the
fourth act—the playwright is engaged in identifications: king and
father, subject and daughter, servants and lord, place and value.
Prior to these recognitions, Cordelia refers to her father as "poor

perdu!" (IV.vii.36), which raises the almost inevitable thought that he who was lost is found.[23]

These matters of identification are met also in the Gloucester story. Apart from the obvious false appearances caused by Edmund's machinations, the old Earl himself has lost his proper persona, a result of his early easy and sliding morality, perhaps also of his failure to second Kent during Lear's initial announcement of abdication. But Edgar has most reason to question his father's identity. Disowned and dispossessed, Edgar knows no cause for the Earl's change from a loving parent to a remorseless persecutor. When first he sees his father, after being forced into disguise and outlawry, Edgar identifies Gloucester as "the foul Flibbertigibbet" (III.iv.114). All chime in at this point to further the theme. Lear looks toward the creature so named by Edgar and cries, "What's he?" (125). Kent follows with the formulaic "Who's there?" (126). Gloucester, no better off in the murk and darkness of fear and suspicion, demands in return, "What are you there? Your names?" (127).[24]

Otherwise an ideal time for Edgar to leap out to reconcile himself with his father, the conditions of the times are such that even the good man submits to identity change; and the son misleads the father with a lengthy description of himself, concluding that he has been Poor Tom, in dreadful plight, for "seven long year" (128–38). Instead of revealing himself, Edgar continues in disguise. As Lear and his party make for Dover to escape the plot on the King's life, Edgar "lurks" behind to "bewray" himself, only "When false opinion, whose wrong thoughts defile thee, / In thy just proof repeals and reconciles thee" (III.vi.111–15).

Edgar discovers, however, that he remained behind for something else as well. When he sees his father blind and poorly

---

23. See G. I. Duthie, *King Lear*, The New Cambridge Shakespeare (Cambridge, Eng., 1960), pp. xx–xxiii. The parable of the prodigal son is in Luke 15.11–32.

24. Exactly as Francisco responds to Bernardo's "Who's there?": "Nay, answer me. Stand and unfold yourself" (*Hamlet*, I.i.1–2).

led, he commits himself to his father's regeneration. Leading the old man to a pasture near the cliffs of Dover, he lets the despairing Earl believe he has fallen from the "dread summit." When Gloucester revives, Edgar must know if the Earl has rediscovered self: "What are you, sir?" (IV.vi.48). The scene is punctuated by the arrival of the mad Lear and by Edgar's query of "who comes here?" (80). The pretended madness of Poor Tom and the near-madness of the distraught Earl are merged into the all-too-real madness of the King, driven so by the kingdom and family who have forgotten who he is. In the same scene a kind of seal is put on Gloucester's restoration with a direct question and a direct answer: Gloucester asks the King, "Dost thou know me?" (135), and although it takes some forty lines, during which the King wanders in and out of lucidity, the identification comes clear and definitive: "I know thee well enough; thy name is Gloucester" (177).

So much for the father. Edgar has still to regain his lost identity. Having given up his name for that of Poor Tom, Edgar responds to the herald of the combat scene appropriately. "What are you?" he is asked. "Know my name is lost," he responds (V.iii.121–23). Edmund is then brought into this kind of labeling: "What's he that speaks for Edmund Earl of Gloucester?" (127). Put into other words, the question demands to know what kind of creature could have supplanted a still-living father, taking his name, his titles, his estates. The single combat is fought; Edgar wins; Edmund lies dying. Evil is everywhere defeated; Goneril is unmasked as Edmund's lover and potential murderer of her husband. Edgar may now reclaim his name with a simple disclosure: "My name is Edgar, and thy father's son" (V.iii.172); as such he is accepted and embraced by Albany: "Methought thy very gait did prophesy / A royal nobleness" (178–79). One must wonder why Shakespeare allows Albany to use the adjective "royal" in address to Edgar. Extremely sensitive to the significance of the epithet— that it must be reserved for members of the reigning house— Shakespeare may be fitting out the King-of-Kings imagery he sometimes attaches to Edgar. If so, extra dimension must be given to Albany's full response: "Let sorrow split my heart, if ever I / Did hate thee or thy father!" (180–81).

Kent is not neglected in these restorations. As the King wrestles with dimming sight and heeds the painful lesson learned—not to trust the senses even when at their best—he wants to hear the man himself make an assertion: "Who are you?" he demands of the Earl; "Are you not Kent?" (V.iii.282, 286). Kent then identifies himself, first by name, second by the service he has rendered as disguised servant.

There remains only the recrowning of Lear, incomplete until Albany abdicates, which he does all too briefly. For moments after he "resign[s]" his "absolute power," Lear dies (303–5).

II

What appear to me the overwhelming Christian issues of the play have not been admitted always and in fact often have been denied vehemently.[25] In the face of this considerable opposition, some critics have persevered to maintain that in this play a statement of considerable scope is wrapped in Christian thought and iconography. Nevertheless, the idea of Cordelia as a Christ figure, though suggested with reasonable frequency, has been opposed fiercely.[26] Stubbornly, I have already gone farther, suggesting that not Cordelia alone but both Cordelia and Edgar carry pronounced features of different aspects of Christ. If Cordelia is Christ sacrificial lamb, Edgar is Christ champion and ultimately Christ victor. Early in the play he undergoes the mortal ministry such as outlawry (see pp. 137–39), temptation by the devil (pp. 138–39, 143), and passion (at least the scourging and crowning with thorns, pp. 137–38). Thereafter, in a way more removed, possibly representative of the Comforter, he works for the salvation of a father

25. For a rehearsal of the debate over a Christian or non-Christian interpretation of *Lear*, see Elton, *King Lear and the Gods*, and footnote 1 above.

26. See John F. Danby, *Shakespeare's Doctrine of Nature* (London, 1961), pp. 114–25; Bethel, *Shakespeare and the Popular Tradition*, pp. 66–68; and M. D. H. Parker, *The Slave of Life* (London, 1955), pp. 141–42.

deep in despair, and, that completed successfully, he puts on the armor of the church militant to combat the dragon error, and, triumphant, plants his foot on evil's neck, restoring the kingdom to goodness as the last of its forces of darkness expire.

The first to meet Edgar after he undergoes his symbolic passion is the fool. Perhaps significance may be attached to the fool's identification of Poor Tom as a "spirit" (III.iv.39), an assertion that is twice more repeated in answer to Kent's "Who's there?" (III.iv.41–42). Surely no word better fits Edgar's subsequent behavior than the word *Comforter*. As Poor Tom, the outcast seems indeed to bring more peace to Lear than either the devoted Kent or the beloved and loving fool. Then, as a series of changing characters—Poor Tom, the fellow "better spoken," the bystander at the base of the cliff, and the Somerset peasant—Edgar brings comfort and grace to his despairing father.

In similar manner, the various plights of the outlawed Edgar reflect the adversities of Christ "led aside of the Spirit into the wildernes" (Matthew 4.1). After forty days of fasting Christ hungered. The beggar/madman who complains that no one gives "anything to Poor Tom" (III.iv.50) and who eats "the swimming frog, the toad, the tadpole,[27] the wall-newt and the water"[28] (128–29) must be

---

27. In swallowing frogs and toads, Edgar reverses the act of Satan in Rev. 16.13. See also footnotes 28 and 33 below.

28. From another point of view, Edgar's consumption of these creatures may be seen as Christ's triumph over Satan. The newt, like the salamander, is a type for Satan since, as Bartholomaeus Anglicus indicates, "*salamandra* is a manner kind of an Ewt [*sic*]" and painters, following Hugo van der Goes and others, render Satan, in the very act of tempting Eve, as a huge salamander (see fig. 28). See *Batman vppon Bartholome His Booke De Proprietatibus Rerum* (London, 1582), Bk. XVIII, cap. 92, and Robert Koch, "The Salamander in van der Goes' *Garden of Eden*," *Journal of the Warburg and Courtauld Institutes* 28 (1965): 323–26. Bartholomaeus claims further that "the *salamandra* . . . corrupteth water, so that he that . . . drinketh thereof, is slayne anone" (Bk. XVIII, cap. 92). Edgar's drinking water would seem to be the habitat of all his amphibians—frogs, toads, tadpoles, and newts combined. That Edgar survives its ingestion may be read as further proof of the fiend's inability to harm him. The witches in *Macbeth* throw "eye of newt" in their cauldron (IV.i.14).

very hungry to take such fare. Christ, after refusing to make bread
of stones to assuage his hunger, is tempted by the devil to suicide
(Matthew 4.3–7). Tom, after complaining of having nothing, reports that

> the foul fiend hath led him through fire and through
> flame . . . hath laid knives under his pillow, and halters
> in his pew, set ratsbane by his porridge.
>
> (III.iv.51–54)

The third temptation of Christ is the devil's offer of the glories of
the world (Matthew 4.8–9)—matters for pride—and Tom follows
his recital of the fiend's attempts to make him suicidal with a history of his former achievements, all amounting to pride "in heart
and mind" (84). Everywhere through this account Edgar has de-
fied the foul fiend, even as Christ. In the very midst of these parallels, Lear likens Poor Tom to one whose flesh has been ripped and
torn like the pelican's, whose young were reported to live off the

Fig. 8. Pelican misericord. SS Peter and Paul, Lavenham, Suffolk.

flesh and blood of their parents (71–74). The iconography of the pelican as Christ is well known (fig. 8).[29] At this juncture Tom recites the oft-noted variations on the Ten Commandments (79–82).[30]

When Poor Tom is appointed one of Lear's commission at the imaginary trial of Goneril and Regan, the beggar breaks into a jingle after first urging that at this judgment they deal "justly":

> Sleepest or wakest thou, jolly shepherd?
> > Thy sheep be in the corn;
> And for one blast of thy minikin mouth,
> > Thy sheep shall take no harm.
> > > > > (III.vi.41–44)

A herder whose flock is in danger suggests strongly the Good Shepherd of John 10.11–15.[31]

29. Florence McCulloch gives the basic texts and interpretations: "The pelican is said to have great love for its young. However, when these begin to grow, they strike their parents in the face. Their parents in turn strike and kill them. After three days their mother pierces her side and sheds her blood over the dead children, thus reviving them.

"Allegorically Christ is the pelican whom mankind struck by serving what has been created rather than the creator. Christ then ascended the cross, where from his side flowed the blood and water of man's salvation and eternal life. . . .

"Here also there is a variation. . . . Instead of the mother's resuscitating the young, it is the father who, regretting his action which had caused their death, pierces his side": *Mediaeval Latin and French Bestiaries*, University of North Carolina Studies in the Romance Languages and Literatures, no. 33 (Chapel Hill, 1960), pp. 155–56. Additional citations may be found in the very comprehensive footnote in the Arden *King Lear*, pp. 118–19. The Arden sources were readily available to Shakespeare and include Geffrey Whitney's *A choice of emblemes* (Leyden, 1586), p. 87 (fig. 8), a work almost certainly a source for Shakespeare's skull imagery in *As You Like It*. See chap. 8, pp. 308–9.

30. See, for example, Coursen, *Christian Ritual*, pp. 307–8, note 2.

31. Muir (Arden Shakespeare), p. 133, argues that the corn is in danger and not the sheep. Although that would seem to be true, the quatrain announces concern for the sheep. The "blast" from the Good

Although the analogy is not close, yet it may be noted that Edgar on the heath, when he first sees his father blind and poorly led, undergoes something akin to Christ's agony in the garden. Like Christ, Edgar addresses deity and then indicates that his spirit has never been tormented more: "O gods! Who is 't can say 'I am at the worst'? / I am worse than e'er I was" (IV.i.25–26). His first reaction to the fantastically arrayed and insane Lear is "O thou side-piercing sight!" (IV.vi.86). The symbolic restoration of Gloucester's sight through miraculous intervention (IV.vi.55, 72–74) has striking similarities to Mark's account of the blind man healed (8.22–25).

The entire second scene of the fifth act has unmistakable associations with Christ and his teachings. Edgar leaves his father in what he takes to be a place of safety until he returns from the battle imminent between the French and English:

> Here, father, take the shadow of this tree
> For your good host; pray that the right may thrive.
> If ever I return to you again,
> I'll bring you comfort.
>
> (V.ii.1–4)

Gloucester is called to come under the shadow of the tree. Tree as substitute for cross is so common in medieval poetry as to need no citation, but perhaps valuable for my purpose is the lovely lyric that concludes

> Nou goð sonne vnder tre,—
> me reweð, marie, ði sone and ðe.[32]

In these verses the pun on *son-sun* produces the shadow mentioned by Edgar. Gloucester's son likens the tree to a host, an un-

---

Shepherd's "minikin mouth" glances obliquely at the judgment trumpet, the more so in that one meaning of *minikin* is *shrill*. See *OED* B.2.

32. Carleton Brown, *English Lyrics of the XIII*th *Century* (Oxford, 1932), p. 1.

usual metaphor if he evokes tree only as hostel or hostel-keeper. Shakespeare reaches for the meaning of *host* as eucharist. Edgar must leave after these lines to aid in the restoration of the true king; but his promise to return if possible is phrased in words highly reminiscent of Christ's promise to his disciples. Edgar says he will "bring . . . comfort"; Christ's words, iterated four times in John 14–16, are closest to Edgar's in 16.7:

> It is expedient for you that I go away: for if I go not away, the Cõforter wil not come vnto you; but if I departe, I wil send him vnto you.

Gloucester prays that "Grace go with" him (4), and when Edgar returns, he has, in a sense, altered from Christ ministrant to Christ militant. As Gloucester lapses again into despair, comfort comes from Edgar exactly in the terms expressed by Christ in John 16.8: "And when he is come, he wil reproue the worlde of sinne, and of righteousnes, and of iudgement." Edgar rebukes his father strongly as the note of judgment, so pervasive throughout the play, brings this drama to one of its two great resolutions:

> What, in ill thoughts again? Men must endure
> Their going hence, even as their coming hither;
> Ripeness is all.
>
> (V.ii.9–11)

Edgar's role as Christ triumphant is rendered in materials that merge with the apocalyptic elements in the play. The champion's appearance follows four blasts of the trumpet—possibly to the four corners of the earth—and he enters "*armed*" (V.iii.111–19). He challenges the creature who has repudiated God and made Nature his goddess, accusing him of being "False to thy gods," and characterizing him as "A most toad-spotted traitor" (137–41). The fight ensues, and Edgar vanquishes the epitome of evil, stands over his fallen foe. The scene carries elements of judgment-day descriptions found in I Cor. 15.24–28 and Rev. 20–21, the toad image being Shakespeare's substitution for the dragon or serpent.[33] Trumpets have been heard everywhere as most of the major figures of the play come to death and implied judgment. Edgar describes Gloucester and Kent in a farewell embrace as the one dies and the other has some sort of mortal stroke: "Twice then the trumpets sounded" (V.iii.221); but the one has died when his "heart . . . burst smilingly," and the other is "tranc'd" as "the strings of life / Began to crack" (200–203, 220–22). The sisters, twinned in evil, die as they pursue their respective evils, one of them a sororicide and suicide, called by her husband a "gilded serpent" (V.iii.86). Evil Edmund is brought by some unknown depth within him to grant forgiveness to the brother who has given him

33. The toad has stood traditionally as one of the many types for Satan or the lesser demons. Scriptural authority is found in Rev. 16. 13–14: "And I sawe thre vncleane spirits like frogges come out of the mouth of the dragon, & out of the mouth of the beast, and out of the mouth of the false prophet. / For they are the spirits of deuils, working miracles, to go vnto the Kings of the earth, and of the whole worlde, to gather them to the battel of that great day of God Almightie." Rabanus Maurus shows that, from as early as the ninth century, iconography identified frogs as amphibians both noxious and evil; on the one hand they comprised the plague of Exodus 8.2–14 and on the other a form of fiendish spirit which he calls *Ranae daemones* (*De Universo*, Patrologia Latinae, 111, 228).

Frogs and toads were almost interchangeable in folklore. A variation of the verses in Revelation, substituting toads, illustrates *OED* definition 1: "Trevisa *Higden* (Rolls) VIII.18. A womman þat hadde a fend wiþ inne her . . . caste up twe blake taddes." That Shakespeare knew this demonological lore is clear from *Macbeth*, whose Second Witch answers to Paddock's call (I.i.9). Muir suggests Reginald Scot as a possible source for the line: "Some say they keepe divels and spirits in the likenesse of todes and cats" (Arden *Macbeth*, p. 4, note).

Of special interest to a reading of *Lear* is the "battel of that great day of God Almightie," associated in Rev. 16.14 with the activities of the froglike demons. Christ's prophecy of "warres, and rumors of warres" is fulfilled in the great battle of Revelation and is matched in *Lear* by the battle between the French and English. The only true victors of the battle in *Lear* are the forces of good, the only true vanquished, the forces of evil. See also footnotes 27 and 28 above.

his death wound. He means "some good . . . to do, / Despite of [his] own nature," and receives the charity of his conqueror, who makes judgmental pronouncements:

> The gods are just, and of our pleasant vices
> Make instruments to plague us.
> (V.iii.169–74, 203–4, 247–48)

Others seem compelled to give an accounting of their lives, such as Albany's apologia to Edgar—"Let sorrow split my heart, if ever I / Did hate thee or thy father!"—and Kent's blunt insistence that his service be recognized—"That from your first of difference and decay / Have follow'd your sad steps" (180–81, 292–93). As the bodies of Goneril and Regan are brought on stage, Albany likens their punishment to the "judgment of the heavens, that makes us tremble" (235), and Kent wonders, "Is this the promis'd end?" (267). Even if it is only an "image of that horror" (268), Albany expects all to "Fall, and cease!" while Lear believes the "heaven's vault should crack" (263). The general imagery is at the verge of that moment when "the first heauen, and the first earth were passed away" (Rev. 21.1) and when "shal the Sōne also him self be subiect vnto him," when "he hathe put downe all rule, and all autoritie and power" (I Cor. 15.28, 24). The latter of these scriptures is fulfilled perhaps in Edgar (the Christ triumphant) refusing the rule offered him by Albany.[34]

    The most important aspect of Cordelia's identification with Christ is the role she plays in the apocalyptic theme. Other parts of her typology have been pointed out.[35] She comes to this symbolism perhaps only after her return to England from France, when she

34. The curtain speech of the play, sometimes given to Albany (as by Kittredge, who follows Q_1), is given by F_1 to Edgar and interpreted by Muir in the Arden *Lear* to be Edgar's answer to Albany's offer that Edgar share the rule with Kent. The sense of Edgar's answer is that he will not take the rule, that Albany speaks out of grief, not out of the fitness of things. But see also F. T. Flahiff, "Edgar: Once and Future King," in *Some Facets of King Lear*, ed. Rosalie L. Colie and F. T. Flahiff (Toronto, 1974), pp. 221–37.

35. See p. 147 above and note 26.

serves as restorer-redeemer-savior to a Lear reborn. Earliest hints of what she is to become echo in France's words, uttered when he refuses to give credence to Lear's "be-monstering" portrait of the formerly "Fairest Cordelia":

> which to believe of her
> Must be a faith that reason without miracle
> Should never plant in me.
>
> (I.i.222–24)

Although matters are reversed, the terms of belief are theological and most applicable to godhead, which may never be established (or in this case disproved) without faith arrived at through miracle.

Nevertheless, an imagery unmistakable attaches to Cordelia, beginning with the unnamed gentleman's description of her receipt of Kent's letters: "There she shook / The holy water from her heavenly eyes" (IV.iii.30–31). The double entendre in her gentle assurance, "dear father, / It is thy business that I go about" (IV.iv.23–24), is, of course, a close echo of Luke 2.49: "knewe ye not that I must go about my fathers busines." Another unnamed gentleman's praise continues the introductory language of symbolic identification:

> Thou hast one daughter
> Who redeems nature from the general curse
> Which twain have brought her to.
>
> (IV.vi.205–7)[36]

More profound apocalyptic imagery attends the actual restoration of Lear. Cordelia's reference to her father as "poor perdu" who has hoveled "with swine . . . / In short and musty straw"

36. These lines, elicited by J. F. Danby, and argued to refer to Adam and Eve (*Shakespeare's Doctrine of Nature*, p. 125), are rejected unimaginatively by Muir (Arden *Lear*, p. 183), who maintains that *twain* refers only to Goneril and Regan. The reader may see where my sentiments lie, but Cordelia's redemptive nature does not rely necessarily on the identification of the twain. Christ redeems daily, even as the sinner partakes daily of the old Adam.

(IV.vii.36–41) has been likened to the parable of the prodigal son.[37] This parable in Luke 15 is followed in Luke 16 with that of Dives and Lazarus. Both parables as well as those others of Luke 15 and 16—of the lost sheep, of the lost coin, of the unjust steward—are parables concerning judgment and are to be read anagogically as warnings of the Last Judgment. The parable of Dives and Lazarus is an almost inseparable part of the great Gothic cathedral portals which present the Last Judgment in their tympana, since most of them include the patriarch Abraham, dandling souls of the blessed in his bosom.[38] Shakespeare was so taken with the parable that he employed it often in plays earlier than *Lear* and for the same eschatological purposes as that which it serves in this play.[39]

As the "poor perdu" awakens from his restorative sleep,

37. See pp. 144–45 above and footnote 23 above.

38. Abraham, whose image appears for the first time in the porch of the judgment portal at Moissac, is part of an elaborate, deep-relief sculpture that tells fully the Dives-Lazarus story. The patriarch is found without the glutton and beggar in such portals as those at Reims, Bourges, Chartres, Laon, and many others. But more important for an Englishman is the series of carved stone panels on the north side of the main portal of Lincoln Cathedral (fig. 25). The entire sequence is of great significance to my argument. First is Dives at table, then follow the death of Lazarus and Dives in hell, Lazarus in Abraham's bosom, the souls of the blessed, the harrowing of hell, and the torments of the damned, in the words of T. S. R. Boase, "a far more reasoned statement on the theme of salvation and damnation than anything we have yet seen in English sculpture": *English Art, 1100–1216* (Oxford, 1953), p. 120.

39. See the sequential use of the elements of the parable in *I Henry IV*, III.iii.31–33; IV.ii.24–26; *II Henry IV*, I.ii.34–35; and *Henry V*, II.iii.9–10, where all are employed in the Falstaff story, plotting his spiritual journey from glutton, doomed to damnation, to surprise death-bed repentance, winding up, after all, in Arthur's bosom. The prodigal-son theme has been seen in the *Henry* plays also. See J. D. Wilson, "Riot and the Prodigal Prince," in *The Fortunes of Falstaff* (Cambridge, Eng., 1944), pp. 17–25. A. R. Humphreys makes the point in this manner: "The Dives-and-Lazarus parable . . . seems, like that of the Prodigal Son . . . to have impressed Falstaff" (Arden *I Henry IV*, p. 21n).

prescribed by the doctor to quell the "great rage" within him, he revives in agony:

> You do me wrong to take me out o' th' grave.
> Thou art a soul in bliss; but I am bound
> Upon a wheel of fire, that mine own tears
> Do scald like molten lead.
>
> (IV.vii.46–49)

The image conveys more than Lear's belief that he is in hell, as several critics have suggested and most have accepted.[40] Lear emerges also from the grave. The picture we get is highly reminiscent of judgment-day scenes from Gothic cathedral portals as well as chancel-arch paintings such as that in the Guild Chapel in Stratford (fig. 9).[41] Lear is like those souls who, will they nil they, arise from their tombs at the sound of the trumpet, and still bewildered ("far wide"), must wonder where they are and where they are headed. Lear, convinced of his sinfulness, believes he is in hell, but like Dives, "being in hel in torments, he lift vp his eyes, and sawe Abraham a farre of, & Lazarus in his bosome" (Luke 16.23). In Lear's case, Lazarus is Cordelia, who must be dead also if Lear himself is dead; yet Cordelia will be on the other side of "a great gulfe set" (16.26). In most judgment-day sculpture and painting, both the damned and the blessed are visible at once, and to my mind, in the Guild Chapel painting, one of the damned does indeed for the moment turn his back to the flaming mouth of hell he

40. See Muir, Arden *Lear*, p. 190n; and J. D. Wilson, New Cambridge *Lear*, p. 257.

41. Although it seems probable that the wall painting was obliterated about one or two years before Shakespeare's birth, its defacement is not certain (fig. 9). See Mary Lascelles, "'King Lear' and Doomsday," *Shakespeare Survey* 29 (1973): 74. In any case, the tableau to which I refer may have been seen by Shakespeare in other such paintings (an extant Last Judgment graces a chancel arch in Suffolk, fig. 10) and in the imagery of the parable itself. Although Lascelles finds parallels between doomsday imagery and *Lear*, she does not draw any of the conclusions reached in this essay.

Painting on the West Face of the Wall
which divides the Nave from the Chancel of the
Chapel of the Trinity at
STRATFORD upon AVON in WARWICKSHIRE

Fig. 9. Copy of chancel-arch Last Judgment. Guild Chapel, Stratford-

upon-Avon. By permission of the Folger Shakespeare Library.

must soon enter and gaze afar off toward the blessed, grouped about the gates of heaven.

The entire episode of Cordelia's death and its Christological analogues has been commented on by Herbert R. Coursen, Jr., although he arrives at conclusions different from those which I suggest here. Coursen elaborates on the passion symbolism in Cordelia's death and argues that it be seen in the context of the crucifixion; but he does not emphasize, as I would, that she dies by hanging.[42] The common late medieval figure for the crucifixion had Christ hanging on a tree.[43] For the purpose of illustrating a point, I have chosen from among many the following fourteenth-century lyric:

> Abyde, gud men, & hald yhour pays
> And here what god him-seluen says,
>   Hyngand on ðe rode.
> Man & woman ðat bi me gase,
> Luke vp to me & stynt ði pase,
>   For ðe I sched my blode.
>
> Be-hald my body or ðou gang,
> And think opon my payns strang,
>   And styll als stane ðou stand.
> Bihald ði self ðe soth, & se
> How I am hynged here on ðis tre
>   And nayled fute & hand.
>
> Behald my heued, bi-hald my fete,
> And of m[o] mysdedes luke ðou lete;
>   Behald my grysely face
> And of ði syns ask aleggance,

---

42. Coursen, *Christian Ritual*, pp. 299–301.

43. Possibly the same tradition prompted the Geneva translators to retain the image in Acts 5.30: "The God of our fathers hathe raised vp Iesus, whome ye slew, & hanged on a tre." The metaphor is repeated in Acts 10.39 and Gal. 3.13.

Fig. 10. Doomsday painting. Painted board, ca. 1500. Chancel arch. St. Peter's, Wenhaston, Suffolk.

> And in my mercy haue affyance
> And ðou sall gett my grace.[44]

This poem brings together two features of Cordelia's death. Not only was she hung from a beam (rood-tree) but also Lear's last words echo the repeated injunction of the fourteenth-century poet: "luke vp to me," "Be-hald," "Bihald," "Behald my grysely face." Lear cries, "Look on her, look . . . / Look there, look there!" (V.iii.315–16). Shakespeare directs us, even as does the author of the medieval poem, to John 19.26: "Ecce Homo."[45]

The plea of Lear, as he enters the room with the dead Cordelia in his arms (an image first of the deposition and then of pietà?), is that something be done to crack the vault of heaven.

44. Carleton Brown, ed. *Religious Lyrics of the XIV*[th] *Century* (Oxford, 1957), pp. 59–60.

45. Without getting deeply into the argument rehearsed by Coursen, pp. 299–307, as to whether Lear dies in a state of joy or dismay, we may say at the very least that he dies with his gaze fixed steadfastly upon the image of a surrogate Christ, while that surrogate fulfills the role of redeemer.

While Coursen sees this imagery as suggestive of the rent in the veil of the temple and of the earthquake concomitant with the crucifixion,[46] certainly in secondary implication we see it also as the destruction of "the first heauen" which gives way to the "new heauen" on the last day (Rev. 21.1). Once again the Christ typology of the play is fused with the apocalyptic theme.

If Lear is redeemed, as he would seem to be, in light of his reconciliation with the Savior/Cordelia and in light of his pledge to Cordelia never to be separated again—

> Have I caught thee?
> He that parts us shall bring a brand from heaven,
> And fire us hence like foxes—
>   (V.iii.21–23)

then he has fulfilled the role that I have assigned him in my hypothetical tetralogy. He is the man evil at the outset of his drama insofar as he has made the great refusal both in state and family; but he has been redeemed by play's end through recognition of his sins, through contrition for them, through confession that he has severed himself unacceptably from rule and from daughter, through satisfaction paid by his suffering and death, and chiefly through the absolution given by Christ himself in the symbolic figure of his daughter with whom he is totally and lovingly reconciled.

46. Coursen, *Christian Ritual*, p. 303.

4. *Macbeth:*
The Great
Doom's Image, II

he last of my hypothetical tetralogy is *Mac-beth*, a play in which the protagonist is a man bad at the outset. As such, Macbeth has two options: he may remain evil and renounce heaven or he may repent of his sins and seek redemption. Because of the unique punishment bestowed upon Macbeth for betrayal of his guest, redemption becomes an impossibility for the murderer early in the play, as we witness him damned upon earth—before the death of his body—in exactly the same manner and for exactly the same crime that Dante condemns Friar Alberigo in *The Divine Comedy*. That Macbeth is evil at play's beginning needs no demonstration. Before he comes into our view in the third scene of the play, riding beside Banquo, he has been tempted clearly to great sin, which though he has not committed neither has he dismissed from mind. We know from Lady Macbeth's earliest meditations that her spouse "wouldst be great"; and though he fears to play false, "yet wouldst wrongly win" (I.v.18, 22). Surely in a field fertile for sin, the witches hope to sow. They mention no meeting with Banquo, only with Macbeth. They seem to

know that Banquo is proof against their temptations, that Macbeth is receptive.

G. Wilson Knight calls *Macbeth* Shakespeare's "most profound and mature vision of evil," an experience of hell.[1] L. C. Knights finds the play "a statement of evil,"[2] and Kenneth Muir "about damnation."[3] All are correct. I cannot read the play tutored by the view of G. R. Elliott, who maintains that in this drama heaven strives "in various ways, to induce Macbeth to repent"; suspense, which might possibly have been killed by the early murder of Duncan, is revived by "the possibility of [Macbeth's] repentance."[4] Instead, I believe that in *Macbeth* Shakespeare presents not only evil, hell, and damnation but also that he shows them in the most complete degrees in which they may be expressed, and that therein he is indebted, possibly, to Dante. Once Macbeth has slain Duncan, he is in an irrevocable state of reprobation, and repentance cannot enter his bosom. In the depth of his iniquity, in the nature of his crime, the evil is "not relative, but absolute"; the murder is "the worst act of evil [that] could well be found."[5] To give it a name is beyond Macduff's powers: "Tongue nor heart / Cannot conceive nor name thee!" (II.iii.64–65). No crime has yet approached it: "Confusion now hath made his masterpiece!" (66). The surest proof of these dramatic assertions lies in Dante, who clearly delineates degrees of evil and the horror of various sins by punishing them commensurately with their depravity in an ever-descending pit and with ever-greater torments, until at the very bottom of hell we find the traitors immersed in ice. The ninth circle of the *Inferno* is a broad lake of four regions: Caina, Antenora, Ptolomaea, and Judecca; as the name of each implies, they punish in narrowing belts of ice the sins of betrayal to kin, to country, to

1. G. Wilson Knight, *The Wheel of Fire* (Oxford, 1930), p. 154; *The Burning Oracle* (Oxford, 1939), p. 54.

2. L. C. Knights, *Explorations* (New York, 1947), p. 32.

3. Kenneth Muir, ed., *Macbeth*, Arden Shakespeare (London, 1951), p. 11.

4. G. R. Elliott, *Dramatic Providence in "Macbeth"* (Princeton, 1958), pp. x, 23.

5. Knight, *Wheel of Fire*, pp. 154, 169.

guests, and to lords. Dante places Judas Iscariot in one of Satan's three mouths as the betrayer of his spiritual lord, Christ; and he places Brutus and Cassius in the other two mouths as betrayers of their temporal lord, Caesar. Surely, any crime that combines the sins of these three deserves the title of evil absolute.

Yet, in one awful act, Macbeth is guilty not only of treason to his lord but also of those other treasons punished in the ninth circle. Betrayal of his country is emphasized in IV.iii., the scene in which Malcolm tests Macduff:

> Let us rather
> Hold fast the mortal sword, and like good men
> Bestride our down-fall'n birthdom. Each new morn
> New widows howl, new orphans cry, new sorrows
> Strike heaven on the face, that it resounds
> As if it felt with Scotland and yell'd out
> Like syllable of dolor.
>
> (2–8)

> Bleed, bleed, poor country!
> Great tyranny, lay thou thy basis sure,
> For goodness dare not check thee; wear thou thy
>   wrongs,
> The title is affeer'd!
>
> (31–34)

> I think our country sinks beneath the yoke;
> It weeps, it bleeds, and each new day a gash
> Is added to her wounds.
>
> (39–41)

> O Scotland, Scotland!
> (100)

But treason to Scotland is implicit in the murder of Duncan, in the usurpation of the crown; and Macbeth is guilty of the sin punished in Dante's Antenora at the very moment that he commits the act punished in Caina, Ptolomaea, and Judecca also:

165

> He's here in double trust:
> First, as I am his kinsman and his subject,
> Strong both against the deed; then, as his host,
> Who should against his murderer shut the door,
> Not bear the knife myself.
>
> (I.vii.12–16)

Kenneth Muir has recorded the relationship of these lines to the *Inferno*,[6] but neglects to show that in betrayal of his lord, Macbeth is guilty of the sins of Judas, Brutus, and Cassius; he has betrayed not only his temporal lord but also, symbolically, his spiritual lord. Duncan has been identified as a Christ-God figure by others.[7] Similarities between the Last Supper and the banquet for Duncan, as well as the eclipse and earthquake that accompany his murder (I.vii.stage directions; II.iii.60–61; II.iv.6–7), have been noticed. To these I would add the imagery of other passages, symbolizing either Duncan's Christlike qualities or his very Godhead:

> Herein I teach you
> How you shall bid God 'ild us for your pains.
>
> (I.vi.12–13)

> The Lord's anointed temple.
> (II.iii.68)

Lady Macbeth's extraordinary hypocrisy as she welcomes Duncan catches my ear as a paraphrase of the offertory common to many

6. Kenneth Muir, "Shakespeare and Dante," *Notes and Queries* 194 (1949): 333. Muir calls attention only to three of the sins of treason—kin, guest, and lord; but in his Arden edition (p. 62), he adds treason to country. He acknowledges Roy Walker's independent findings in *The Time Is Free* (London, 1949), p. 54. Walker cites actually but two of the sins: murder of guest and lord. He makes no point of the similarity to the *Inferno*, never suggesting that Shakespeare might in this detail be indebted to Dante.

7. See esp. S. L. Bethell, *The Cultural Revolution of the Seventeenth Century* (London, 1951), pp. 79–81; Muir, Arden *Macbeth*, p. 37; and F. N. Lees, "A Biblical Connotation in *Macbeth*," *Notes and Queries* 195 (1952): 534.

Christian services and originating in I Chronicles 29.14: "all things come of thee: and of thine owne hand we haue giuen thee":

> Your servants ever
> Have theirs, themselves, and what is theirs, in compt,
> To make their audit at your Highness' pleasure
> Still to return your own.
>
> (I.vi.25–28)

But more important is the continuation of Macbeth's "double-trust" speech:

> this Duncan
> Hath borne his faculties so meek, hath been
> So clear in his great office, that his virtues
> Will plead like angels, trumpet-tongu'd, against
> The deep damnation of his taking-off;
>
> . . . .
>
> or heaven's cherubin, hors'd
> Upon the sightless couriers of the air,
> Shall blow the horrid deed in every eye,
> That tears shall drown the wind.
>
> (I.vii.16–25)

When we connect this part of Macbeth's soliloquy to the first part quoted above, we find the rather striking parallel that Shakespeare names the crimes involved in the very order that Dante uses in the ninth circle: kinsman (Caina), subject (Antenora), guest (Ptolomaea), and lord (Judecca). The identification of Macbeth's crime is now complete: the most wicked act that the greatest poetic imagination of the Middle Ages could formulate, working upon a philosophical structure of the ethics of Aristotle. Macbeth is not seeking still his "third and worst crime" when he plans the assassination of Lady Macduff and her children; he has not chosen "evil as evil" for the first time with that deed.[8] His decision for evil was made perhaps before the play opens. But he needed to "screw [his] cour-

---

8. Elliott, *Dramatic Providence*, p. 24.

age to the sticking place" (I.vii.61), and with Duncan's murder his act overtakes his intention; his desire is consummated; his will was free. His evil is an abomination; his damnation is already accomplished. The murders of Banquo and Macduff's family are evil without remorse; the murder of the family is even without reason; and beyond these crimes, the hardened Macbeth makes "Each new morn / New widows howl, new orphans cry" (IV.iii.4–5). His first crime, the murder of Duncan, is the worst; there can be none greater. All that follow are only the acts of an obdurate demon.

In the *Inferno*, the punishment assessed all four crimes of treason is immersion in the frozen lake of Cocytus. Both Muir and Walker have called attention to the porter, who will "devil-porter it no further" because "this place is too cold for hell" (II.iii.16–17).[9] But they have not, nor has any other commentator, mentioned another peculiarity of punishment that goes with one of Macbeth's crimes.

In Canto 33, the last of the *Inferno* but one, Dante meets Friar Alberigo:

> O, diss' io lui: Or sei tu ancor morto?
>   Ed egli a me: Come il mio corpo stea
>   Nel mondo su, nulla scienza porto.
> Cotal vantaggio ha questa Tolomea,
>   Che spesse volte l' anima ci cade
>   Innanzi ch' Atropòs mossa le dea.
> E perchè tu più volentier mi rade
>   Le invetriate lagrime dal volto,
>   Sappi che tosto che l' anima trade,
> Come fec' io, il corpo suo l' è tolto
>   Da un demonio, che poscia il governa
>   Mentre che il tempo suo tutto sia volto.
> Ella ruina in sì fatta cisterna.
>
> $$(121-33)^{10}$$

---

9. Muir, Arden *Macbeth*, p. 62; Walker, *The Time Is Free*, p. 74.
10. *Tutte Le Opere Di Dante*, ed. E. Moore (Oxford, 1909), p. 76:

> "O," I said to him, "are you dead already?"
> And he: "What the condition of my body

Through the unique punishment of sending the soul to hell before the body dies, Dante emphasizes the utter depravity of murdering one's guests. More than any other, the guest is misled by his
betrayer's hypocrisy, by the fair offers and the smiling greeting.
Shakespeare does not overlook the added perfidy. His most pointed
addition to Holinshed is to place the murder carefully within the
doors of Macbeth's castle.[11] At the very point that Duncan identifies
Lady Macbeth with the role of "honor'd hostess" (I.vi.10), she is
her most hypocritical, asserting pervertedly the very reasons why
she should love her guest, thereby deepening her guilt:

> All our service
> In every point twice done, and then done double,
> Were poor and single business to contend
> Against those honors deep and broad wherewith
> Your majesty loads our house. For those of old,
> And the late dignities heap'd up to them,
> We rest your hermits.
>
> (I.vi.14–20)

In every respect, Lady Macbeth is as guilty as her husband; all the
torments he undergoes or is yet to reap are her portion also. Both
merit the punishment of Ptolomaea. Both lose their souls to that

---

> In the world is, I have no way of knowing.
> Such advantage has this Ptolomaea
> That often a soul plunges into it
> Long before Atropos gives it a push.
> And, that you may more readily erase
> From my face the tears that are like glass,
> Know that the moment any soul betrays,
> As I did, its body is snatched from it
> By a demon, who then dominates it
> Till its allotted time has run out
> And it tumbles down into this cistern."

Trans. Louis Biancolli, *The Divine Comedy*, 3 vols. (New York, 1966), 1 : 140.
   11. *Shakespeare's Holinshed*, ed. W. G. Boswell-Stone (London,
1896), p. 25: "he slue the king at Enuerns, or (as some say) at Botgosuane."

region before their bodies die. For those bodies to function, they must be invested by devils, even as Dante describes in the story of Friar Alberigo.[12] Of course, for realistic drama and tragedy based on history, the substitution of devil for soul must be a symbolic or mystical one, an allegorism that Dante would call anagogical. Therefore the substitution is handled symbolically; I know of no play in the Shakespeare canon where the imagery of substitution—or rather investment and possession, as I shall call it—is so prevalent.

Before the crime is committed, we are prepared for the idea of false-covering, the pleasing facade that masks a spotted interior. The eleventh line of the play tells us "Fair is foul, and foul is fair." Duncan, speaking of Cawdor, emphasizes the point: "There's no art / To find the mind's construction in the face" (I.iv.11–12). Lady Macbeth informs us clearly that whatever holds sway within her body and her husband's must be replaced. She fears that Macbeth is "too full o' th' milk of human kindness," and that she must pour her spirits into his ear (I.v.17, 26). What are her spirits? We are told through one of the most significant speeches of the play and in the appropriate investment/possession imagery:

> Come, you spirits
> That tend on mortal thoughts, unsex me here,
> And fill me from the crown to the toe top-full
> Of direst cruelty! Make thick my blood;
> Stop up th' access and passage to remorse,
> That no compunctious visitings of nature
> Shake my fell purpose, nor keep peace between
> Th' effect and it! Come to my woman's breasts,

12. This concept may be found elsewhere as well. Chaucer's Man of Law addresses Donegild:

> Fy, feendlych spirit, for I dar wel telle,
> Thogh thou heere walke, thy spirit is in helle!
> (Robinson's *Chaucer*, p. 70)

The idea may be seen also in *The Legend of Good Women* (p. 511). Scriptural authority usually cited is John 13.27 and Ps. 55.15.

And take my milk for gall, you murd'ring ministers,
Wherever in your sightless substances[13]
You wait on nature's mischief! Come, thick night,
And pall thee in the dunnest smoke of hell.

(I.v.40–51)

The "smoke of hell" surrounds symbolically the spirit that comes to her, because it comes from hell to invest the empty body that her soul, dropping to Ptolomaea, will leave behind.

I believe no one has noticed that Lady Macbeth's invocation is an anti-hymn, paralleling, as at a black mass, the *Veni Creator Spiritus* of the Pentecostal service. The *Veni Creator* had been a part of the Use of Sarum throughout the sixteenth century. It was one of the Sequences that followed the Gradual of every mass celebrated during the church year. At the Council of Trent (1545–63) all but four Sequences were abolished. One of the four, the *Veni Creator*, is used still on Whitsunday. The Book of Common Prayer, from the first of 1549 to that in use today, has retained one or another English translation of the hymn, always as an adjunct to the order for consecration of priests as well as bishops. In Shakespeare's time, the ordinal was published separately from the Prayer Book, under the title of *The forme and manner of makyng and consecratyng of Archebishoppes Bishoppes, Priests and Deacons.* In this volume the hymn is called for in consecrating either priests or bishops. Some form of the hymn, both in Latin and English, was available in England throughout Shakespeare's lifetime.

The verses pertinent to Lady Macbeth's invocation are as follows:

13. W. C. Curry's annotation on "sightless substances" is helpful to my argument: "Certain aspects of Lady Macbeth's experience indicate that she is possessed of demons. . . . The murdering ministers whom she invokes for aid are described as being sightless substances, *i.e.*, not evil thoughts and 'grim imaginings' but objective substantial forms, invisible bad angels, to whose activities may be attributed all the unnatural occurrences of nature": *Shakespeare's Philosophical Patterns* (Baton Rouge, 1937), p. 86.

Veni creator spiritus mentes tuorum visita /
   imple superna gratia que to creasti pectora.
. . . .
Accende lumen sensibus infunde amorem cordibus /
   infirma nostri corporis virtute firmans perpetim.
Hostem repellas longius pacemque dones protinus /
   ductore sic te preuio vitemus omne noxiam.
(Folio XXX^r)

[Come creator spirit, the hearts of thy faithful visit.
Fill with heavenly grace, what thou didst create, our
   hearts.
. . . .
Kindle light in our senses, infuse love in our hearts.
The weaknesses of our bodies with virtue
   perpetually confirm.
The enemy repel far off and peace give us at once.
Thou our leader, thus, thou before us we shall avoid
   all harmful.]
(F₃^v) [14]

These phrases echo Lady Macbeth's cry that evil spirits come to her, fill her (especially her breasts) with cruelty instead of grace, kindle her fell purpose instead of bringing light and love, keeping out remorse and compunctious nature instead of repelling the enemy and bringing peace. Furthermore, the light prayed for by the hymnodist is replaced by Lady Macbeth with a call for thick night and smoke of hell.

    She stands at this point either as a counterpart to the disciples as the Paraclete comes to them on the first Pentecost or as a counterpart to any priest or bishop as he receives ordination. Anti-disciple or anti-priest, she functions as a proselytizer and converts Macbeth to her purpose.

    To continue to list the guest-investment-possession imagery would be to record something from almost every scene of the play,

    14. For the Sarum Use see *Expositio hymnorum secundum usum Sarum* (1509); for the Edwardian Ordinal see *The forme and manner . . . Deacons* (1549).

but several passages bear emphasis to show that Macbeth undergoes the same transformation as his lady. I take to be most significant the lines in which Macbeth announces hypocritically to the horrified spectators outside the dead Duncan's chamber that the world without this king is a graceless place; the ambiguities that comment on the state of Macbeth's soul are quite to the point:

> Had I but died an hour before this chance,
> I had liv'd a blessed time; for, from this instant,
> There's nothing serious in mortality;
> All is but toys. Renown and grace is dead;
> The wine of life is drawn, and the mere lees
> Is left this vault to brag of.
>
> (II.iii.92−97)

With the soul out of the body, indeed "There's nothing serious in mortality"; in this series of metaphors *wine* is the soul, *toys* and *lees* are the body. Later, when Macbeth laments that all his evil labor is likely to benefit Banquo if Banquo and his son live, he reminds himself that he has given his "eternal jewel / . . . to the common enemy of man" (III.i.67−68).

Further than this, the possession concept fits well with Macbeth's boast, "I dare do all that may become a man; / Who dares do more is none" (I.vii.47−48). When Macbeth commits his inhuman act, he will in fact be a man no longer; the spirit that invests his body after Duncan's murder will make of him a fiend. Shakespeare employs this very equivocation in *Hamlet* when the gravedigger denies that Ophelia is a woman. She is only "One that was a woman, sir, but, rest her soul, she's dead" (V.i.135−36). Iago also is merely a body-shell invested by another demon; thus Shakespeare uses the same device in *Othello*: Emilia describes a creature which she dubs "some eternal villain," and Iago responds, "there is no such man; it is impossible" (IV.ii.132−36).

Macbeth is described as a fiend several times throughout the play: "black Macbeth" (IV.iii.52); [15] "Not in the legions / Of horrid

15. See chap. 2, p. 90, for a discussion of *black* and its association with the devil.

hell can come a devil more damn'd / In evils to top Macbeth"
(IV.iii.55−57); "Devilish Macbeth" (IV.iii.117); "Turn, hell-hound,
turn!" (V.viii.3); and the exchange between Macbeth and young
Siward: "My name's Macbeth. / The devil himself could not
pronounce a title / More hateful to mine ear" (V.vii.7−9). Lady
Macbeth is not excluded from this sort of label: "fiend-like queen"
(V.viii.70).

As the souls of Macbeth and his lady leave their bodies immediately after the murder of Duncan, Macbeth describes part
of the transformation; Lady Macbeth indicates her plight to be
identical:

> What hands are here? Ha! They pluck out
>   mine eyes.
> Will all great Neptune's ocean wash this blood
> Clean from my hand? No, this my hand will
>   rather
> The multitudinous seas incarnadine,
> Making the green one red.
>
> LADY MACBETH
> My hands are of your color; but I shame
> To wear a heart so white. (*Knock.*) I hear a
>   knocking
> At the south entry. Retire we to our chamber.
> A little water clears us of this deed.
> . . . .
>   (*Knock.*) Hark! More knocking.
> Get on your nightgown.
>   (II.ii.57−68)

Almost every line of this dialogue contributes to the concept of
preemption of the soul and possession by a fiend. Since from
the moment of the murder the soul no longer can be redeemed,
Macbeth has no opportunity in the life remaining to his body to
cleanse the soul no longer there; thus the seas cannot wash off the
blood. Lady Macbeth is sin-spotted in the same way; we know from
a later passage that she cannot rid herself of her bloodstains either

(V.i.34–51). In the passage above occurs the first indication of the knocking which I take to be the appearance at hell's gate of the departing souls of these two murderers. The investment image of putting on nightgowns concludes the acts of the evil spirits, as they don the bodies of Macbeth and his lady like robes. An image reciprocal to the fiends taking over the bodies of the guest-betrayers is that of goodness flying out of the possessed clay. Menteith explains Macbeth's alleged madness (V.ii.13) as the desertion of elements that will not remain in the company of evil—in the company of the demon within the body:

> Who then shall blame
> His pester'd senses to recoil and start,
> When all that is within him does condemn
> Itself for being there?
> (V.ii.22–25)

Macbeth's own statement about what holds mastery within him supplements Menteith's by avowing that his intellect and courage are not like those of ordinary men; they fit better the faculties of the visitors from hell:

> The mind I sway by and the heart I bear
> Shall never sag with doubt nor shake with fear.
> (V.iii.9–10)

The infernal intellect thinks never "to do aught good," and the hellish heart need never "shake with fear," being already a denizen of hell with nothing further to lose. The general image of flight as well as of imprisonment—the good escapes but the evil is confined, both the spirit that supplies the soul's place, locked in the body, and the evil soul itself, locked in hell—is implemented in the desire of Macbeth's retainers to flee: the doctor and the soldiers—

> . . . none serve with him but constrained things
> Whose hearts are absent too.
> (V.iv.13–14)

The concept of possession that I trace from Dante's ninth circle was quite familiar to Elizabethans from contemporary sources as well. Pierre le Loyer asserts in *IIII Livres des Spectres* (1586), giving the Catholic position, that "a disembodied spirit may assume a body in order to appear visibly to men, without being united to it as men are." Furthermore, "When one from the dead appears it may . . . be a devil who has taken the body of a corpse."[16] Mystically, the moment the souls of Macbeth and Lady Macbeth leave their bodies to go to Ptolomaea, those bodies are corpses, free for devils to invest. But possession is not limited to corpses. Sixteenth-century prints showing demons being exorcised from the bodies of the possessed are commonplace (fig. 11). The Protestant position is represented by Reginald Scot ("we credit . . . assuming of bodies by soules and spirits"),[17] who, however, rejects possession, along with other superstitions, which he labels Popish beliefs. A clear Protestant statement occurs also in King James's *Daemonologie* (1599). King James lists, as the third of four kinds of devils that walk the earth, those that "enter within the living and possess them." Those most susceptible to possession are men "guiltie of greevous offences" whom "God punishes by that horrible kinde of scourdge."[18] W. C. Curry says of *Macbeth* that "The whole drama is discovered to be saturated with the malignant presences of demons or fallen angels; they animate nature and ensnare human souls by means of diabolical persuasion, by hallucination, infernal illusions, and possession."[19]

That the murder of Duncan may be associated immediately with eschatological matters is borne out by the imagery attendant upon the King's death. Although some events such as the supper and the earthquake have been associated with the last days of

16. Digested in Lewes Lavater, *Of Ghostes & Spirites Walking By Nyght* (1572), ed. J. Dover Wilson and May Yardley (Oxford, 1929), pp. 230–31, 234.

17. Scot, *A Discourse of Diuels and Spirits* (1584), pp. 532–33.

18. King James, *Daemonologie*, ed. G. B. Harrison (London, 1924), pp. 57, 62–63.

19. Curry, *Shakespeare's Philosophical Patterns*, p. 97.

Fig. 11. Possession and exorcism. Pierre Boaistuau, *Histoires prodigieuses*.
Paris, 1597.

Christ, others match well with various signs that late medieval writers believed would accompany the last days of the world.[20] Shakespeare evokes these same images at the death of King Hamlet and at the abdication of Lear; they are appropriate to the fall of kings always insofar as the kings' subjects submit to an emotional belief that the world must end if their anointed king, the surrogate for God, has ended his rule on earth. Yet in *Macbeth* the association of apocalypse with Duncan's death is even more fitting since immediate damnation for the souls of Macbeth and Lady Macbeth is in reality their judgment day.

As Macduff enters the King's bedchamber where he will discover Duncan's body, Lennox describes the "unruly" night:

> . . . chimneys were blown down, and, as they say,
> Lamentings were heard i' th' air; strange screams of
> death,
> And prophesying, with accents terrible
> Of dire combustion and confus'd events
> New hatch'd to th' woeful time. The obscure bird
> Clamor'd the livelong night. Some say the earth
> Was feverous and did shake [fig. 12].
>
> (II.iii.55–61)

Eight separate events are reported by Lennox; seven of them are among the fifteen signs that medieval tradition proclaimed were to forerun judgment day. These signs, by attribution, were first recorded by St. Jerome, but no scholar has ever found the Jeromite source. They have been reproduced by innumerable writers from Bede through Vincent of Beauvais, the authors of the *Legenda Aurea* and the *Cursor Mundi*, to anonymous rimers in many independent lyrics. They are found in thirteenth-century sculpture, stained-glass, and illustrations in Bible picture books such as the *Holkham Bible*.[21] They persisted in widespread profusion into

20. See chap. 3, pp. 129–32 and note 14.

21. See the modern edition with excellent reproductions of the illustrations, ed. W. O. Hassall (London, 1954); discussion and bibliography pertinent to the fifteen signs are on pp. 148–49 and 152–55.

Cities and all buildings shall be ouerturned.

*Stones shall tūble
together, and make a
huge noise.*

*Terrible earthquakes
shall make mē hide
themselues.*

Vallyes shall be filed & hils brought low.

Fig. 12. Sixth (top), seventh (left), eighth (right), and ninth (bottom) signs preceding doomsday. *Queen Elizabeth Prayer Book.* Press of John Day, London, 1581.

Shakespeare's lifetime, being described with great elaboration, for instance, in a continuing series of editions of *The craft to liue well and to die well*, issuing from the presses of Wynkyn de Worde and Richard Pynson in the first decade of the sixteenth century (fig.13, also see figs. 3, 4, and 12). All are accompanied by primitive wood-block illustrations. Spinoffs from these blocks can be found in all editions of the famous *Queen Elizabeth Prayer Book*, more accurately entitled *Christian Prayers and Meditations in English, French, Italian, Spanish, Greeke, and Latine*, published first in 1569, but with subsequent editions until at least 1581. The fifteen illustrations in this volume published by John Day are not accompanied by a text such as that in Wynkyn de Worde's *craft*, but rather each picture has subjoined captions which prove fully as explanatory as the much expanded materials in the earlier work.

Equally available to Shakespeare were literary versions of the fifteen signs: eighty-eight verses by John Lydgate called "The Fifftene Toknys Aforn the Doom" and an insertion in the Chester Cycle—in the XXIInd play, *The Prophets and Antichrist*—prefaced with a Latin rubric: *Signa quindecim magna quae, secundum opiniones doctorum, extremum precedunt judicium.* . . . In any or all of these independent versions of the omens attendant upon judgment day, Shakespeare could find seven of the eight observations made by Lennox. The eighth can be attributed to expanded accounts of the apocalyptic event. Let us excerpt the eighth first and then proceed to the other seven.

The prophesying that Lennox has overheard is echoed among the episodes that accompany the birth and usurpations of Antichrist. Present in all the Antichrist plays of the various mystery cycles and present also in Wynkyn's *The craft to liue well and to die well*, the prophecies have their ultimate source in Christ's warnings to his disciples. Asked by them "what signe shalbe . . . of the end of the worlde," Christ admonishes them to

> Take hede that no man deceiue you. For manie shal come in my Name, sayīg I am Christ, and shal deceiue manie. And ye shal heare of warres, and rumors of

Fig. 13. Fifteen signs preceding doomsday. The third sign is from *The craft to liue well and to die well*, press of Wynkyn de Word, 1505. All others are from *The book intytulyd the Art of good lywyng & good deying*, press of Antoine Vérard, Paris, 1503. Signs 1–5. (Figure 13 continues on pp. 182–83.)

Fig. 13. Signs 6—10.

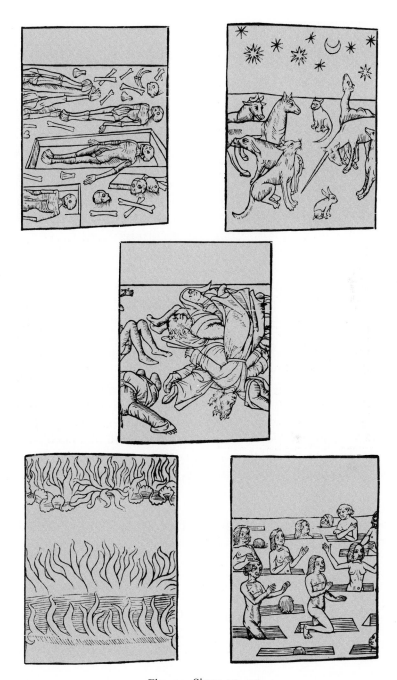

Fig. 13. Signs 11—15.

warres. . . . And manie false prophetes shal arise. . . .
For there shal arise false Christs, & false prophetes.
(Matt. 24.4–24)

Among the seven other occurrences Lennox describes are
the toppled chimneys, an event accounted for on the sixth day
of the fifteen signs (most versions of the fifteen signs relate a different event on fifteen successive days; thus the sixth sign is often
introduced as the sixth day). As Lydgate has it, "Grete Castellys,
tours maad of lym and stoon / Playn with the Erthe to grounde /
shal doun falle."[22] The Chester play produces an image closer
to common dwellings: "buylded thinges to ground shall fall—
/ church, cittie, house, and wall."[23] The author of the Wynkyn de
Worde treatise supplies a very similar image—"all the buyldynges
aboue ye erthe/as townes/cytes & all other buyldynges shall fall and
tomble at y^t daye vnto ye erthe"—as well as the scriptural source:
"Nõ relīquetur lapis super lapidē qui non destruatur" (Matt. 24.2).[24]
The woodblock for the sixth day in Wynkyn (folio Cxli^r) shows several chimney-like towers toppling over, as does the illustration in
Queen Elizabeth's Prayer Book (folio 59^v) (figs. 12 and 13).

The "Lamentings heard i' th' air" by Lennox as well as the
"strange screams of death" are accounted for easily in the general
dismay and destruction that attend all the terrifying events of the
last days and in the death that shall come to all creatures alive still
at the sounding of the trumpets. As the author in Wynkyn's art of
living and dying well puts it, "for ye shal wepe & your songes &
lawghynges shal be cõuerted in to wepynges, lamentacyons/cryes
& waylȳges at ye day of ye iugemēt generall" (folio Cl^r).[25] The thirteenth day or sign will be that in which "all mē womē & chyldren

---

22. *The Minor Poems of John Lydgate*, ed. H. N. MacCracken (London, 1911), p. 118.
23. *The Chester Mystery Cycle*, ed. R. M. Lumiansky and David Mills
(London, 1974), p. 406.
24. *The craft to liue well and to die well*, trans. A. Chertsey (1505),
folio Cxli^v.
25. Pagination in this edition of Wynkyn is hopelessly corrupt.

y^t than shal be lyuȳge on the erthe shal dye . . . . & ymagen ye pyteous playntes/& syghes y^t shal be in y^t place where all ye creatures lyuynge . . . shal be sodaynly stryken" (folio Cxlii^r).

On both the fourth day and the fourteenth "dire combustion" shall accompany first the burning of "sea and water . . . / agaynst kinde," and then "both yearth and eke heaven."[26] All versions of the fifteen signs include these two separate days and signs of burning.

Lennox's obscure bird which clamors all night long is glossed usually as an owl, as indeed it probably is meant to be. But owl or otherwise, on the third day, all "Foul . . . shal tremble in certeyn, / Compleynyng in ther hydous moone / Vp the skyes; this noyse nat maad in veyn, / For what they mene, God shal knowe alloone" (see owl in fig. 13, fifth sign).[27] Again, all accounts refer to the distress of birds, although in Wynkyn and the Chester play, the clamoring of the fowls accompanies the fifth token, and most accounts assert that the screeching of the birds will be understood by God alone. I emphasize the mystery of their moan as a possible explanation of Lennox's "obscure bird."

All the upheavals of the last days may be gathered under Lennox's "confus'd events," but the feverous and shaking earth of which he reports is assigned specifically to the eighth day in all versions of the fifteen signs that I have examined. The treatment in Wynkyn, for example, refers the reader to Apocalypse 15 in these words: "Et factus ē tremotus magnus qualis nō fuit ex quo hoīes [*sic*] esse ceper̄t [*sic*]" (folio Cxlii^v).[28] Geneva translates:

> . . . & there was a great earthquake, suche as was not since men were vpon the earth, euen so mightie an earthquake.
>
> (Rev. 16.18)

26. *The Chester Mystery Cycle*, pp. 406–7.
27. "The Fifftene Toknys Aforn the Doom," p. 118.
28. Latin quotations in Wynkyn often vary widely from the standard Jeromite text and are riddled with other errors. In modern editions this passage is found in Apoc. 16.18.

The absolute singularity of the apocalyptic tremors is captured in Lennox's youthful wonder: "My young remembrance cannot parallel / A fellow to it" (II.iii.62–63). The very youth of Lennox hardly makes the earthquake the greatest in the history of mankind, but Shakespeare adds the testimony of a very old survivor:

> Threescore and ten I can remember well,
> Within the volume of which time, I have seen
> Hours dreadful and things strange, but this sore
>   night
> Hath trifled former knowings.
>
> (II.iv.1–4)

In *Lear*, where the fifteen signs also accompany a judgment-day motif, similar uniqueness is claimed. Kent marvels,

> Since I was a man,
> Such sheets of fire, such bursts of horrid thunder,
> Such groans of roaring wind and rain, I never
> Remember to have heard. Man's nature cannot carry
> Th' affliction nor the fear.
>
> (III.ii.45–49)

Immediately after the several signs rehearsed by Lennox, Macduff bursts out of the murder chamber to liken the death of Duncan to "The great doom's image" (II.iii.78). Surrounding his words are further evocations of judgment day. Macduff, noting the sleepy confusion of those about him, identifies them with the dead who must arise at the last day:

> Banquo and Donalbain! Malcolm! Awake!
> Shake off this downy sleep, death's counterfeit,
>
> . . . .
>   Malcolm! Banquo!
> As from your graves rise up, and walk like sprites,
> To countenance this horror!
>
> (II.iii.75–80)

Lady Macbeth equates the alarum-bell that Macduff has caused to
ring with the horn at judgment day that wakes the dead and summons them to sentence: "What's the business, / That such a hideous trumpet calls to parley / The sleepers of the house?" (81–83).
The sleepers have been likened already to the rising dead. Trumpets and resurrection are such commonly encountered elements
of doomsday that we need hardly go to Lydgate to find that "alle
bodyes shal that day aryse" (fig. 14).[29] Several scriptural passages
provide authority for the trumpets; most often cited is Matthew
24.31: "And he shal send his Angels with a great sounde of a
trumpet, and they shal gather together his elect, from the foure
windes & from the one end of heauen vnto the other."

The porter scene, which serves of purposes aplenty, follows the departure for hell of the souls of Macbeth and Lady
Macbeth and introduces Lennox's description of the ominous signs.
Placed as he is among judgment-day events, the Porter, as "keeper
of the gate opposite to St. Peter's,"[30] functions then not only as
everyday porter of hell gate but also as doorman on doomsday itself.

Ross and the old man of seventy add events that continue
even as Lennox tells of those already transpired:

ROSS

     Ha, good father,
  Thou seest the heavens, as troubled with man's
    act,
  Threatens his bloody stage. By th' clock 'tis
    day,
  And yet dark night strangles the traveling
    lamp.

  . . . .

29. "The Fifftene Toknys Aforn the Doom," p. 120.

30. Emilia is called such in *Othello*, IV.ii.91–92. In many judgment
portals of the great Gothic cathedrals, an imp appears to play this role. So
also may such a figure be found in various paintings and block illustrations available to Shakespeare. See, for example, the demons of the judgment portal at Bourges Cathedral and their counterparts in the chancel
painting in the Guild Chapel in Stratford-upon-Avon (see fig. 9).

Fig. 14. (a) Doomsday trumpet raising the dead. *Hore presentes ad vsvm Sarvm*. Press of Philippe Pigouchet, Paris, 1502.

Fig. 14. (b) Dead rising from the earth, detail from doomsday painting, ca. 1500. Chancel arch, St. Peter's, Wenhaston, Suffolk.

OLD MAN
        A falcon, tow'ring in her pride of place,
        Was by a mousing owl hawk'd at and kill'd.

ROSS
        And Duncan's horses—a thing most strange
           and certain—
        Beauteous and swift, the minions of their race,
        Turn'd wild in nature, broke their stalls, flung
           out,
        Contending 'gainst obedience, as they would
        Make war with mankind.

OLD MAN
                'Tis said they eat each other.
                                (II.iv.4–18)

The eclipse, reported in Ross's imaginative way, is included regularly in events of the last days, chiefly because of Christ's own prediction in Matthew 24.29: "And immediately after the tribulatiõs of those dayes, shal the sunne be darkened." A fine woodblock illustration of eclipse accompanies the fifteen signs in the *Queen Elizabeth Prayer Book*, although not one of the fifteen (fig. 3). Shakespeare's image of man's bloody stage suggests that the ultimate source for the entire passage is Revelation. In 6.12, "the sunne was as blacke as sackecloth of heere, and the moone was like blood"; and 16.3–6 seems to coat the entire earth with blood. Revelation 19.17–18 would appear to suggest Shakespeare's flesh-eating owl and horses and perhaps also contention against mankind:

> an Angel . . . cryed . . . to all the foules that did flye by the middes of heauen, Come, and gather your selues together vnto the supper of the great God,
> That ye may eat the flesh of Kings, & the flesh of hie Capitaines, and the flesh of mightie men, and the flesh of horses.

Additionally, the flesh-eating horses may reflect the pale horse, with the pale rider (6.8), who, immediately prior to the bloody eclipse (6.12), is given power "to kill with sworde, and with hõger, and with death, and with the beasts of the earth" (fig. 15). Revelation 9 in its entirety contains horse imagery of a most violent nature, as, for instance, verse 17: "& the heads of the horses were as yᵉ heads of lyons."

Macbeth seems to see himself as some great Antichrist, some great herald of doomsday, who, if he cannot rule, welcomes destruction of both heaven and earth. As his evil reign begins to fall apart, as he fears no long continuance, chiefly because of the prophecy that places Banquo's issue on the throne, he calls for an end to the created universe; if he cannot rid it of his rebuker (III.i.55), "let the frame of things disjoint, both the worlds suffer" (III.ii.18). That he fears no judgment when such a time comes supports further the idea that he endures his punishment already. With the same words in which he calls for the world's dissolution, he reports that his nightly sleep is one of terrible dreams, that every waking moment he undergoes a "torture of the mind," a "restless ecstasy" (III.ii.6–24). When he revisits the witches to de-

Fig. 15. The Four Horsemen of the Apocalypse. Albrecht Dürer, 1498.
Florida State University Library.

mand further prophecies, he again will have the end of the world,
and apparently he knows the tradition of the fifteen signs:

> Though you untie the winds and let them fight
> Against the churches, though the yesty waves
> Confound and swallow navigation up,
> Though bladed corn be lodg'd and trees blown
> down,
> Though castles topple on their warders' heads,
> Though palaces and pyramids do slope
> Their heads to their foundations, though the
> treasure
> Of nature's germains tumble all together,
> Even till destruction sicken, answer me
> To what I ask you.
>
> (IV.i.52–61)

Clearly Macbeth calls for a great tempest, reminiscent of the apocalyptic storm in *Lear* and of Lear's appeal to the forces of destruction that "all germains spill at once" (*Lear*, III.ii.8). Wynkyn's version of the fifteen signs opens with a preface unusual to the genre.
Neither in the Chester play nor in Lydgate's poem nor in the wood-
blocks of the *Queen Elizabeth Prayer Book* is there anything similar.
Yet Wynkyn's anonymous author makes mention of additional
signs: "after yᵉ doctours I fynde that iiii. tokens shall fyrst come
before/& after yᵉ sayd .iiii. tokens there shal come other .xv. tokens"
(folio lxxxxviiᵛ). As the fourth of the preliminary signs, an elaborate expansion of Christ's reference to wars and rumors of wars
gives a picture of universal discord which surely is the source in
Lear of Gloucester's dismay, expressed to Edmund in I.ii., and beginning, "These late eclipses in the sun and moon" (line 106). The
Wynkyn author concludes, "For there shal be scarcenes in yᵉ erth yᵗ
shall bere no fruyte ne other thynge necessary & couenable for yᵉ
lyf. so grete moeuynges of the erth shal be made ayenst yᵉ comune
cours of nature & maner accustumed yᵗ many cytees/toures &
castelles shal be distroyed & beten downe/in yᵉ oce[an] & in the
waters shall be greter tēpestes & cōmocyons than in tymes past/yᵉ

ayre shall be replynysshed wᵗ pestylēces & wᵗ infeccions wherof shal come pestylences/mortalytees & corrupcyōs innumerables as well in men as in bestes/thondres/lyghtenynges/tēpestes wyndes & stormes shal be impyteous more thā euer they were in suche wyse yᵗ yᵉ men shall be brought & put in meruayllous fere and drede" (folio lxxxxviiiᵛ). The spilling of Lear and Macbeth's germains would produce that scarcity of fruits and other things necessary for life, and the general pestilences mentioned in Wynkyn suggest to Macbeth the sickness even to destruction.

A third and final time Macbeth calls for the dissolution of the globe:

> I 'gin to be aweary of the sun,
> And wish th' estate o' th' world were now undone.
> Ring the alarum-bell! Blow, wind! Come, wrack!
> (V.v.49–51)

Though briefer than his other evocations of doomsday, the passage has the necessary ingredients: a request for the obscured sun, tempest, and destruction, an end to the world. As Macbeth rushes out to seek such fate, Macduff causes trumpets to be blown: "Make all our trumpets speak! Give them all breath, / Those clamorous harbingers of blood and death" (V.vi.9–10).

Yet in all these horrors Macbeth goes about like a man with no feelings of them, like someone not really there. My argument is, of course, that he is there in body only; the wine of life—the spirit—is drawn. The porter scene, believed so un-Shakespearean by Coleridge,[31] shows us symbolically, at a moment immediately posterior to the murder of Duncan, the descent into hell of the souls of his slayers. Although Shakespeare must present the porter scene after the murder scene, he causes the knocking to be heard by Macbeth and Lady Macbeth at the moment the murderer cries that his soul is being plucked out through his eyes and the murderess says, "Get on your nightgown" (II.ii.68), the moment for

31. *Shakespearean Criticism*, ed. T. M. Raysor, 2 vols. (Cambridge, Mass., 1930), 1:75.

each of judgment, punishment, and possession. The act of entry into an afterlife accompanied by sound-summons has been prepared for by Shakespeare, ironically I think, when Macbeth hears the bell he has ordered struck:

> the bell invites me.
> Hear it not, Duncan, for it is a knell
> That summons thee to heaven or to hell.
> (II.i.63–65)

Note that the bell invites Macbeth, and one of the alternatives allowed to Duncan is the hell for which Macbeth is destined. Coleridge's dismissal of the porter scene long has been reversed, but J. W. Hales puts it most interestingly:

> "If a man were porter of hell-gate." But is this man not so? What then is hell? and where are its gates? and what is there within them . . . ? Knowing what we know of the hideous transactions that night has witnessed in his castle, may we not well say "How dreadful is this place! This is none other but the house of the devil, and this is the gate of hell."[32]

Similar to the suggestion that the porter guards the gate of hell are the statements of G. Wilson Knight that the Macbeth "universe" is desolate and dark, "where all is befogged, baffled, constricted by evil," that "the greater part of the action takes place in the murk of night," and that "*Macbeth* . . . expresses its vision . . . of the abysmal deeps of a spirit-world untuned to human reality, withdraws the veil from the black streams."[33] Thus, at the moment the souls of Macbeth and Lady Macbeth go down to hell, mystically or anagogically the place where the living demons reside becomes

---

32. J. W. Hales, "On the Porter in Macbeth," *New Shakespeare Society Transactions*, ser. 1, no. 2, p. 264. Sir Arthur Quiller-Couch echoes this sentiment in *Cambridge Lectures* (Cambridge, Eng., 1943), pp. 159, 164.

33. Knight, *The Wheel of Fire*, pp. 155, 159, 174.

hell. The castle at the porter's back is hell, and, by extension, when Macbeth becomes King of Scotland, all Scotland is hell. Pointedly, Shakespeare describes the nation as it is under the tyrant in an evocation of Dante's vision of hell:

> Alas, poor country,
> Almost afraid to know itself. It cannot
> Be call'd our mother, but our grave; where nothing,
> But who knows nothing, is once seen to smile;
> Where sighs and groans and shrieks that rend the
>   air
> Are made, not mark'd; where violent sorrow seems
> A modern ecstasy.
>
> (IV.iii.164–70)

The grave image suggests a subterranean location, and the sighs, groans, and shrieks echo *Inferno*, III.22–26:

> Quivi sospiri, pianti ed alti guai
>   Risonavan per l'aer senza stelle,
>   Perch' io al cominciar ne lagrimai.
> Diverse lingue, orribili favelle,
>   Parole di dolore, accenti d' ira.[34]

The entire porter soliloquy has its analogy to the *Inferno* in general. Just as Dante, by his journey down the terraces to the center of the earth, catalogues sins and sinners, so too the porter lets in first a suicide, then a liar, and last a cheat; but he has broken off because it is too cold; he "had thought to have let in some of all

---

34. *Tutte Le Opere*, p. 31:

> Here sighs, complaints, and piercing shrieks
> Resounded through the air devoid of stars
> With such great effect that at first I wept.
> Diverse languages and hideous discourse,
> Anguished words and accents of great wrath.
>
> *The Divine Comedy*, 1:9.

professions that go the primrose way to th' everlasting bonfire" (II.iii.17–19). The porter's complaints against the cold are unusually appropriate; for even as he speaks, the souls of Macbeth and Lady Macbeth enter the frozen regions of Cocytus.

When the bodies of Macbeth and his lady are inhabited by demons, certain things are forbade these creatures. King James writes, "there are diuers symptoms, whereby [possession] may be discerned . . . such as . . . their not abiding the hearing of God named, and innumerable such like vaine things."[35] Macbeth, as he emerges from the murder chamber, tells his wife that one groom cried out "God bless us!" and the other "Amen!" He wonders why he could not add his voice:

> But wherefore could not I pronounce "Amen"?
> I had most need of blessing, and "Amen"
> Stuck in my throat.
>
> (II.ii.29–31)

Lady Macbeth's answer, "These deeds must not be thought / After these ways; so, it will make *us* mad" (my italics), indicates her inability also to ask blessing.[36]

35. King James, *Daemonologie*, p. 70.

36. At this point may be brought together additional evidence for the Dante-*Macbeth* relationship. W. C. Curry sees in Lady Macbeth's sleepwalking further sign of investment: "the violence of her reactions indicates that her state is what may be called 'somnambuliform possession' or 'demoniacal somnambulism'" (*Shakespeare's Philosophical Patterns*, p. 89). Macbeth's second meeting with the witches takes place "at the pit of Acheron" (III.v.15), appropriate symbolically since the tyrant's soul is already in hell. Kenneth Muir, G. Wilson Knight, and Roy Walker cite in reference to the witches and Hecate that they have resemblances to Medusa and the Furies of *Inferno*, 9. Added to this kind of support might be the name of the familiar spirit of the third witch: Harpier, perhaps a verbal echo from the harpies of *Inferno*, 13. G. R. Elliott calls attention to "Be lion-mettled, proud" (IV.i.90) and cites the lion of the *Inferno*. Two wolf images may be added (II.i.54–55; IV.i.22), Dante's third animal, which keeps sinners from the right way and is symbolic of sins of fraud, among which are the sins of the ninth circle.

The fearsome transformation of two mortals into something difficult to define causes an audience perhaps to wonder about such monstrous creations. Shakespeare, intent upon their evil, emphasizes both the malignancy and the mystery. Using the device he found so efficacious in *Hamlet* and *Lear*, he gives it even greater force in *Macbeth*. In both other plays, and always in the ambiance of evil, one character or another cries out, "Who's there?" fearful to find, perchance, some terrifying enemy whose nature is beyond his strength or faith. Illustrative in *Hamlet* is the opening challenge of Bernardo (I.i.1), hasting forward to what he hopes will be the friendly company of Francisco but also "distill'd / Almost to jelly" (I.ii.204–5) because he approaches a noise that may momently confront him with the ghost that twice before he has encountered. Following the first three knockings on the castle gate, Macbeth's porter cries out, "Who's there?" Spaced as these knockings are, the porter's response provides a refrain, and shouted so as to be heard outside on what proves to be a stormy night, the phrase takes on dramatic power. Furthermore, attached to the knocking, which we have seen exactly coincidental with the possession of the guest-slayers' bodies, "Who's there?" jogs the mind to wonder at the nature of such murderers. In fact, the fourth time the porter questions his visitor, he alters the refrain to "What are you?" (II.iii.16).

Shakespeare has prepared for this moment in a telling scene just prior to the murder. A sleepless Banquo walks the inner courtyard of Macbeth's castle. The moon is down, denoting the witching hour—past midnight. The stars are obscured. In most ambiguous terms, Banquo likens his insomnia to "A heavy summons [that] lies like lead" (II.i.2–6) upon him. Deeply depressed to find himself in a terrain of spiritual darkness and evil, he prays for strength to resist the very temptations that at the same moment assault Macbeth: "Merciful Powers, / Restrain in me the cursed thoughts that nature / Gives way to in repose!" (7–9). Figures eerily illuminated by a torch approach, and Banquo calls for his sword: "Who's there?" Macbeth emerges from the gloom, his nature in its last few minutes of humankind. In the scene that follows, Macbeth comes downstairs from some upper chamber where he has just killed Duncan, descending symbolically (II.ii.16) and heralded by the owl, "the fatal bellman, / Which gives the stern'st good-night" and the crickets who foretell death.[37] His own spirit, entering its new and eternal abode, itself cries out to the first creature it meets, "Who's there?" (II.ii.3–8). The creature is, of course, Lady Macbeth, changed likewise and fellow with him in Ptolomaea.

Two additional qualities that go along with Dantean possession are joylessness in the fruits of the crime and a feeling of tediousness that comes from the unchanging state of sinfulness and the knowledge that everything will be the same for all eternity. It hardly needs proof that Macbeth and Lady Macbeth take no joy in their rule. A central part of the theme as well as of the plot is Macbeth's awareness that he is to be replaced on the throne by a long line of kings issuing from the loins of Banquo: "Macbeth's agony is not properly understood till we realize his utter failure to receive any positive joy from the imperial magnificence to which he aspired."[38] Almost immediately after the murder of Duncan, Macbeth is fretted by the witches' prophecy:

> They hail'd him father to a line of kings.
> Upon my head they plac'd a fruitless crown,
> And put a barren scepter in my gripe,
> Thence to be wrench'd with an unlineal hand,
> No son of mine succeeding. If 't be so,
> For Banquo's issue have I fil'd my mind;
> For them the gracious Duncan have I murder'd.
>   (III.i.59–65)

Banquo's murder, which follows, is therefore clearly not a further step into deepening sin, as some critics have seen it; it is only an attempt by an obdurate demon to secure what he has gained so foully. But Fleance escapes, and the murder of Banquo proves pointless. Macbeth must carry still the comfortless knowledge that Banquo's progeny may yet succeed him on the throne. Manifestly,

37. Muir, Arden *Macbeth*, p. 54n.
38. G. Wilson Knight, *The Imperial Theme* (London, 1931), pp. 131–32. Knight, however, does not connect this condition to Dante.

Lady Macbeth has never had joy of her crime either. Her sleep-walking establishes that her mind has been disturbed since the murder, that it dwells upon nothing else. She lives again the moment of the slaying and, no doubt, again and again and again:

> Out, damned spot! Out, I say! One—two—why, then
> 'tis time to do 't. Hell is murky.—[39] . . . who would
> have thought the old man to have had so much blood
> in him.
>
> (V.i.34–39)

Macbeth's own sleeplessness is well documented also:

> Methought I heard a voice[40] cry "Sleep no more!
> Macbeth does murder sleep," . . .
>
> Still it cried "Sleep no more!" to all the house;
> "Glamis hath murder'd sleep, and therefore
> Cawdor
> Shall sleep no more; Macbeth shall sleep no more."
>
> (II.ii.33–41)

The whole of the fourth scene in Act III is perhaps less a visit of the ghost of Banquo than a continuing reminder that Macbeth lives continuously with shades and torments. In such a sense his being "cabin'd, cribb'd, confin'd, bound in" denotes not only the pervasive wretchedness of his being but also the spiritual dungeon in which he resides presently and from which he will never emerge.

---

39. Note that her direct statement—"Hell is murky"—establishes the whereabouts of her soul.

40. Macbeth seems truly to hear this voice somewhere outside the confines of his own brain. Twice he reports its precise words. When Lady Macbeth asks, "Who was it that thus cried," we wonder with her, and we feel strongly that they both shall never again be without attendant tormenting spirits. The voice is joined shortly by hands that pluck at Macbeth's eyes. Lady Macbeth's bravado that these are merely "painted" devils leads us to speculate that they may be real.

The great and awful tedium that pervades Dante's hell at-taches itself to Macbeth as early as III.iv. He does not hesitate to kill Macduff or Macduff's entire clan. Bloodletting is to him so daily and familiar an enterprise that what harrows the audience is to him merely irksome: [41]

> I am in blood
> Stepp'd in so far that, should I wade no more,
> Returning were as tedious as go o'er.[42]
> (III.iv.137–39)

This condition continues in Macbeth to the end: "I have liv'd long enough" (V.iii.22); "I 'gin to be aweary of the sun" (V.v.49); and, of course, the grinding "sound and fury" that is nothing but nothing, that "Tomorrow, and tomorrow, and tomorrow / Creeps in this petty pace from day to day / To the last syllable of recorded time" (V.v.19–21).

41. Another illustration that his damnation is not progressive but absolute from the moment of his first and greatest crime.

42. I owe to Mrs. Denise Katheder the suggestion that the river of blood implicit in these lines may be likened to the river Phlegethon in the *Inferno*. Dante describes these waters as "La riviera del sangue, in la qual bolle / Qual che per violenza in altrui noccia" (Moore ed. *Inf.* 12.47–48). Plunged in blood to varying depths are the "tiranni / Che dier nel sangue & nell' aver di piglio" (12.104–5), and among whom are Alexander the Great and the English connection, Guy de Montfort, who "fesse in grembo a Dio / Lo chor che in sul Tamigi ancor si cola" (12.107, 119–20). Inter-esting is the conjunction at this point in *Macbeth* of Hecate's reference to Acheron only twenty-one lines after the river-of-blood passage. The first reference in the play to Macbeth as "tyrant" is only forty-four lines be-yond that. Perhaps also of considerable interest is that Dante's arrival at Phlegethon immediately follows reference to an earthquake (12.40–43), which Dante indirectly associates with chaos. The earthquake at Duncan's death, which I identify with other of the fifteen signs preceding dooms-day, is pertinent. One edition of Dante even illustrates *Inf.* 12.40–43 with French miniature illuminations of Revelation 7.12–16, one of the sources for the earthquake and other imagery mined for the fifteen signs. See *Tutte Le Opere Di Dante*, Fratelli Fabbri Editori, 6 vols. (Milano, 1965).

All that remains is to bring to an end the days of Macbeth's mortal part, his body. Involved in these last things is the triumph of Christ over evil or Satan on judgment day, putting a natural seal upon the other doomsday imagery of the play. The figure of Edward the Confessor is used symbolically to plant his foot upon the head of the serpent to crush out his life as hell's doors are closed forever. Edward is established as a "holy king" (III.vi.30) to whose court it requires some "holy angel" (46) to fly. Later he is referred to as a "healer"; for "There are a crew of wretched souls / That stay his cure" (IV.iii.141–42). In terms even more unmistakable, "Such sanctity hath heaven given his hand— / They presently amend" (144–45). Specifically, the disease that Edward cures is "call'd the evil" (146), and I take to be significant Shakespeare's omission of the modifier, *king's*.[43] Edward does not go to Scotland (hell) in person to put an end to evil (Macbeth) there, but his ministers carry "the grace of Grace" (V.viii.73) with them. Present, perhaps, in person, is Satan. Hard to overlook is the probable pronunciation of the name of the last retainer to be at Macbeth's side: Seyton.[44] His appearance is timed magnificently:

> Seyton!—I am sick at heart
> When I behold—Seyton, I say!—This push
> Will cheer me ever, or disseat me now.
> (V.iii.19–21)

In a sense, he takes over Macbeth's final moments. When the tyrant asks for his armor, Seyton says, with some authority, "'Tis not needed yet" (34). And Seyton goes out at the cry of women to attend the death of Lady Macbeth, for he returns with the news that "The Queen . . . is dead" (V.v.16).

Macbeth at his end is, of course, unrepentant. As in my argument concerning Iago, no amount of prayer can possibly mat-

---

43. L. C. Knights complains that previous critics "have slurred the passages in which the positive good is presented by means of religious symbols": *Explorations*, p. 45.
44. A point made by Roy Walker, *The Time Is Free*, p. 185.

ter.[45] Damned already, Macbeth tries with his great bluff to drag Macduff with him to hell: "damn'd be him that first cries 'Hold, enough!'" (V.viii.34). Since immediately thereafter we are told that young Siward "parted well, and paid his score, / And so, God be with him!" (52–53), we are meant clearly to contrast their ends. In fact, we are meant also to contrast Macbeth's end with his predecessor's. The first Thane of Cawdor, much like the second, betrays his king; but to emphasize the almost incredible evil of Macbeth, the evil that includes betrayal when the betrayed is a guest, Cawdor is allowed redemption. He dies a model death, following the steps of the sacrament of penance and putting into practice the lessons of the *Ars moriendi*:

> he confess'd his treasons,
> Implor'd your Highness' pardon, and set forth
> A deep repentance. Nothing in his life
> Became him like the leaving it. He died
> As one that had been studied in his death
> To throw away the dearest thing he ow'd,
> As 'twere a careless trifle.
>
> (I.iv.5–11)

Apart from his contrition and confession, his satisfaction (paid with his life), he observes the cardinal rule of the *Ars moriendi*: he has conned the art of dying well and seeks not to hang on to the worthless trifle of life. Many versions of the English *Ars moriendi* collate well on this point. Here is Caxton's:

> eueryche synner verily contryte ought not to be soroufull ne trouble hym of the temporall or bodyly deth . . . for what some euer mater or cause be layd to hym, but he oughte to suffre and receyue it pacyently and in thankis and gladly inconformyng him selfe playnli, And in comyttynge hooly his proper will to goddys wylle. . . . For well to deye is gladly to deye. . . . and if he soo doo in suffrynge pacyently the payne of

45. See chap. 2.

Fig. 16. Dying man distracted by worldly possessions. *The craft to liue well and to die well.* Press of Wynkyn de Worde, London, 1505.

deth, he satysfyeth for all his venyalle synnes, And that more is he bryngeth some thynge for to satysfye for the dedely synnes [fig. 16].[46]

46. *The arte & crafte to knowe well to dye* (1490), Sigs. A₁ᵛ, A₄ᵛ. I have used the Caxton rather than the Wynkyn edition used elsewhere in this chapter because the Wynkyn copy is imperfect, lacking those pages that correspond to this passage in Caxton.

Macbeth, unrepentant, knows now that "juggling fiends" (V.viii.19) have deceived him; but he will not yield, curses the man he has "avoided" because his "soul is too much charg'd / With blood" of Macduff's already, and determines to "try the last," while calling for damnation to light upon the loser (4–34). With his own death, the fiends that inhabit his body no longer have a place of residence in the world and, presumably, return to hell to keep company with the damned soul whose housekeeping they had taken over.

Macbeth then is a play preeminently about last things, and in its very special presentation of possession, damnation, and location shows marked similarities to Dantean concepts. Sometimes closeness in imagery and symbolism suggests more than a vague familiarity with the *Inferno*. But I should not want to go so far as to state categorically that Shakespeare knew Dante firsthand. Some of the analogies may have come about by accident; some through a common body of theology, superstition, and convention; some from only a vague or secondhand knowledge of Dante on Shakespeare's part. Yet, whatever may be the explanation to these multiple correspondences, I think that a reading of *Macbeth* that keeps in mind the *Inferno* cannot go very far astray, and the reading we are left with is of Macbeth and his lady, who, in the murder of their king, a kinsman-guest, commit a crime so black, so profound, so abominable that further degradation cannot take place. Opportunity for redemption no longer exists for these two; they are damned eternally from the moment of the act. *Macbeth* is a portrait of damnation and a landscape of hell.

5. *Romeo and Juliet:*
Some Shall Be Pardoned

ervasive in Shakespeare's mature plays is his dismay that otherwise good men can be destroyed, even to damnation, by a sliver of fate or by an unhappy moment's failure in judgment. Hamlet's father—in Horatio's view a "goodly king" (I.ii.186), and in his son's a man the like of whom shall not be met readily again (187–88)—is taken unprepared for death. The manner of his leave may be called accidental: "The serpent . . . did sting thy father's life" (I.v.40). Insofar as the disposition of King Hamlet's soul is concerned, it matters little that the slain ruler was caught unawares by a true adder or by the serpent that "now wears his crown." Truly, heaven alone knows how the dead King's audit stands, but equally true is our thought and Hamlet's: "'Tis heavy with him" (III.iii.84).

That Shakespeare was appalled by happenstance which might take off not life only but soul also we perceive in Hamlet's rueful musings about justice and judgment:

So, oft it chances in particular men,
That for some vicious mole of nature in them,

As in their birth—wherein they are not guilty,
Since nature cannot choose his origin—

. . . .

Carrying, I say, the stamp of one defect,
Being nature's livery, or fortune's star,
His virtues else, be they as pure as grace,
As infinite as man may undergo,
Shall in the general censure take corruption
From that particular fault.

(I.iv.23–36)

To construe "general censure" as a figure for judgment day[1] reveals a Shakespeare who laments that one sin alone may damn a man—if he die unhouseled and unaneled—a Shakespeare who grieves that one sin alone disappoints him of heaven, "His virtues else, be they as pure as grace, / As infinite as man may undergo."

Othello, a good man, acting upon an uncharacteristic lapse in judgment, is betrayed even to damnation by an evil force he cannot see. Iago has "ensnar'd . . . *soul* and body" (V.ii.310, my italics) of a man who "nought . . . did in hate, but all in honor" (V.ii.303). His accusers, if they "set down [nothing] in malice," may say of him only that he "lov'd not wisely but too well" (V.ii.352–53). In such a view *Othello* becomes Shakespeare's most profound, most pessimistic tragedy. In *Hamlet* the good man's inability to pierce in time the disguises of evil leads only to mortal destruction; in *Othello* the otherwise flawless man's blindness to the demonic enemy leads to eternal damnation.[2]

Shakespeare works his way out of this black view in the redemptive forgiveness of the final romances, but the dark mood lin-

---

1. See p. 70 above. In various spiritual encyclopedias of the Middle Ages, *general* is the common adjective denoting *universal*. Wynkyn de Worde's *The craft to liue well and to die well* (London, 1505), for example, carries a running title of *The greate Jugement generall* for its doomsday section, and the word *judgment* or its synonyms rarely occurs without the said adjective throughout the entire text.

2. See chap. 2.

gers in *Measure for Measure,* in Escalus's anguish over Angelo's refusal to forgive Claudio: "some [are] condemned for a fault alone"
(II.i.40). Lucio, of the same opinion, expresses it more lewdly: no
life "should be . . . foolishly lost at a game of tick-tack" (I.ii.191–
92); "a ruthless thing is this . . . , for the rebellion of a codpiece to
take away the life of a man!" (III.ii.111–12). Escalus and Lucio refer only to the law that makes a capital offense out of human
indiscretion, but the Christian framework of *Measure for Measure*
suggests strongly an allegorical reading: the Duke, who, in Shakespeare's growing light, stands for mercy, would, like God of whom
he is a pattern, forgive.

These matters may be seen adumbrated in *Romeo and Juliet.*
Considerable discomfort among critics is attributable to what some
call the ethical problems of the play.[3] Impossible for them to reconcile is the apparent approval that Shakespeare gives to the young
lovers even as they break those commandments against idolatry,
filial irreverence, and murder (self-murder as well as that of Tybalt
and Paris). In truth, Shakespeare has everywhere softened character and action from what he found them in Brooke. In such manner
the playwright diminishes the faults of these golden children, but
that he means for his audience to consider the theological conse-
quences of the lovers' actions seems indisputable. Rather than force
us to believe, however, that Romeo and Juliet are damned, Shakespeare raises the issue he considers so profoundly and movingly in
Hamlet, Othello, and *Measure for Measure*: can it be that otherwise
good and loving souls are "condemned for a fault alone," that be
their virtues else "as pure as grace, / As infinite as man may undergo" they "Shall in the general censure take corruption / From
that particular fault"?

In order to face the matter squarely, Shakespeare, rather
than brush aside, compels theological considerations. Franklin
Dickey and Joseph A. Bryant, Jr.,[4] among others, have made simi-

3. For a fine resumé, see Joseph A. Bryant's "Introduction" to the
Signet *Romeo and Juliet* (1964), pp. xxiii–xxvi.
4. Franklin Dickey, *Not Wisely But Too Well* (San Marino, 1957),
pp. 63–117; Bryant, "Introduction," *Romeo and Juliet.*

lar assertions, Dickey at some length and quite persuasively; but unnoticed to date is a judgment theme, which in almost pure allegory—one is tempted to say parable—demands that the audience review the final audit of the souls of the two lovers.

Shakespeare's use of *memento-mori* materials is demonstrated everywhere throughout this book.[5] Quintessentially, the *memento-mori* device paints a harrowing picture of death and bodily dissolution as an allegory to the greater horrors of hell. When the genre is taken up in Christian art, grisly corruption of the flesh warns of punishment, the lot of the sinner turned from God (fig. 17). *Memento-mori* poetry exhorts the reader to seek for grace and to eschew further iniquity.

Romeo and Juliet encompasses one of Shakespeare's lengthiest employments of the *memento-mori* theme. The significance is inescapable. Hardly any literary motif is more bound to eschatology. When one of the two protagonists of this tragedy of love is exposed pointedly and repeatedly to the monitory words and images of promised judgment, we must conclude that Shakespeare nudged, if not constrained, his audience to thoughts of retributive justice.

When Friar Laurence probes to find the pith of Juliet's courage, the furthest verge to which she will go to escape marriage with Paris, the girl catalogues those things most fearful in her imagination. The least of these is to die. Worse are wanderings in "thievish ways," lurkings with "serpents," imprisonings with wild animals. Worst is the insistent nightmare, the deranging visions of sepulcher and rot:

> . . . hide me nightly in a charnel house,
> O'er-cover'd quite with dead men's rattling bones,
> With reeky shanks and yellow chapless skulls;
> Or bid me go into a new-made grave
> And hide me with a dead man in his tomb.
>
> (IV.i.81–85)

5. See especially the appendix.

Fig. 17. *Memento mori*. Title page of *The glasse of vaine-glorie*. Press of J. Windet, London, 1587.

These hideous imaginings compared to a conventional *memento-mori* lyric such as John Skelton's "Vppon a deedmans hed" (fig. 18) illustrate readily the use to which Shakespeare intends them:

> No man may hym hyde
> From Deth holow eyed,
> With synnews wyderyd,
> With bonys shyderyd,
>
> . . . .
>
> Oure eyen synkyng,
> Oure bodys stynkyng,
> Oure gummys grynnyng,
> Oure soulys brynnyng.

The one essential ingredient of all Christian *memento-mori* art is the reminder that escape is found only through redemption. As Skelton puts it: "To whom, then, shall we sew, / For to haue rescew, / But to swete Jesu."[6]

Memento-mori art, then, exhorts the spectator to stare steadfastly at his end, and Shakespeare opens this theme predictably early with Tybalt's challenge to Benvolio: "Turn thee . . . look upon thy death" (I.i.67). In the final scene, all remaining principals are commanded by the Prince: "Look, and thou shalt see" (V.iii.213). They gaze upon death, which has taken the youngest and loveliest among them. Speaking, no doubt, for all, Lady Capulet recites the lesson, learned woefully late:

> O me! This sight of death is as a bell
> That warns my old age to a sepulcher.
>   (V.iii.206–7)

Shakespeare envelops his play with two tableaux in each of which characters are enjoined to peer at death. Clearly, one of the chief concerns of the play is that vision. Everywhere in between, characters and audience are forced to contemplate death, not only in the

6. *The Poetical Works of John Skelton*, ed. Alexander Dyce, 2 vols. (London, 1843), 1:18–19.

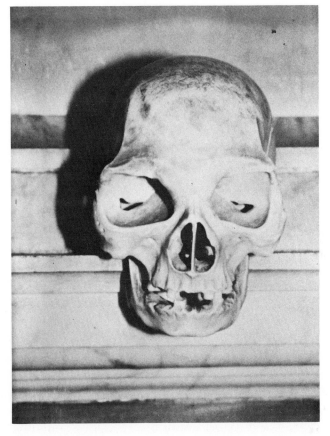

Fig. 18. Marble skull. Funerary monument to John, 8th Earl of Rutland (d. 1679). Church of St. Mary, Bottesford, Leicestershire.

actual killings of Mercutio, Tybalt, and Paris but also in the relentless grave that yawns beside the lovers' marriage bed.

Implicit in death and very much a part of all Christian *memento-mori* art is judgment. As in other of his plays, Shakespeare employs in *Romeo and Juliet* a specific judgment-day motif prominently among the devices that support his eschatological concerns. Reassigning Freetown, in Arthur Brooke's *Romeus and Juliet* the Capulet castle, Shakespeare makes it Verona's "common judgment-place" (I.i.102). The sentence—forfeit of life and pain of death—

threatened by the Prince (I.i.97, 103) there where the civil brawl broke out will be with all judgmental solemnity reissued at the judgment-seat and, if necessary, the doom handed down and executed.

The young lovers come all too quickly under a prospect of fearful sentence, although first they are established separately as gracious children. In sequential scenes, Juliet expresses complete obedience to authority in her parents—"But no more deep will I endart mine eye / Than your consent gives strength to make it fly" (I.iii.99–100), and Romeo submits himself to God:

> my mind misgives
> Some consequence yet hanging in the stars
> . . . .
> But He that hath the steerage of my course
> Direct my suit!
>
> (I.iv.106–13)

However, once they meet, each substitutes the other as highest, in fact, as only authority. The sin is labeled clearly idolatry. It begins, along with love, at first sight. In startling and rapid progression, Romeo likens Juliet first to a shrine and then to a saint (I.v.95, 102–4). On next view, she has become the sun (II.ii.3) and then "bright angel" (26). Romeo offers to "be new baptiz'd" (50) in what is manifestly his new religion with Juliet as goddess. Juliet, equally smitten, creates Romeo "the god of [her] idolatry" (114).

Idolatry is the overriding sin of both. It gives rise to all other acts. What they call love they have elevated to some sort of faith, complete with new gods (themselves) and new cosmographies. Each has become for the other not only god but also earth and heaven; each sees absence from the other as being cast into outer darkness. Juliet interprets mistakenly the nurse's report of Tybalt's death as the death of Romeo. Confusion grows and she thinks both Tybalt and Romeo are dead:

> Then, dreadful trumpet, sound the general doom!
> For who is living, if those two are gone?
>
> (III.ii.67–68)

Although Juliet momentarily includes Tybalt, we learn shortly that thought of any other than Romeo is totally empty of feeling. And when the terrible news is corrected, when Romeo is known to be alive, Juliet finds his banishment of equal devastation:

> "Romeo is banished," to speak that word,
> Is father, mother, Tybalt, Romeo, Juliet,
> All slain, all dead. "Romeo is banished!"
> There is no end, no limit, measure, bound,
> In that word's death.
>
> (III.ii.122–26)

Both these passages describe judgment day. Life for every living thing has ceased for Juliet if her entire world—and that is Romeo— no longer exists.

Romeo reacts to banishment in exactly the same way: "What less than doomsday is the Prince's doom?" (III.iii.9). Having made Juliet sun and god, he converts her surroundings into paradise: "Heaven is here / Where Juliet lives" (29–30). Who or whatever can reach to her presence may "steal *immortal* blessing" (37, my italics). She is also the entire world and all that lives:

> There is no world without Verona walls,
> But purgatory, torture, hell itself.
> Hence "banished" is banish'd from the world,
> And world's exile is death.
>
> (III.iii.17–20)

> O friar, the damned use that word [banished]
>   in hell;
> Howling attends it.
>
> (47–48)

Memento mori emphasizes the inevitability of death:

> If none can scape deaths dreadfull dart,
>   If rich and poore his becke obey,

If strong, if wise, if all do smart,
  Then I to scape shall have no way.[7]

In the classical period, the reminder of death urged that man's brief span be spent in joy; in the Christian, it pleads that, even in joy, man be mindful of the pangs of death and the torments of damnation. Shakespeare fuses elements of joy and death in a marriage-grave/*memento-mori* motif that permeates the play and produces one of its greatest ironies. With horrifying accuracy, Juliet initiates a theme of which she, as her beloved Romeo, remains, even into the tomb itself, tragically unaware:

  If he be married,
My grave is like to be my wedding bed.
      (I.v.135–36)

Her simple meaning does not include what the sentence holds for everyone familiar with the story of these doomed children: especially if Romeo marries Juliet will her wedding sheets be made into her shroud cloth: "Our wedding cheer to a sad burial feast, / . . . / Our bridal flowers serve for a buried corse" (IV.v.87–89).

At least fifteen additional times Shakespeare employs the marriage-grave image, directly and in subtle variations.[8] Always it registers with wrenching irony; always it supports the *memento-mori* theme (fig. 19). Moreover, it blends into additional elements in the larger judgmental statement of the play. One of these is the traditional *memento-mori* lyric itself, developed by Shakespeare into a dramatic counterpart. Juliet's tearful appeal to her mother opens the "detestable maw" itself:

  Delay this marriage for a month, a week;
  Or, if you do not, make the bridal bed
  In that dim monument where Tybalt lies.
        (III.v.200–202)

7. *The Poems of Robert Southwell, S.J.*, ed. J. H. McDonald and Nancy P. Brown (Oxford, 1967), p. 74.
  8. Prol. II.i; II.ii.183; II.iii.83–84; III.ii.136–37; III.iii.3;

Fig. 19. Death and the lover, c. 1520. St. Mary Magdalene,
Newark-on-Trent, Nottinghamshire.

Juliet's desperate courage, wherein she assures Friar Laurence that
she is capable of hiding in a charnel house, already has been
noted. Later, when she lies alone in bed, having dismissed her
nurse, fears engulf her. In the longest set-piece of *memento-mori*

III.iii.66–70; III.v.140; III.v.201–2; IV.i.107–8; IV.iii.22–23; IV.v.35–
39; IV.v.78–90; IV.v.84–89; V.i.34; V.iii.73; and V.iii.155.

imagery in Shakespeare, Juliet summons up fearful sights of the "rotten jaws" and "womb of death":

> How if, when I am laid into the tomb,
> I wake before the time that Romeo
> Come to redeem me? There's a fearful point!
> Shall I not then be stifled in the vault,
> To whose foul mouth no healthsome air breathes in,
> And there die strangled ere my Romeo comes?
> Or, if I live, is it not very like,
> The horrible conceit of death and night,
> Together with the terror of the place—
> As in a vault, an ancient receptacle,
> Where, for this many hundred years, the bones
> Of all my buried ancestors are pack'd;
> Where bloody Tybalt, yet but green in earth,
> Lies fest'ring in his shroud; where, as they say,
> At some hours in the night spirits resort—
> Alack, alack, is it not like that I,
> So early waking, what with loathsome smells,
> And shrieks like mandrakes' torn out of the earth,
> That living mortals, hearing them, run mad—
> O, if I wake, shall I not be distraught,
> Environed with all these hideous fears,
> And madly play with my forefathers' joints,
> And pluck the mangled Tybalt from his shroud,
> And, in this rage, with some great kinsman's bone,
> As with a club, dash out my desp'rate brains?
>   (IV.iii.30–54)

All her terrors flood in upon the chance that Romeo fail to arrive on time. The special word she employs is *redeem*, and with it we remember that Romeo may be thought of as a bridegroom. Though truly husband, Romeo is so newly wedded that the name of bridegroom hangs upon him still. Yet, he is not the only bridegroom of the play. Paris, having been accepted by Capulet and consented to by Juliet (IV.ii.17–35), is called specifically a bride-

groom by Friar Laurence (IV.i.107). Capulet plans a feast to celebrate the marriage. With these observations, we perceive a great
complex of images and symbols cohering to make an eschatological
statement that permeates the entire play. The marriage-grave motif
is not merely a commentary on the shattering ironies in this tragic
love; it is also an element in the judgment theme, since Shakespeare
couples it with the idea of a redeemer-bridegroom. Willful disobedience by these children, focused in their self-arranged and
idolatrous marriage, requiring rebellion against their parents,[9]
threatens them with spiritual death.

No metaphor is more common to scripture than that of
marriage and its accompanying feast. Christ is the bridegroom
(John 3.29), and "The kingdome of heauen is like vnto a certeine
King which maried his sonne" (Matt.22.2). Perhaps best known is
the parable of the ten virgins:

> Then the kingdome of heauen shalbe likened vnto
> ten virgins, which toke their lampes, and went to mete
> the bridegrome [fig. 20].
>
> (Matt. 25.1)

Shakespeare employs the parable of the wise and foolish virgins
as a means of awakening to the figure of the redemptive Christ
the sleeping will of Juliet. The likely agent of this lesson is Friar
Laurence, but the good, old man is woefully somnolent himself to
its meaning. Purposing only good for Juliet, he indicates merely
the folly of his counsel:

> Now, when the bridegroom in the morning comes
> To rouse thee from thy bed, there art thou dead.
>
> (IV.i.107–8)

Any sixteenth-century auditor of a prelate's words that included
bridegroom, morning, rouse, bed, and *dead* who did not call to mind

---

9. We may assume that Montague outrage would equal Capulet if
Romeo's father were aware of his son's new alliance.

Fig. 20. Foolish virgin. South porch, Lincoln Cathedral. By permission of the Dean and the Chapter of Lincoln Cathedral.

readily the parable of the ten virgins was, like Juliet and Friar Laurence, missing the good news:

> Now while the bridegrome taryed long, all slombred
>   and slept.
> And at midnight there was a crye made, Beholde,
>   the bridegrome cometh: go out to mete him.

Then all those virgins arose, & trimmed their
    lampes.

                            (Matt. 25.5–7)

These three verses account only for *bridegroom, morning, rouse,* and
bed; but the parable is prefaced with its application in which the
virgins are compared with heaven. The conclusion is likewise anagogical: the bridegroom of heaven "knowe[s] not" (25.12) the five
unprepared virgins. Spiritually they are dead. The warning to
Juliet—"there art thou dead"—should overwhelm her, but it does
not. In every way, the tag to this parable accords with the purpose
of *memento-mori* verse, which in the lyric version of Thomas Lord
Vaux, a poem with which Shakespeare's gravedigger in *Hamlet* is
plausibly familiar, is rendered in the feeling cry: "Leave off these
toys in time." [10] *Time* is the key word, for as the parable has it,
"Watche therefore: for ye knowe nether the day, nor the houre,
when the Sonne of man wil come" (25.13).

    Early echoes of the parable can be found in III.iv. A sense
develops that time is fleeting for many of these people, but marriage and feast require considerable time for proper preparation:

CAPULET
    Things have fall'n out, sir, so unluckily,
    That we have had no time to move our
        daughter.
    Look you, she lov'd her kinsman Tybalt dearly,
    And so did I. Well, we were born to die.
    'Tis very late, she'll not come down tonight.
    I promise you, but for your company
    I would have been a-bed an hour ago.
PARIS
    These times of woe afford no times to woo.
                     (III.iv.1–8)

10. *Tottel's Miscellany (1557–1587),* ed. Hyder Rollins, 2 vols. (Cambridge, Mass., 1928), 1:166.

Bedtime, wedding, lateness of the hour (enforced by repetition of "no time[s]") are all elements that begin to cohere as ingredients in the parable. Furthermore, they are linked in this very passage to the *memento-mori* motif by Capulet's crocodile tears for Tybalt and the pious reminder that "we were born to die." Shortly thereafter, Lady Capulet is commanded specifically, *before she go to bed*, to see Juliet and "Prepare her . . . against this wedding-day" (31–32). Once again we are reminded, this time with two intensifiers, "it is so very late" (34).

When Lady Capulet carries out her husband's injunction, she stipulates that a bridegroom comes for whom neither she nor Juliet watched:

> a sudden day of joy,
> That thou expects not, nor I look'd not for.
>
> . . . .
>
> The County Paris, at Saint Peter's Church[11]
> Shall happily make thee there a joyful bride.
>   (III.v.109–15)

In other lines focusing on these matters, further warnings are given to the lateness of the time: III.iii.164, 172; III.v.66; IV.i.1. The bridegroom himself announces his intention to arrive before Juliet wakes: "on Thursday early will I rouse ye" (IV.i.42). She has been warned to prepare on every side.

As time grows late, haste and impetuosity increase. The rashness that is already a well-established theme, and clearly the quality of youth that plunges the lovers into their predicament, races Mercutio to his death. The feverish contagion, spreading like wildfire, has engulfed Friar Laurence and now claims the previously sober Capulet. When Juliet returns from the Friar, happy with his desperately dangerous plot, she is most dissemblingly dishonest with her secular father. The sinfulness of her deceit is

11. St. Peter's Church may be considered the church universal. Marriage in that church carries greater sanctity than the rite performed in Laurence's cell.

underscored heavily by the girl's own recognition of a need for atonement at the very moment she deceives: "I have learn'd me to repent the sin / Of disobedient opposition / . . . . / Henceforward I am ever rul'd by you" (IV.ii.17–22). Capulet, coming under the hectic of a worldly desire to have his will fulfilled—to have his daughter fortunately bestowed—hastes forward the wedding to the next morning. He will "stir about" and "not to bed tonight" (IV.ii.24–42). Yet, when morning comes, Capulet crying still commands of "stir," "make haste," and ticking off the hours with "The second cock hath crowed, / The curfew-bell hath rung [with all the heavy symbolic burden of *curfew*], 'tis three o'clock . . . Good faith, 'tis day" (IV.iv.3–21), they are not ready for the bridegroom:

> Go waken Juliet, go and trim her up.
> . . . Hie, make haste,
> Make haste. The bridegroom he is come already;
> Make haste, I say.
> (IV.iv.25–28)

Trim is the new and potent word in this flying scene. Shakespeare carries it over from the parable, whose virgins rise and *trim* their lamps. But Juliet does not rise, and others are asked to trim her up. When she cannot be awakened, even to greet the bridegroom, Capulet's common response suggests yet another meaning: "For shame . . . her lord is come" (IV.v.22).

But Juliet had rejected the bridegroom previously in sharp and unmistakable terms of despair. In the medieval *psychomachia*, the virtue paired with the vice *desperatio* is *patientia*, although, more often, the vice paired with *patientia* is *ira* (fig. 21). Not Tybalt, Mercutio, nor finally Romeo is able to subject his wrath to patience:

TYBALT
> Patience perforce with willful choler meeting
> Makes my flesh tremble in their different
> greeting.
> (I.v.90–91)

**The.iii.heed of the beeſt of helle is Ire
oꝛ wrath Ca. ☙☙☙ .xxb.**

Fig. 21. *Patientia* and *Ira. The boke named royall.* Press of Wynkyn de Worde,
London, 1507.

MERCUTIO
   Tybalt, you rat-catcher, will you walk?
        (III.i.74)

ROMEO
   Away to heaven, respective lenity,
   And fire-ey'd fury be my conduct now!
        (III.i.122–23)

Ira kills the first two and precipitates the tragedy of the last.
Romeo's fury gives way to despair, and he kills himself. But he be-
haves no differently from his lady:

   Shall I be married then tomorrow morning?
   No, no, this shall forbid it.
        (IV.iii.22–23)

The suicide-knife she then lays ready to hand, if used, cuts her off from marriage as the bride of Christ. And yet, immediately after this movement away from grace, she has that second vision of the fearful tomb in which she summons up "the horrible conceit of death and night" that she will encounter if she awakes without the bridegroom "Come to redeem" her (IV.iii.30–58). Both in contemplation of the bridegroom's visit and in preparation for the bridegroom's arrival, Juliet is deficient.

One final time in her mortality Juliet looks toward waking at a bridegroom's coming, the one she wants, the one for whom she hazards all. And one final time Juliet fails her spouse. She wakes too late and once again outsleeps a chance for holy marriage. I select the word *chance* by careful choice. Much has been written of the chance or fate, the accident or crossing-star that foils the joy of the two youths; but no element of the play places the main theme more squarely in the Christian framework that some critics would put aside. Christ's warning in the parable of the virgins exhorts the person who would live in hope of heaven so to conduct his life that no chance of fate may steal away his soul: "Watche therefore: for ye knowe nether the day, nor the houre."

The parable of the wise and foolish virgins is widespread in all medieval and Renaissance art. The very origins of Gothic sculpture, attributed generally to the influence of Suger in his reconstruction of St.-Denis, emphasized the west entrance as the *porta caeli*. As such it was a montage of Christ in majesty, presiding at the last judgment: right were ascending angels and the blessed; left, demons and the lost. Beneath the throne were those newly awakened dead, emerging from tombs and graves, making their way to be judged. In the opposed uttermost corners of the half-circle that forms the tympanum were one each of the wise and foolish virgins; the other eight were arranged appropriately on the right and left jambs of the portal (fig. 22). Doomsday as a sculptural theme had preceded the figures at St.-Denis, but Suger's immense political and ecclesiastical influence gave it such great emphasis that it assumed overwhelming proportions in subsequent Gothic cathedral sculpture. Allowing for variation, Suger's sculptural program can be found in all the great cathedrals of northern France, the subordinate theme of the ten virgins accompanying judgment-day portals at Notre Dame de Paris, Amiens, Sens, Auxerre, and Chalons-sur-Marne, to name but a few.

In English cathedral art, the figures in the parable are found both in the glass and in the sculpture at Lincoln. The sculpture is also part of the judgment porch, located on the south side of the Angel Choir. In the third outermost voussoir, the figures are small but, in common opinion, are among the most elegant at Lincoln (fig. 20).

Karl Young prints the text of a twelfth-century play about the wise and foolish virgins, called the *Sponsus*.[12] "It was clearly associated with the idea of final Judgment for it ended with demons emerging to seize the Foolish Virgins, rejected of Christ, as they knelt before the locked doors of heaven, perhaps vainly grasping the handles in the despairing attitude shown on the Judgement tympanum of S. Denis, Paris."[13] Clearly, the parable was in wide deployment in Anglo-Norman art.

Romeo is the figure in the play most aware of destiny, but an act of will, which he labels defiance (V.i.24),[14] spurs him to the apothecary's shop. He does not crumble under a malevolent fate but fashions his own in repudiation of what the stars have thus far omened for him. Nor does he blame his course on powers malign—heavenly orbs or heavenly steerer; instead he acknowledges that his free choice has been to turn his back on good. "Put not another sin upon my head," he cries to Paris (V.iii.62), who would keep him from the tomb. But several other sins he still commits: defies authority, murders a man, and kills himself.

In the light of this assessment against his soul, we escape with difficulty a fear that Romeo, as Juliet, lies damned, each self-killed in disobedient arms, dying upon forbidden kisses. But we must not forget that Shakespeare has softened all. Arthur Brooke's scheming

12. Karl Young, *Drama of the Medieval Church*, 2 vols. (Oxford, 1933), 2:361–69.

13. Mary D. Anderson, *Drama and Imagery in English Medieval Churches* (Cambridge, Eng., 1963), p. 30.

14. I follow Q_1's *defie* as do most editors, but the point remains unchanged with Q_2's *denie*.

Fig. 22. West portals of St.-Denis. Florida State University Library.

older girl in Shakespeare's hands is "a stranger in the world; / [that] hath not seen the change of fourteen years" (I.ii.8−9). Glowingly praised by all until her domestic defection, after her seeming death, Juliet receives epitaph as "the sweetest flower of all the field" (IV.v.29). Clearly some similar eulogy will grace the "statue in pure gold" so that "whiles Verona by that name is known, / There shall no figure at such rate be set / As that of true and faithful Juliet" (V.iii.299−302). No less in Veronese esteem is Romeo. His father's enemy is author of the common view: "Verona brags of him / To be a virtuous and well govern'd youth" (I.v.68−69). By play's end these views, perhaps strangely, have not altered. Prince, both fathers, and friar lament over great loss. It behooves us not to damn these lovers summarily.

Before the aborted marriage with Paris, Juliet had already engaged in another. Everything about the actual marriage, except for parental consent, shows the lovers to be seeking a holy union. Juliet must know that Romeo's "bent of love be honorable, / [His] purpose marriage," or she must beseech him "To cease [his] strife, and leave [her] to her grief" (II.ii.143−52). Romeo offers nothing less, and indeed they marry sacramentally. Even an accompanying feast commemorates the marriage. Although not intended to celebrate the marriage of Romeo and Juliet, it proves to be the feast that brings the lovers indissolubly together. The feast itself is preceded by a strange scene in which Shakespeare devotes over a hundred lines merely to show several young men—Benvolio, Mercutio, Romeo, and others—rollicking toward the Capulet banquet. Other than to introduce Mercutio and to let him recite his lengthy Queen Mab speech, even dubbed by Romeo "nothing," the scene seems to juxtapose Romeo's determination for virtue alongside Juliet's. It follows Juliet's humble acceptance of her parent's authority with Romeo's own submission to Him "that hath the steerage" of his course. But in this scene also are some thirty-odd lines the main subject of which has to do with torches.

Romeo, a reluctant companion to the others, argues that to attend is foolish: "'tis no wit to go" (I.iv.49). He has had a dream, his mind misgives, he fears that going will bring untimely death. Yet, despite his demurrers, he consents to go, putting his life in his

God's hands. He fears no death. Presumably he believes himself in grace; and the imagery of the torches, worked out as a preface to the later use of the parable of the wise and foolish virgins, supports this idea. Three times Romeo insists that he will be a torchbearer (I.iv.11, 35, 38). He dissociates himself from the pure pleasure-seeker:

> Let wantons light of heart
> Tickle the senseless rushes with their heels.
> (35–36)

Common interpretation of the foolish virgins indicates that they wasted their oil in revelry and wantonness. A striking canvas, executed in 1570 by Hans Eworth, presents, through multiple scenes within the 24-square-inch panel, the entire allegory of the ten virgins. Eworth was official portraitist for Queen Mary and apparently was out of favor with Elizabeth until 1572, when he is known to have designed settings for a series of fetes given by the Queen. Although this painting is now in the Royal Museum of Fine Arts in Copenhagen, Eworth's known residence in London from 1549 to at least 1572 proves England as the provenance of the panel. Its five foolish virgins are indeed wanton (fig. 23).[15]

All the young men in the scene desire, as Romeo, to be as full of probity as the wise virgins. Mercutio is mindful that they waste their torches: "Come, we burn daylight" (43). When Romeo points out that it is nighttime, Mercutio responds in a vein that sounds very much to me like the message of a parable:

> I mean, sir, in delay
> We waste our lights in vain, like lamps by day.
> Take our good meaning, for our judgment sits
> Five times in that ere once in our five wits.
> (44–47)

15. Biographical information on Eworth may be found in Roy Strong, *The Elizabethan Icon: Elizabethan and Jacobean Portraiture* (London, 1969), pp. 83, 99.

DVM STERTVNT FATVÆ MEDIA DE NOCTE PVELLÆ VOX SONAT H
PRVDENTES. QVARVM RVTILA LVX LAMPADE FVLGET. OCCVRRVNT
PANDITVR EXCELSI SVBLIMIS IANVA CŒLI ET SVBEVNT
ACCVRRVNT FATVÆ SED IANVA CLAVDITVR ILLIS. QVI SAPIT IS S

Fig. 23. Wise and Foolish Virgins. Hans Eworth, 1570. By permission of the Royal Museum of Fine Arts, Copenhagen.

Benvolio, as well, does not want to miss the feast: "Supper is done, and we shall come too late" (105).

The feast itself would seem aflame with light. Three times Capulet calls for more light, more torches (I.v.28, 88, 126). The room apparently has heated so from the torches that he orders the fire quenched. But most refulgent of all is Juliet: "O, she doth teach the torches to burn bright" (45). When Romeo addresses Juliet and she responds in the famous dialogue-sonnet, many directors of the play have their actors engaged in the general dancing. But such is not so. Juliet expressly identifies Romeo as "he . . . that would not dance" (133). What transpires instead of dancing would seem to be a most religious experience in which both parties—identified as saint and pilgrim—cleanse each other of sin:

> ROMEO
>> Thus from my lips, by thine, my sin is purg'd.
>
> JULIET
>> Then have my lips the sin that they have took.
>
> ROMEO
>> Sin from my lips? O trespass sweetly urg'd!
>> Give me my sin again.
>
> (108–11)

The ambiguity that the sin is present still on one set of lips or the other is part of the rich doubts of the play.

Two other symbolic moments give us further pause before we condemn the luckless pair. One is Romeo's second dream, not the one that caused him doubts about the wisdom of attending the Capulet feast, but the dream that he reports immediately prior to receiving news of Juliet's death:

> I dreamt my lady came and found me dead—
>
> . . . .
>
> And breath'd such life with kisses in my lips
> That I reviv'd and was an emperor.
>
> (V.i.6–9)

Something of resurrection resides in these lines, a rebirth that Romeo attributes to a shadow of love, a shadow that stands for love itself:

> Ah me, how sweet is love itself possess'd,
> When but love's shadows are so rich in joy!
> (10–11)

The second of these resurrection-moments pertains to Juliet, thus redeeming both:

> Within this three hours will fair Juliet wake.
> . . . .
> Poor living corse, clos'd in a dead man's tomb!
> (V.ii.25, 30)

Three hours may glance at Christ's three days in the sepulcher, but whatever the sojourn, the living creature will wake, escaping from both the body and the tomb.

With as much symbolic action directing acquittal as that sup-posing guilt, we may neither damn the lovers easily nor exonerate them completely. Both have sinned because of one particular flaw. Their virtues else seem as pure as grace, as infinite as youth may undergo. Like Othello, nothing they did was in hate or malice; all their error budded because they loved "too well." In *Romeo and Juliet* Shakespeare probes early matters dwelt on so profoundly in *Hamlet* and *Othello*. We may not put aside last things. Judgment is an issue: can God cast into outer darkness the sinner whose guiding fault was love? In *Othello* an older Shakespeare says yes, but mourns the pity of it. In *Romeo and Juliet* a younger Shakespeare, innocently surer of the power of love, has hopes of livelier mercy. Surely God is no more severe than a merciful Renaissance prince. Surely God, as the Prince, is struck with woe by the story of these tragic chil-dren; and in heaven above, as on earth below, although some shall be punished, surely "Some shall be pardon'd" (V.iii.308).

6. *A Midsummer Night's Dream:*

So Quick Bright Things Come to Confusion

ime and the moon have given readers of *A Midsummer Night's Dream* nothing but trouble from the earliest commentators to the most recent. Dr. Johnson wondered why the playwright should "so carefully inform us" that the lovers enter the woods on the night before May Day and then give the play a midsummer title. Farmer and Malone are both of the opinion that the title had nothing to do with "the precise time of the action." H. H. Furness sums up all arguments anterior to 1895 by urging happily that Shakespeare wove together in "one potent glamour" all the "shadowy realm" of *Walpurgisnacht* (eve of May Day) and *Johannisnacht* (eve of the feast of St. John the Baptist, June 24).[1] C. L. Barber makes all things possible by proving that references to May games might be made all summer long: "people went Maying at various times, 'Against May, Whitsunday, and other time' is the way Stubbes [*Anatomie of Abuses*, 1583] puts

---

1. All these earlier observations are digested in *A Midsommer Nights Dreame*, A New Variorum Edition of Shakespeare, ed. H. H. Furness, 4th ed. (Philadelphia, 1895), pp. v–viii.

it. This Maying can be thought of as happening on a midsummer night, even on Midsummer Eve itself."[2]

Mishandling of the moon, which, without exception, critics attribute to Shakespeare, began at least as early as 1709, when the illustrator for Rowe's edition etched into his frontispiece a full moon, shining down upon a fairy ring (fig. 24). John Dover Wilson asserts that the confusion began when in one of two separate revisions Shakespeare rewrote the play's opening: "the trouble all arises from I.i.1–11, which was probably added at the time of a revision."[3] Within these lines is a clear call for a new moon:

THESEUS
> Four happy days bring in
> Another moon; but, O, methinks, how slow
> This old moon wanes! . . .

HIPPOLYTA
> Four nights will quickly dream away the time;
> And then the moon, like to a silver bow
> New-bent in heaven, shall behold the night
> Of our solemnities.
>
> (I.i.2–11)

Wilson neglects line I.i.83, in which Theseus reiterates precise lunar time: "by the next new moon." But perhaps Wilson would gather that line in also merely by repeating his claim of revision. His argument presents a first draft of the play set on a stage bathed constantly by a full moon, much as the illustrator of Rowe's edition conceived and much as every subsequent writer concurred. Wilson's phrase in 1924 is "the whole play is bathed in moonlight."[4] Ernst Schanzer, as late as 1965, believes an important visual effect

2. C. L. Barber, *Shakespeare's Festive Comedy* (Princeton, 1959), p. 120.

3. *A Midsummer-Night's Dream*, ed. Sir Arthur Quiller-Couch and John Dover Wilson (Cambridge, Eng., 1924), p. 122.

4. Quiller-Couch and Wilson, *A Midsummer-Night's Dream*, p. 121. The phrase remains unaltered in all subsequent printings of the play, down to the latest of 1968.

Fig. 24. Frontispiece, *A Midsummer Night's Dream.*
Nicholas Rowe edition. London, 1709.

is achieved, a "unity of atmosphere . . . by flooding the play with
moonlight."[5] C. L. Barber echoes Wilson: "Shakespeare does not
make himself accountable for exact chronological inferences; the

5. "*A Midsummer-Night's Dream,*" *Shakespeare: The Comedies,* ed.
Kenneth Muir (Englewood Cliffs, N.J., 1965), p. 29, trans. by the author
from a longer version in *Oeuvres Completes de Shakespeare,* ed. P. Leyris and
Henri Evans (Paris, 1958).

moon that will be new according to Hippolyta will shine according to Bottom's almanac."[6] David P. Young, in a book-length study of the play, agrees with Kittredge that "No audience would notice the discrepancy, for the night in the enchanted forest is long enough to bewilder the imagination."[7] All these commentators settle for easy solutions. To suggest that Shakespeare played fast and loose with time is to reject the overwhelming testimony of almost every piece that he wrote, each of which witnesses the poet's near obsession with "devouring time." To forget that age when the sun was day's and the moon night's timepiece is to lose a great tool for critical pronouncement as well as for natural observation.

To think that Shakespeare, in whose work regard for time is always prominent, should so far forget himself that in revision he would botch one of his main concerns or that he would count on the swift two hours' traffic of the stage to cover careless time references or that he would attempt to "bewilder the imagination" of his audience to hide from them a faulty chronology is unthinkable.

So few of Shakespeare's contemporaries, like Touchstone, were able to pull a dial from their pokes that sun and moon were their only clocks; country boys like Shakespeare, with little or no opportunity to hear the chimes of London or to read "the bawdy hand of the dial," learned to note time by the orbs in the sky. To think they forgot the trick in London is unthinkable.

A third thought unthinkable is that a playwright who uses the word *moon* with all its variants such as *moonlight, moonshine*, and *moonbeam* forty-nine times should ever so forget himself as to call for dark of the moon in the first eleven lines of his play and then flood his stage with moonlight thereafter.

Instead we should think that there are no inconsistencies in any of the various references to the moon, in the title, or in the

6. Barber, *Shakespeare's Festive Comedy*, p. 120; Wilson's phrase is, "Shall we say that Shakespeare cared nothing for astronomical exactitude . . . ?" Quiller-Couch and Wilson, *A Midsummer-Night's Dream*, p. 122.

7. *A Midsummer Night's Dream*, ed. George Lyman Kittredge (Boston, 1939), p. ix, reprinted and approved by Irving Ribner in the 2d ed. (1966), pp. xvi–xvii; David P. Young, *Something of Great Constancy* (New Haven, 1966), pp. 86–87.

time-plan of the play. We should see that all three of these elements coalesce to show a meticulous craftsmanship, undertaken to underprop one of the main statements of the comedy.

More and more cognizance has been taken of what Harold Jenkins perceived in *As You Like It*. Shakespeare's "mature comedy . . . permits . . . criticism of his ideal world in the very centre of it. . . . he dares to speak in Arcadia, where one can never grow old, of Time's inevitable processes of maturity and decay."[8] In the bright, gay, happy, and golden forest of Arden, not only does the clock tick away to produce images of inevitable decrepitude but also the minutes are observed to carry the lovers, fresh in beauty, youth, and love, all the way to the tomb, so that Death may say, "et in Arcadia ego."[9] A similar theme may be perceived in *A Midsummer Night's Dream*, chiefly through calendar references, and a calendar, at that, dominated by the phases of the moon.

Had *A Midsummer Night's Dream* been composed in the period of the so-called golden comedic trilogy of *Much Ado About Nothing*, *Twelfth Night*, and *As You Like It*, it would have as much right to a carefree appellative as any of them. Yet Death holds his court in the woods outside Athens just as surely as he does in the palace of Richard II, and the poet means to remind us, after the fashion of *memento-mori* verse, that Death, with his little pin, may bore through the armor of youth, beauty, and love as easily as through the stone in castle walls.

Various components of the play contribute to a thematic underscoring that although these young lovers, as well as the mature Duke and his Amazon bride, are, at play's end, merely setting foot on the threshold of married love, they have begun also time's swift consumption of their joys.

First, as it comes first, we might consider the title of the play, accepting at the outset C. L. Barber's proof that the rite of May "can be thought of as happening . . . on Midsummer Eve itself."[10] Midsummer Night has two distinctions: it is the eve of the feast of

8. Harold Jenkins, *"As You Like It," Shakespeare Survey* 8 (1955): 45.
9. See chap. 8.
10. See note 2 above.

St. John the Baptist and the eve of the summer solstice. As the Saint's feast day is a fixed holy day, falling always on June 24, but the summer solstice varies one or two days, in the Julian calendar falling earlier and earlier over the centuries, June 24 is only the nominal Midsummer Day, but, as such, midsummer festivities were celebrated always as an adjunct to the Saint's day.

The point to be made about the solstice is that it provides for the northern hemisphere the year's longest day and shortest night. Our play, in its chief action, unfolds on Midsummer Night, and we are told by the title to consider the happenings merely a dream; thereby we are forcibly informed that the duration of young love is no more than the ephemeral joy of a happy night-vision, beheld on the shortest night of the year. The playwright has told us elsewhere to "reason thus with life": "Thou hast nor youth nor age, / But as it were an after-dinner's sleep, / Dreaming on both" (*Measure for Measure*, III.i.6, 32–34). How much shorter then is that part of life during which lovers have their youth, beauty, and fresh delight in each other.

The Epistle in the Propers for St. John's Day in all editions of The Book of Common Prayer from the first of 1549 to that in use today is from Isaiah 40, centering on the brevity of life:

> all fleshe is grasse, and . . . all the goodlyness therof is
> as the floure of the fedle. The grass is withered, the
> floure falleth awaye. Even so is the people as grasse,
> when the breath of the Lorde bloweth upon them.
>
> (ed. of 1549)

The lesson from the Epistle in conjunction with a feast day that falls near or upon the summer solstice emphasizes a reality that was not lost on the celebrants of Midsummer Eve: from the moment of solstice onward, the sun declines from the northern hemisphere. As a symbol of man's life, the sun's decrease in heat and vigor presages man's ultimate winter or death. The festivities on Midsummer Eve are the last great burst of life, of joy and high spirits, before the long winter draws on, even as those of Mardi Gras hold off for one more day the Lenten severity that culminates in another death. The peak of young love is that moment when pursuit is over and the lover obtains his beloved; it is the solstitial moment—in a marriage masque, the wedding night—after which the long decline of married love inevitably follows.

Any piece of literature that celebrates marriage and takes to itself a title associated with the shortest night of the year must chime for the reader certain tinkling moments in Spenser's great marriage hymn, exactly contemporary with *A Midsummer Night's Dream*. Sir Arthur Quiller-Couch, because of similarities between stanza 19 of Spenser's *Epithalamion* and Puck's evocation of a fearful nighttime (V.i.370 ff.) and because of the obvious matrimonial material in both works, made "little doubt that Shakespeare had Spenser's very words in mind as he wrote."[11] Considering the controversy over the date of composition of *A Midsummer Night's Dream*, I hesitate to be as certain as Quiller-Couch. Yet, without making firm assertions, I find it profitable to draw additional comparison between the two works, notably between the title of Shakespeare's play and Spenser's bright bit of self-directed humor:

> This day the sunne is in his chiefest hight,
> With Barnaby the bright,
> From whence declining by degrees,
> He somewhat loseth of his heat and light,
>
> . . . .
>
> But for this time it ill ordained was,
> To choose the longest day in all the yeare,
> And shortest night, when longest fitter weare:
> Yet neuer day so long, but late would passe.[12]

Saint Barnabas's Day is June 11, and Spenser is exactly correct to call it the longest day and shortest night, although that is

---

11. Quiller-Couch and Wilson, *A Midsummer-Night's Dream*, p. xi.

12. *The Works of Edmund Spenser*, A Variorum Edition, ed. Greenlaw, Osgood, Padelford, and Hefner, *The Minor Poems*, ed. C. G. Osgood, H. G. Lotspeich, and Dorothy Mason (Baltimore, 1947), 2:248.

the claim that I am making for Midsummer Day. The spring equinox occurred on March 25 when the Julian calendar was established. By 1582, because of its inaccuracies, the equinox fell on March 11. Pope Gregory XIII, issuing that year the calendar bearing his name, suppressed ten days in order that the equinox fall on March 21, its date at the time of the Council of Nicea (325 A.D.). But England did not adopt the Gregorian calendar until 1752; and the summer solstice in England, like the spring equinox, was ten days earlier in 1595 than it was at the Vatican, or on June 11, St. Barnabas's Day. Nevertheless, in the folk mind all the associations of Midsummer Day were identified with the feast of St. John. June 24 was to be thought of as the day the sun did its turnabout, even though the almanacs of the 1590s indicate clearly "Sol in Cancer" on either the eleventh or twelfth of June.[13]

Apart from having in common the celebration of a wedding on the shortest night of the year, *Epithalamion* and *A Midsummer Night's Dream* both illustrate an awareness that even at the moment the young lovers—Spenser and his bride as well as the nuptial-intended of the play—first set out on a hoped-for long life of harmonious pairings, their feet touch the sill of shade. For Spenser's golden gift works its measured way to a close wherein the loving poet bestows his "goodly ornament," predicting that it will be "an endless moniment" for what he knows is the "short time" of youth, beauty, and love. Such also is the argument I here put forward for *A Midsummer Night's Dream*. Whether Shakespeare knew the *Epithalamion* or Spenser *A Midsummer Night's Dream* does not really matter. One so used the other that the inheritor could not miss the bequeather's sobering truth: "all stories, if continued far enough, end in death, and he is no true-story teller who would keep that from you."[14] Shakespeare was incapable, apparently, even in

13. Thomas Buckminster, *An Almanack and Prognostication for the Year 1598*, ed. and intro. E. F. Bosanquet, Shakespeare Assoc. Facs., no. 8 (London, 1935).

14. Ernest Hemingway, *Death in the Afternoon* (New York, 1932), p. 122.

the happiest of his creations, of forgetting for the moment that "nothing 'gainst Time's scythe can make defense."

To be rejected then are those arguments that the title of *A Midsummer Night's Dream* has no more significance than that of *The Winter's Tale*.[15] The title so well fits Shakespeare's intention that perhaps more than in most of his plays the title announces a major theme of the work: not only does young love endure no longer than a dream but also a dream no longer than the shortest night of the year allows.

Once the theme of the brevity of youth, beauty, and love is perceived, so also is Shakespeare's careful deployment of moon imagery. Rather than an oversight through revision or any other act of nodding, the moon in its waning days is the playwright's symbolic statement equivalent to that of the play's title. If we equate the moon with the love of the young people and then note that its appearance is just as brief and ephemeral as a midsummer night's dream, we shall be rid successfully of the greatest crux of this play. At the same time we shall exonerate Shakespeare of the charge of careless work, either in composition or revision, and refute the critics, at least those of *A Midsummer Night's Dream*, who claim that Shakespeare did not hold himself strictly accountable for time schemes.

When Theseus says, "Four happy days bring in / Another moon," we are faced with Shakespeare's use of *new moon*. *New moon* refers both to dark of the moon, a phase when no moon is visible to the earthbound because its setting coincides with the sun's, and also to the first new crescent visible on the day following dark of the moon. Hippolyta's subsequent elaboration indicates we are dealing with the latter usage: "then the moon, *like to a silver bow / New-bent* in heaven" (I.i.9–10, my italics).

If we calculate Theseus's four days to include the day he speaks, the lovers, who steal forth the night following, meet in the forest three days before the new crescent appears (or since, as will

15. An idea suggested by both Farmer and Malone. See the Variorum Shakespeare, p. vi.

be seen, I argue that they meet well after midnight, two calendar days). The *actual* day of the weddings (moved up one day from the announced four) is dark of the moon, and the *intended* day of the weddings is new moon. Thus the night the lovers wander in the woods is the last night on which a waning crescent is visible. Since Shakespeare causes these phases of the moon to coincide with the summer solstice, the briefest display of moon on the briefest night of the year is the setting the lovers have chosen for cementing their loves.

The moon is symbolic of and identified with love implicitly in the opening statements of Theseus and Hippolyta, but it is explicitly named the medium through which a pair of the young lovers become mesmerized, one with the other:

> This man hath bewitch'd the bosom of my child.
> . . . .
> Thou hast by moonlight at her window sung
> . . . .
> With cunning hast thou filch'd my daughter's heart.
> (I.i.27, 30, 36)

Also, the moon sets the time Lysander and Hermia will meet, for no hour or other indication of time is given:

> Tomorrow night, when Phoebe doth behold
> Her silver visage in the wat'ry glass,
> Decking with liquid pearl the bladed grass,
> A time that lovers' flights doth still conceal,
> Through Athens' gates have we devis'd to steal.
> (I.i.209–13)

Furthermore, in Lysander's words, moonrise is a traditional ally of lovers, providing light bright enough for elopement yet soft enough for concealment.

Some forty-odd additional references to moon and moonlight have caused commentators, almost without exception, to as-

241

sume that the boards are daybright with moonshine. Some pale light is there of course, but not the klieg light of full moon.[16] That some moon is required, other than to supply the playwright's imagery, is apparent to anyone who has tried to walk the woods at night with sky overcast or at dark of the moon. What small glimmer stars may give in deep woods on a cloudless and moonless night is diminished all the more by close-set trees of ancient height. Would Lysander ask Hermia, his beloved, to meet him in the woods, she having to travel alone that portion of the way before they get together, before the moon is available to illuminate her steps? Since they mean to travel a fair way after they get together (the aunt to whom they fly lives seven leagues distant [I.i.159]), surely they would prefer that the sun rise soon after they meet. They cannot want to travel so far afoot by dark, nor sleep out an entire night in the forest, when pursuit may be sent after them if Egeus finds his daughter missing soon after she leaves. Clearly the moon has a practical function in the play, and many of the references to it serve to set the time, a time convenient for flight. Shakespeare, though he wants moonshine, does not want a nightlong display; rather he wants a moon that will designate an hour of meeting, an hour late enough to hide departure, late enough to give way to

16. The only reference to *moon* in the entire play that might be seen by some as troublesome is Quince's assertion, "Yes, it doth shine that night" (III.i.51). This apparent contradiction might be dealt with in several ways. (1) Quince's assertion is one of the blockhead mistakes made by the rustics. After all, is it not Quince who calls the tragedy of Pyramus and Thisbe a "most lamentable comedy" (I.ii.11–12)? He makes the very same mistake the lovers make, not seeing that young love, symbolized by the very moon he thinks will always be there, will not always be there, will not always end happily. (2) Quince cannot know, although the almanac promises moonlight, that the sky will not be overcast, thus casting doubt over any such assertions. (3) I confess there is *some* moonlight, and Quince does no more. (4) In actual fact, the rustics are compelled to provide their own moon, indicating that there is not enough for their purposes. Probably an equal number of additional explanations may be made to explain away Quince's moon; the most telling argument against it is all the rest of this chapter.

morning soon after in order that flight may continue in the companionable light of day. For Hermia to meet Lysander at the rising of the full moon evoked by the Rowe illustrator and so many of his followers would cause her to leave her home at about 7:00 P.M., hardly in time to rise from the supper table and surely before old Egeus retires, much less any of the servants.

Of greater importance still is the symbolic function served by this least of waning moons. Identified with love, it says, metaphorically, that bright young fancy has life as long as the briefest show of moon, that last sliver we see an hour before it is outshone by the rising sun, that last presence which is followed next night by dark of the moon. In short, the moon of *A Midsummer Night's Dream* makes exactly the same statement as the play's title: youth, beauty, and love are fitful as a short dream, brief as a waning moon. If we fail to observe the symbolic action, Shakespeare spells it out for us:

> . . . if there were a sympathy in choice,
> War, death, or sickness did lay siege to it,
> Making it momentany as a sound,
> Swift as a shadow, short as any dream,
> Brief as the lightning in the collied night,
> That, in a spleen, unfolds both heaven and earth,
> And ere a man hath power to say "Behold!"
> The jaws of darkness do devour it up.
> So quick bright things come to confusion.
>
> (I.i.141–49)

No critic has overturned successfully the all-too-clear inconsistency between the four-day delay announced by Theseus in the opening lines and the passage of but three before the marriage ceremony is performed. Rather than to prove by fantastical argument that four days really pass or to accept the discrepancy as an irreconcilable inconsistency, let us suppose that Shakespeare knows exactly what he is doing, that there is no error through revision or any other means, and then ponder the poet's intention in telling us one thing and doing another.

As common to young love as its brief tenure is the rash haste of lovers. Shakespeare investigated this impetuosity in the tragic mode in *Romeo and Juliet*, composed close in time to *A Midsummer Night's Dream*. For him to look at the same theme from another angle and in the comic mode is not at all untypical. Therefore, the undue haste that leads Romeo and Juliet to the tomb leads Theseus and Hippolyta, as well as the young lovers, only to an earlier arrival at the altar and consequently to the earlier consummation of their desires. The marriage may be presumed set forward one day because Theseus would wait no longer. But what right do we have to make such an assumption?

As late as the beginning of the fourth act, Oberon's new accord with Titania reveals that no change in plans has occurred:

> Now thou and I are new in amity,
> And will *tomorrow midnight* solemnly
> Dance in Duke Theseus' house triumphantly
> And bless it to all fair prosperity.
> *There shall the* pairs of faithful *lovers be*
> *Wedded, with Theseus.*
> (IV.i.86−91, my italics)

A scant twelve lines later, Theseus refers puzzlingly to an "observation" performed (103). The Duke and his lady listen briefly to the music of his hounds before they stumble upon the sleeping lovers. Theseus speculates that the four young people,

> hearing our intent,
> Came here in grace of our solemnity.
> (IV.i.132−33)

"Intent" might well refer to a hasty change in plans, a desire to speed forward union of the lovers. Three other times in the play *solemnity* or *solemnities* alludes unmistakably to the marriage. If the ceremony has been updated, "observation" refers perhaps to some premarital lustration. In the lines immediately following, Theseus asks Egeus, "Is not this the day / That Hermia should give answer of her choice?" (134–35). This query should give us no pause. Hermia's decision was tied to the Duke's wedding, whenever that might fall. In a play that includes a judgment theme, such as this does, Hermia's fateful answer might well be called for upon a day and in an hour that she looked not for.[17]

A second decision enforces the Duke's growing eagerness:

> Fair lovers, you are fortunately met.
> Of this discourse we more will hear anon.
> Egeus, I will overbear your will;
> For in the temple, by and by, with us
> These couples shall eternally be knit.
> And, for the morning now is something worn,
> Our purpos'd hunting shall be set aside.
> Away with us to Athens.
>
> (IV.i.176–83)

Everything in this unusual speech smacks of changed plans, of haste, of the Duke's giving his "sensual race the rein." The lovers are fortunate in that they might be married immediately. Theseus will take no time to hear their discourse. Egeus will get no chance to argue his case but is incontinently overborne. Although John Dover Wilson has proved that *by and by* does not mean immediately, as most have glossed the phrase, nevertheless, taken with the Duke's decision to set aside his purposed hunting, taken with his urgent "Away," *by and by* tokens clearly a quickened pace toward the altar.

Furthermore, in the same way that we can show an unusual frequency of such words as *haste, rashness, impatience* and the like in *Romeo and Juliet*, so also can we in *A Midsummer Night's Dream*. Once again, the opening lines establish a theme so pervasive in the play that to claim them a product of late and careless revision seems misguided:

17. See the entire treatment of the marriage element in the parable of the ten virgins discussed in the preceding chapter.

THESEUS

> Now, fair Hippolyta, our nuptial hour
> Draws on *apace*. Four happy days bring in
> Another moon; but, O, methinks, how *slow*
> This old moon wanes! She *lingers* my desires,
> Like to a step-dame or a dowager
> *Long withering out* a young man's revenue.

HIPPOLYTA

> Four days will *quickly* steep themselves in night,
> Four nights will *quickly* dream away the time.
>
> (I.i.1–8, my italics)

As is his use, Shakespeare, within the first few lines of his play, announces through one device or another a major thematic concern. Here he uses paradox to indicate impatience in love. Actual time is described as swift in three of the instances italicized above; seeming time ("methinks"), time as it appears to one in love, is three times described as laggard. To lovers anticipating the fulfillment of desire, the four days stretch tediously before, and, apparently, even the mature Duke with eagerness puts forward the wedding service, the quicker to embrace Hippolyta.

A Midsummer Night's Dream is crammed with phrases indicating the furious haste with which the lovers pursue their joys: "Lysander and myself will fly this place" (I.i.203), "My legs can keep no pace with my desires" (III.ii.445), etc., all of which are given emblematic form in Helena's reminder that Cupid has wings but no eyes, figuring "unheedy haste" (I.i.237). Counter observations are equally plentiful to show that youth races toward its delights not quite so fast as love and beauty fly from them, backward in time: "How chance the roses [in her cheeks] do fade so fast" (I.i.129), "hasty-footed time" (III.ii.200), etc. The double sense of time is caught up in several oxymorons such as "tedious minutes" (II.ii.112), "long age of three hours" (V.i.33), "tedious brief" (V.i.56), etc., all leading to the paradox inescapable in the long-sought moment: "The iron tongue of midnight hath told twelve. / Lovers, to bed" (V.i.358–59). In view of the significance of title and moon, time proves a double-edged force that with iron insistence marches toward the last midnight and lays "Golden lads and girls . . . All lovers young" (*Cymbeline*, IV.ii.263, 275) in a bed from which there is no rising.

To list the words and phrases that have to do with haste and the ultimate stillness to which the swift course of life brings the lovers is to record something from almost every page of the play, all illustrating the text: youth and its pursuits are but a midsummer night's dream. But though the language is everywhere present, another form of the statement is the pace of the young people, more appropriate to drama insofar as it is conveyed in action on the stage. As we enter the forest along with the lovers, we see in their movements something of a ballet in which the tempo at the outset is *presto*. Two lovers are running away, a third tries to overtake them, a fourth to overtake the third. If possible, the dance-time quickens, for the lovers are maddened. The two men rush with fury in pursuit of each other; Helena flees in terror of her life; and Hermia hastes after, fearful to be left. The pace is such that of course it cannot be maintained. In fact, it comes to a dead stop. The action onstage reflects the impact of the play's language: young love in vigorous race will wear down. As each youth expends the strength of youth, each utters one of those phrases that give a larger cast to the episode:

LYSANDER

> fallen am I in dark uneven way,
> And here will rest me.

. . . .

DEMETRIUS

> Faintness constraineth me
> To measure out my length on this cold bed.

. . . .

HELENA

> sleep, that sometimes shuts up sorrow's eye,
> Steal me awhile from mine own company.

. . . .

HERMIA

I can no further crawl, no further go;
My legs can keep no pace with my desires.

(III.ii.417–45)

With these speeches we become aware most fully that a
memento-mori underprop supports the time themes of *A Midsummer
Night's Dream*. Not only must youth, love, and beauty pass away but
also all time must have a stop; life itself must cease. Beyond visual
presentation of the youths coming to the immobility of the grave,
Shakespeare is at pains to employ also the imagery of the *memento-
mori* tradition. Oberon's instructions to Puck evoke the afterworld
("The starry welkin cover thou anon / With drooping fog as black
as Acheron" [III.ii.356–57]), identify sleep with death ("lead them
thus, / Till o'er their brows death-counterfeiting sleep / . . . doth
creep" [363–65]), and employ *memento-mori* imagery ("leaden legs
and batty wings" [365]).[18]

18. For general *memento-mori* imagery and treatment to be found
in the English lyric, see the appendix. The larger pictorial tradition
makes clear that any creatures from the graveyard (or presumed from the
graveyard by early, if faulty, naturalists), such as bats, worms, toads, liz-
ards, snails, etc., serve the *memento-mori* purpose. In this connection, note
the unusual conjunction of the *memento-mori* lyric with another widespread generic poem of the Middle Ages and Renaissance, the lullaby, the
song with which her fairies lull Titania to sleep (II.ii.9–23). All the creatures warned off by the singers can be found in engravings, drawings, and
paintings of the *memento-mori* tradition: "spotted snakes," "thorny
hedgehogs," "newts and blindworms," "weaving spiders," "long-legg'd
spinners," "beetles black," "worm nor snail." See F. P. Weber, *Aspects of
Death and Correlated Aspects of Life in Art, Epigram, and Poetry*, 4th ed. (London, 1922), pp. 477–79. I have noted also the "leaden legs" as an evocation of the tomb such as we find three times in Spenser's *Shepheardes Cal-
ender:* "Nowe dead he is, and lyeth wrapt in lead" ("June," line 89); "all the
worthies liggen wrapt in leade" ("October," line 63); and "Dead, and lyeth
wrapt in lead" ("November," line 59). Richard Barnfield's finest piece, "As
it fell upon a day," numbers among its finest lines, "King *Pandion*, he is
dead: / All thy friends are lapt in Lead."

Puck's response is laden with reminders of the terrible rapidity of time's passage and additional graveyard imagery that denote the latter end to which time conveys all mortals:

> My fairy lord, this must be done with haste,
> For night's swift dragons cut the clouds full fast,
> And yonder shines Aurora's harbinger,[19]

19. At this point may be brought together evidence to indicate that every bit of the play's action from II.i.i to IV.i.100 takes place in less than an hour. If, as I argue, the lovers as well as the rustics do not meet in the forest until the moon appears, and if the moon shining on that night is the last waning crescent before dark of the moon, then the action cannot begin until shortly before 5:00 A.M. Astronomical charts will show that the moon loses from thirty to fifty-odd minutes to the sun every twenty-four hours. On the night of that day when Theseus opens the play with all his talk about new moon, the moon would rise between seventy to one hundred minutes before the sun. On the night the fairies, rustics, and Athenian youths all gather in the woods, the moon would be up for less than an hour before the sun rose to outshine it.

We are barely into II.i. when Oberon determines to punish Titania. Required is the "western flower." Oberon enjoins Puck to make the trip in less time than "leviathan can swim a league," and Puck boasts that he can "put a girdle round about the earth / In forty minutes" (II.i.174–76). Again, when Oberon intercedes in behalf of Hermia, he emphasizes the haste required by admonishing Puck: "And look thou meet me ere the first cock crow" (II.i.267).

All the fairy-revelry should be understood to consume no more than fairy-time. Titania, giving a series of prodigious tasks to her fairy band, limits the execution to "the third part of a minute" (II.ii.2–8). The play that the rustics rehearse in this same half hour to an hour is carefully described by Philostrate as "some ten words long, / Which is as brief as I have known a play" (V.i.61–62). Of course, Quince and company practice but a portion of their opus when Puck takes a part.

We are back to Puck's reminder to his fairy lord that they must correct with haste the errors made concerning Lysander, Demetrius, and the magic herb, since the dawn begins to glow in the east (III.ii.378–80). Oberon concurs; "haste; make no delay. / We may effect this business yet ere day" (394–95).

At whose approach, ghosts, wand'ring here and there,
Troop home to churchyards. Damned spirits all,
That in crossways and floods have burial,
Already to their wormy beds are gone.
For fear lest day should look their shames upon,
They willfully themselves exile from light
And must for aye consort with black-brow'd night.

(III.ii.378–87)

Puck's warning is the admonition of all *memento-mori* verses: death will come; unless the mortal be prepared, he will spend eternity with the "Damned spirits all."

Lysander seems in some danger; for as he pursues Demetrius, his intention is "revenge" (III.ii.420). Indeed may he say, "fallen am I in dark uneven way." But he goes to sleep praying for light: "Come, thou gentle day!" (418). So it is with all the young lovers. Demetrius's "cold bed," where he measures out his length, evokes faintly the grave; yet he also wants to see day. Helena, on the shortest night of the year, hints at eternal night, "O weary night, O long and tedious night, / Abate thy hours!" (III.ii.431–32), and cries for "comforts, from the east" (432). Hermia, "Never so weary, never so in woe," will lie down "till break of day" (442–46). Reminded all by darkness, night, and the fearful spirits one might meet on *Johannisnacht*—the spirits Puck raises for our view—all wish for day; all reach toward light.

When Theseus comes upon the sleepers, although he is accompanied by Hippolyta, Egeus, "and all his train," any one of whom might bend down, gently to nudge the youths awake, he rouses them in an unusual manner: "Go, bid the huntsmen wake them with their horns" (IV.i.137). Both Quarto and Folio indicate *They all start vp* as though trumpets have announced judgment day (see fig. 14), and the first words spoken thereafter by one of them are, "Pardon, my lord" (140). Lysander continues, as though "compell'd, / Even to the teeth and forehead of [his] faults, / To give in evidence" (*Hamlet*, III.iii.62–64), with an exact confession of his transgressions, "for truly would [he] speak" (148). Theseus, made God by having the trump of doom be blown, with God-like powers dismisses their evil disobedience to authority ("Egeus, I will overbear your will") and admits the lovers into grace:

> For in the temple, by and by, with us
> These couples shall *eternally* be knit.
> (IV.i.178–80, my italics)

That these matters may be seen as anagogical is suggested, although with delightful self-satire, by Theseus, who sees "The poet's eye, in a fine frenzy rolling, / . . . glance from heaven to earth, from earth to heaven" (V.i.12–13). When Hippolyta pronounces what many have taken to be a key to the play—a pronouncement that argues with her new husband—we note that he accepts her view through his silence:

> But all the story of the night told over,
> And all their minds transfigur'd so together,
> More witnesseth than fancy's images
> And grows to something of great constancy;
> But, howsoever, strange and admirable.
> (V.i.23–27)

Hippolyta's view is eschatological; for the story of the night is that which overwhelms us unless our minds are so transfigured as to see that fancy's (love's) images are of short duration, and to see that God's strange (inscrutable) design is admirable and constant (from everlasting to everlasting).

Follows then the lamentable tragedy, which, though it serves of purposes aplenty, serves eschatologically as well. The play of Pyramus and Thisbe is Shakespeare's substitute in *A Midsummer Night's Dream* for what he had investigated in *Romeo and Juliet*: the tragedy to which rashness, haste, and impetuosity may bring young lovers. Although we need not assert that Romeo and Juliet are damned because of filial disobedience and suicide, yet we recog-

nize that such is a distinct possibility. But, reprobate or in grace, all
lovers must die:

> Dead, dead? A tomb
> Must cover thy sweet eyes.
>
> . . . .
>
> Lovers, make moan.
> (V.i.325–31)

And the moon, which brought the lovers together—not only
Pyramus and Thisbe but also Lysander and Hermia—will shine
on golden without them: "Moonshine . . . [is] left to bury the
dead" (345).

We leave the seeming lunacy of the rustics only to go through
the same statement again, this time in its application to the lovers
watching the play:

> The iron tongue of midnight hath told twelve.
> Lovers, to bed; 'tis almost fairy time.
> I fear we shall outsleep the coming morn
> As much as we this night have overwatch'd.
> This palpable-gross play hath well beguil'd
> The heavy gait of night. Sweet friends, to bed.
> A fortnight hold we this solemnity,
> In nightly revels and new jollity.
> (V.i.358–65)

Although the time is lovers' bedtime, it arrives on the iron tongue
of the church-tower bell that tolls time's passage. Fairy time it is,
but caution must be taken not to outsleep the morn that comes to
all; the meaning of the night must not be beguiled (is there a pun
on *gait-gate*, the gate of night being that which swallows up all
those who outsleep the morn?). In any case, the nightly revels and
new jollity will be allowed a fortnight; in the vastness of time, how
much more than a fortnight may be deemed the entire lives of the
lovers?

When all the newly married exit, in comes Puck to level a final *memento-mori* admonition, emphasizing what awaits tardy lovers on that morning they awake to find all life has been an after-dinner or midsummer night's vision, "swift as a shadow, short as any dream" (I.i.144):

> Now the wasted brands do glow,
>> Whilst the screech-owl, screeching loud,
> Puts the wretch that lies in woe
>> In remembrance of a shroud.
> Now it is the time of night
>> That the graves, all gaping wide,
> Every one lets forth his sprite,
>> In the churchway paths to glide.[20]
>
> (V.i.370—77)

But, of course, the play is a silvered epithalamion, and these are not to be the last words; they are followed by promise of joyous beginnings: "we fairies . . . Now are frolic" (378-82). The king and queen of the realm of happy spirits come to bless the marriages, sealing fidelity and unblotted issue to all; and so the play should end. But, even in their beneficent intentions, the fairies are not altogether fortunate bestowers. Shakespeare must have last things to be last things. Puck's spell, "Not a mouse / Shall disturb this hallowed house" (382—83), well intended, nevertheless takes from the inhabitants a reminder they had best heed. The mouse is "a time-

---

20. This is the passage cited by Quiller-Couch, from which he concludes Shakespeare's indebtedness to Spenser's *Epithalamion*. Without reproducing Spenser's entire stanza, we may cite the pertinent words and images: "deluding dreames," "Pouke," "evill sprights," "hob Goblins," "shriech Oule," "deadly yels," "damned ghosts." Spenser's stanza, like Shakespeare's countertheme, is not as Quiller-Couch calls it, "a merry Καθαρσις, a pretty purgation, of those same goblin terrors which Spenser would exorcise from the bridal chamber" (p. xi); it is a *memento-mori* passage, supporting Spenser's own awareness that his marriage-joy is but for "short time."

honored and very well-known symbol for all-devouring time."[21] As we leave the play, its characters must yet work out their destinies, to seek comforts more durable than love, youth, and beauty, "so quick bright things come to confusion."

21. Erwin Panofsky, "Et in Arcadia Ego," in *Philosophy and History,* ed. R. L. Klibansky and H. J. Paton (Oxford, 1936), p. 233.

7. The *Henry* Plays:
Prince Hal, Apostle
to the Gentiles

everal critics have emphasized the importance of time as a theme in both parts of *Henry IV*.[1] Two have tied their discussions to St. Paul's epistle to the Ephesians, one concluding that "reading the plays with Ephesians in mind almost gives one the illusion that Shakespeare set out to confirm St. Paul's epistle."[2] The significance of time and Pauline thought in these plays is thus well documented, but the vein opened has not been mined fully, and the complete interdependence of the theme of time with Pauline purpose has not been made clear.

1. Paul A. Jorgensen, "'Redeeming time' in *Henry IV*," in *Redeeming Shakespeare's Words* (Berkeley, 1962), pp. 52–69; Joseph A. Bryant, Jr., "Prince Hal and the Ephesians," in *Hippolyta's View* (Lexington, Ky., 1961), pp. 52–67; L. C. Knights, "Time's Subjects: The Sonnets and *King Henry IV, Part II*," in *Some Shakespearean Themes* (London, 1959), pp. 45–64; B. T. Spencer, "*2 Henry IV* and the Theme of Time," *University of Toronto Quarterly* 13 (1944): 394–99.

2. Both Jorgensen and Bryant determine the critical verse to be 5.16. The quoted words are Bryant's, *Hippolyta's View*, pp. 52–53.

Quite correctly, Ephesians has been linked with important determinations of the plays:

> Take hede therefore that ye walke circum-
> spectly, not as fooles, but as wise,
>   Redeming the time: for the dayes are euil.
>
> (5.15–16)

Previous emphasis has been to apply these verses almost solely to Prince Hal, seeing through them both a need and a program for the Prince's reformation.[3] But we must make use also of the phrase that identifies the days as evil, keeping in mind the young Prince who, in his first soliloquy, knows that he will be someday King of England, and that meanwhile he is the "sweetest hope" the country owns.[4] Hal's vow to redeem the time must be construed not as an oath to reform personally but as the obligation of an heir apparent, fated to be an anointed ruler. Not enough has been written as yet about Shakespeare's sovereigns who are also high priests of their kingdoms. The playwright sometimes implements this theme through Christ symbolism,[5] as in *Richard II*, *Measure for Measure*,

---

3. Jorgensen, "'Redeeming time,'" passim; Bryant, *Hippolyta's View*, pp. 60–67. Bryant, however, in a wider-ranging essay, makes considerable application to Falstaff as well.

4. The line that follows these words of Vernon—(*I Henry IV*, V.ii.68) "So much misconstrued in his wantonness"—is further evidence to prove that the Prince is misunderstood by critics as well as by contemporaries in that he was never prodigal but only seeming so.

5. Hal himself appears typologically a Christ figure in several respects: Christ not Paul awaits the "perfectness of time"; Christ not Paul is the "Apostle and high Priest" of Hebrews 3.1; Christ more than Paul smothers his glory to move among those he means to save in a lower world ("From a God to a bull? .... It was Jove's case" [*II Henry IV*, II.ii.165–66]). Yet these similarities to Christ do not make Hal any less the apostle to the gentiles. Paul's own example, like Peter's, is to "folowe his steppes," or in Paul's words, "He therefore gaue some to be Apostles. . . . Til we all mete together . . . vnto a perfite man, & vnto the measure of the age of the fulnes of Christ" (Ephesians 4.11–13).

or *The Tempest*. In fact, Henry IV's angry words to his son carry considerable irony: "As thou art to this hour was Richard then" (*I Henry IV*, III.ii.94). The usurping King unconsciously likens his son to an anointed king. Henry IV is not, but Hal carries already the oil of holiness: "This in the name of God I promise here" (III.ii.153).

Paul's Epistle to the Hebrews[6] identifies Christ as "Apostle and high Priest of our professiō" (3.1). All true rulers are surrogates for Christ, "God's substitute, / His deputy anointed in His sight" (*Richard II*, I.ii.37–38). If Christlike then also priestly, and all true rulers have a priestly function to redeem their people from evil. Nowhere is this theme more engaged than in *Hamlet*,[7] unless it be in these *Henry* plays. Hamlet is another prince who exercises a priestly concern while he appears to be only heir apparent.[8] The priest labors for the redemption of those in his cure by urging repentance. Hamlet, in two extended scenes, leads both Ophelia and Gertrude through the steps of the sacrament of penance,[9] as in like manner he is briefly instrumental in the atonement of Laertes.[10] Like a good "Persoun of a toun" he twice-over precedes his parishioners in the sacrament himself, "To drawen folk to hevene . . . / By good ensample."[11]

To see Hal also as priest/king, if only in anticipation of succession to the throne, underscores more boldly the significance of time in the *Henry* plays, as well as the Prince's Pauline role. For Hal—and perhaps Shakespeare's eye caught the word *Apostle* as well as the phrase *high Priest* in Hebrews 3—is better suited in

6. Few scholars attribute Hebrews to Paul, but the epistle is presented commonly as part of the Pauline statement.

7. See chap. 1, pp. 53–57.

8. Hal is somewhat different from Hamlet, since, as I argue throughout chapter 1, Hamlet is the true king of Denmark from the moment of his father's death.

9. III.i.104–52; III.iv.19–203.

10. Laertes' penance is self-instigated, but presumably because he recognizes Hamlet's grace. See chap. 1, p. 58.

11. Hamlet's own acts of penance show the way to Ophelia at III.i.123–30 and to Gertrude at III.iv.179–84.

apostleship than in Christ symbolism; he is more like Paul exhorting the churches Ephesus and Corinth than like the sacrificial lamb, bowing under scourge and cross. Redemption of time by a ruler requires not only turning his people from sin to be worthy as high priest but also expunging evil from the land so to be efficacious as apostle. Hal must attempt both the redemption of Falstaff, Poins, and Francis and the suppression of rebellion in the figure of Hotspur.

To deal at once with the obvious problem of a Hal already at I.ii. a pure and priestly leader, we must reject the widely held view that the education of a prodigal prince is a major theme of these plays.[12] Suspense, dramatic vigor, and developmental action are not thereby killed off in the *Henry* plays any more than they are in *Measure for Measure*, where the Duke is a constant figure throughout. The excitement of the play consists in the success or failure of this monk/duke (priest/king) to redeem Vienna and various citizens therein: Isabel, Angelo, Lucio, Claudio, even Barnardine. The theme of time and the redemption of the times in the *Henry* plays is applicable to England, and not only to the nation but also to specific subjects of whom perforce that nation is made up. Fully to value Shakespeare's use of the verses from Ephesians, we must observe the ways in which characters other than the Prince spend their short "time of life," the ways in which the Prince deals with *them*, and the ways in which the "days" are redeemed.

Among others, Jorgensen has noted numerically the presence of the word *time* in the *Henry IV* plays.[13] Unfortunately he did not have available a good concordance to do the counting for him. His forty-one count for *time* in Part I should be forty-five according to the Oxford Shakespeare Concordances, and if we add *times* and *time's*, in senses appropriate, forty-seven. His thirty-four count for Part II proves to be forty-three. His further mention of "some

12. Most critics take the view from John Dover Wilson's otherwise excellent book, *The Fortunes of Falstaff* (Cambridge, Eng., 1944). See especially chapter 2, pp. 17–25, "Riot and the Prodigal Prince." Even Bryant succumbs. Jorgensen insists, however, that Hal "has not radically changed his status in the eyes of God. . . . only the other characters . . . are surprised by their later perceptions" ("'Redeeming time,'" p. 68).

13. Jorgensen, "'Redeeming time,'" p. 52.

sixty-four references to units of time in the two plays" must neglect spans such as *day*, which word alone appears in both parts ninety times, as well as *minutes, hours, weeks, months, years*, and other "rags of time." It would be unnecessarily tedious, even with the help of the Concordances, to gather all time references, including such adverbs as *while, now, then*, etc., which have often important time-theme significance, as well as specific *two o'clocks, Tuesdays, Michelmases, Peascod times*, and others which clearly serve the theme. Perhaps we achieve what is necessary by noting that the word *time* appears first in line two of Part I and the word *year* but five lines from the end of Part II and that hardly a page anywhere in between fails us with some time reference or other.

Part I opens with King Henry, who first employs the word *time*. With his aides, in lengthy speeches of scene one, he gives ample evidence that "the dayes are euil." Although the King acknowledges that he has a journey to make to the Holy Land (as do all men), he allows the sickness of his land to delay his pilgrimage, but in the postponement lies his own sickness. Cure of the realm may seem a holy and religious thing for him to attempt, but since he is the usurper and instigator of the assassination of an anointed king, physic for the state requires first that Henry purge himself. Aware as the King is of his own guilt, he yet defers making the satisfaction that would season his repentance:

> And for this cause *awhile* we must neglect
> Our holy purpose to Jerusalem.
> (I.i.100–101, my italics)

Similarity between Henry's tardiness and Falstaff's is manifest; both fit well the lineaments of those in Dante's Ante-Purgatory called the late-repentant. Henry may be seen as one of the preoccupied, a group of kings, among whom is a namesake-predecessor, Henry III.[14] Falstaff may be seen as one of the indolent. Henry would purge higher on the mountain than Falstaff, as the preoccupied do above the indolent; for Harry intends all along to make

14. "Purgatorio," 7.130–32, *Tutte Le Opere Di Dante*, ed. E. Moore (Oxford, 1909).

his way to the heavenly city; Falstaff tries always to shut it from his thoughts.

Even as the last words of scene one—Henry's words—mark the King as procrastinator, so the first words of scene two tag Falstaff as one unheedful of the hour: "Now, Hal, what time of day is it, lad?"[15] Although the question itself seems to contradict the claim of Falstaff's unconcern, Hal supplies immediate prospective for viewing the wayward knight: in drunkenness ("fat-witted with drinking of old sack"), in gluttony ("unbuttoning . . . after supper"), in sloth ("sleeping upon benches after noon" [the indolent]), and in lechery ("leaping-houses"), Falstaff has been wasting hours, weeks, years, life itself, so that the Prince may say,

> What a devil hast thou to do with the time of the
> day? . . . I see no reason why thou shouldst be so
> superfluous to demand the time of the day.
>
> (I.ii.5–12)

In another sense, Falstaff and his cohorts are thieves of time, or as he puts it himself, "thieves of the day's beauty" (I.ii.25).[16]

15. Falstaff is not the only person in the play forgetful of the clock. Gadshill (II.i.33), the sheriff (II.iv.518–20, where he is corrected by Hal), and, under the terms indicated, the King (*II Henry IV*, III.i.33) lose track of the sand in the hourglass. Francis's heart lies right, but he has some trouble noting the precise moment (*I Henry IV*, II.iv.42, 54, and 96–97).

16. To Carisse Mickey, I owe the observation that as such Falstaff is one of "Diana's foresters" (I.ii.25), a further identification as an Ephesian of the old church:

> Moreouer ye se and heare, that not alone at Ephesus,
> but almoste through out all Asia this Paul hathe persuaded,
> & turned away muche people, saying, That they be not
> gods which are made with hands,
> So that not onely this thing is dangerous vnto vs,
> that the state shulde be reproued, but also that the temple
> of the great goddesse Diana shulde be nothing estemed, and
> that it wolde come to passe that her magnificence, which all
> Asia and the worlde worshippeth, shulde be destroyed.
>
> (Acts 19.26–27)

Falstaff, as advocate of disorder, yearns, of course, for days of evil, which St. Paul delineates as times of "fornication, & all vnclennes, or couetousness . . . filthines . . . foolish talking . . . jesting" (Ephesians 5.3–4). Falstaff's constant hope, which the fat knight thinks falsely to be realized at Hal's accession, is that "the laws of England are at [his] commandment" (*II Henry IV*, V.iii.138). He hopes the true prince will turn false thief, "for the poor abuses of the time want countenance" (I.ii.152–53). As time waster and promoter of misrule, Falstaff is dead center of St. Paul's target: a profligate to be redeemed, an architect of evil days.

Hotspur, even as every other major character of the play, has time on his mind and on his tongue at all appearances. He neither wastes time as Falstaff does, nor delays in making the most of time as Henry; but his use of time is distorted. He is given the most moving and most direct utterances about time of any character in the play. He knows "the time of life is short" (V.ii.81) and wishes not to use it basely. Time spent other than in pursuit of his brand of honor is of no concern to him: "O, let the hours be short / Till fields and blows and groans applaud our sport!" (I.iii.301–2). But his concept of honor is of earthly achievement, which he shuns selfishly to share with any corrival. He is concerned that it might "for shame be spoken in these days, / Or fill up chronicles in time to come" (I.iii.170–71) that his family honor has been sullied. He sees time as a squire holding the reins of the horse Honor ("Yet time serves"), which are to be relinquished into his firm grasp in order that he may struggle solely to regain "the good thoughts of the world" (I.iii.180–82). But a man can dazzle the world only in the time of his life, whereas

> life, time's fool,
> And time, that takes survey of all the world,
> Must have a stop.
>
> (V.iv.81–83)

Seeking only an earthly reward, Hotspur inherits no more than "two paces of the vilest" (V.iv.91). Dying with only proud words on his tongue, he is unregenerate.

Other and lesser characters think often about time and ac-

cording to their persuasions utter noteworthy assessments. Most of
the rebels in the two *Henry IV* plays see time as something to seize
at its most unstable moments in order to gain vantage in rebellion
and insurrection. The King describes such "discontents" as "moody
beggars, starving for a time / Of pellmell havoc and confusion"
(V.i.76, 81–82). Worcester views the times when "wanton" as
opportunity for evil and other "injuries" (V.i.50). The King will,
says Worcester twice over, find a "time to pay us home" (I.iii.288), a
"time / To punish this offense in other faults" (V.ii.6–7). Worcester,
for the rebels, seeks that moment "When time is ripe" (I.iii.294) for
the abetment of revolt. Northumberland calls for "The ragged'st
hour that time and spite dare bring" (*II Henry IV*, I.i.151), but will
not join the higher-minded Archbishop Scroop "Till time and vantage" (II.iii.68) give him better hope to turn the kingdom topsy-
turvy. Hastings believes the rebels will prevail because "the times
do brawl" (I.iii.70); and when the Archbishop seconds this view by
lamenting that little "trust" may be found in "these times," that
"Past and to come seems best; things present worst" (100, 108),
Hastings counsels action; clearly the evil of the time is helpful to
their cause: "We are time's subjects, and time bids be gone" (110).[17]

Supporters of the King know well the need to take time by
the forelock in order to counter insurrection. Westmoreland rebukes Falstaff with gentle self-inclusion: "'tis more than time that I

17. For an extensive treatment of time in Shakespeare, see Wylie
Sypher, *The Ethic of Time* (New York, 1976). Chapter 2, "Political Time," is
especially provocative in respect to the *Henriad*, but I must differ from
Sypher's conclusions that find "The Lancastrians [as] creatures of time
who can manipulate the occasion" (p. 31), much the charge I am making
against the rebels. Individual Lancastrians must be differentiated in their
use of time, even as all characters in the play. If Hal employs time in the
Pauline sense argued in this chapter, he differs greatly from his father.
What Sypher sees as Hal's "outrageous imperialism . . . his invasion into
France" (p. 30) is merely Sypher's own post-Vietnam geopolitical view.
The first scenes of *Henry V* are elaborate in Shakespeare's "patriotic" de-
termination to establish the King's invasion as a just and religious claim
(I.ii.10), second to those "thoughts" "to God, that run before" his "busi-
ness" in France (I.ii.302–3).

were there, and you too" (*I Henry IV*, IV.ii.53–54). Warwick knows the late hour and informs a king whom time overtakes:

> Many good morrows to your Majesty!
>
> KING
> Is it good morrow, lords?
>
> WARWICK
> 'Tis one o'clock, and past.
>   (*II Henry IV*, III.i.32–34)

Warwick emerges as the one man in either play aware that the Prince has been about the redemption of the realm at all times; Hal "but studies his companions" and "in the perfectness of time" will "Cast off his followers" (IV.iv.68, 74–75).[18]

And so we come to the Prince himself. To the passage from Ephesians, now add the fifth verse from Colossians 4: "Walke wisely towarde them that are without, and redeme the time."[19] Ephesians turns the addressee, perhaps, inward; Colossians clearly out. When we understand the Prince's redemption of time to in-

---

18. Although I associate the Prince with St. Paul rather than with Christ, the Christlike qualities in St. Paul, and thus in Hal (see footnote 5 above), help to dispel one of the two strongest aversions that have been directed at Hal. One, of course, is the rejection of Falstaff, dealt with elsewhere in this chapter (see p. 279); the other is a proclaimed hypocrisy in the Prince's determination to "awhile uphold / The unyok'd humor of . . . idleness" (I.ii.189–90). Why does Hal wait and hide his "sun"-like glory? is the usual question. One answer is Warwick's surmise that Hal attends upon the perfectness of time, a belief that finds echo in several of Christ's prophecies that His "time is not yet come" (John 7.6). See also, for instance, Matthew 27.18; Acts 1.7; 7.17; 7.26; and I Cor. 4.5. The fullest parallel to Hal's behavior is found in Acts 17.30–31:

> And the time of this ignorãce God regarded not: but now he admonisheth all men euerie where to repent,
> Because he hathe appointed a day in the which he wil iudge the worlde in righteousnes.

19. Already noted by Bryant, *Hippolyta's View*, p. 52.

clude the regeneration of those in his pastoral care, Colossians assumes greater importance, and I Corinthians supplies the Apostle's own formula toward those "without." Attempts to explain the upshot of Hal's "honorable action" with Francis and the other drawers have produced the most impoverished explication of any passage in *I Henry IV*:

> I am now of all humors that have show'd themselves
> humors since the old days of goodman Adam to the
> pupil age of this present twelve o'clock at midnight.
>
> (II.iv.92–95)

These words stand as a signpost. Poins has just asked the Prince, "what's the issue?" Hal's answer provides one meaning to the entire play, but, more immediately, meaning to a lengthy scene—over one hundred lines—in which the Prince has sojourned first with a leash of drawers among the hogsheads and then with Francis just outside the fat room. With the varied labors that have gone into tracing scriptural analogues in Shakespeare, it surprises me that no one has caught hitherto in Hal's rejoinder to Poins an echo of the memorable and moving lines in St. Paul:

> For thogh I be fre frō all men, yet haue I made
> my self seruant vnto all men, that I might winne
> the mo.
> And vnto yᵉ Iewes I become as a Iewe, that I
> may winne the Iewes: to them that are vnder the
> Lawe, as thogh I were vnder the Law, that I may
> winne thē that are vnder the Law:
> To them that are without lawe, as thogh I were
> without law (whē I am not without Law as perteining
> to God, but am in the Law through Christ) that I may
> winne them that are without Law.
> To the weake I become as weake, that I may
> winne yᵉ weake: I am made all thīgs to all men, that I
> might by all meanes saue some.
>
> (I Cor. 9.19–22)

264

If the correspondence between "I am made all thīgs to all men" and "I am now of all humors" remains unconvincing, we may work out the entire Pauline intention.

Noteworthy first is the attention that Shakespeare calls to Corinthians even as later he invokes Ephesians.[20] Asked by Hal what company Falstaff keeps, the page of *II Henry IV* replies, "Ephesians, my lord, of the old church" (II.ii.142). Asked by Poins, "Where hast been, Hal?" the Prince explains that he has tarried with "loggerheads," sounding the "very basestring of humility," so that they take it, "upon their salvation," he is "no proud Jack like Falstaff, but a Corinthian" (*I Henry IV*, II.iv.3–11). Of course Hal is no such thing. That is the claim of the lads in Eastcheap. Rather than "boon companion," which most texts give as the gloss for *Corinthian*, Hal is the apostle who has gone among his churches, hoping to be heard as well among the Laodiceans as among the Colossians (Colossians 4.16). He exhorts Corinthians as well as Ephesians, weak as well as lawless, as we shall see.

The Epistle to the Corinthians indicates that Paul has become as four different "humors" in order to "saue some." For convenience, let us reverse Paul's list, dealing first with Francis, one of the loggerheads who initiates these considerations; let us consider the weak. That the apprentices are the weak of the kingdom Hal adequately denotes when he becomes proficient in their way of life in "one quarter of an hour," and when he inveighs against Francis for having "fewer words than a parrot" (II.iv.4, 17–18, 98–99). Hal has become one of them (in order to save some) by sounding the "basestring of humility" (5–6). He is accepted as "sworn brother" and shall "command all the good lads in Eastcheap" (6, 13–14). The "issue" of the Francis diversion has been misrepresented somewhat to Poins who might not understand or otherwise cooperate. Although the Prince has engaged Poins to help "drive away the time till Falstaff come" (27–28), the Prince, in his own Pauline purpose of redeeming time and saving some, works upon Francis (who takes it "already upon [his] salvation") to

20. Bryant's commentary on the way in which Shakespeare evokes Ephesians is of great value. See Bryant, *Hippolyta's View*, pp. 60–61.

confirm the boy in righteous ways. The entire Francis episode is framed and riddled through with the ticking clock, Francis's refrain-like response of "anon, anon, sir" providing an important thematic statement.

Dialogue begins with a query on Francis's number of indentured years. The poor wretch displays a certain vagueness: "five years, and as much as to—." In the midst of his tale of life he is summoned, but his reply is "Anon, anon, sir" (41–44). We should begin to feel that something like allegory has taken over; we watch wavering indecision, very much like that of the Hollow Men in T. S. Eliot's poem. As Francis unravels his tedious life, the Prince tests the boy's susceptibility to evil. Francis is tempted to flee his apprenticeship when another summons comes, which once again the boy delays with another promise of "Anon, sir" (52). Each question the Prince puts to the fellow hinges on some turn of time: "How old art thou, Francis?"; "Ask me when thou wilt"; "tomorrow, Francis; or, Francis, a-Thursday." Always the summons interrupts; always the promise is "anon." The final and critical question is "Wilt thou rob this . . . Spanish-pouch?" (53–71). As Francis recoils from immediate villainy, the Prince happily encourages the boy to "stick it out":

> Why, then, your brown bastard is your only drink; for
> look you, Francis, your white canvas doublet will sully.
> In Barbary, sir, it cannot come to so much.[21]
>
> (73–76)

The Prince applauds Francis's virtue, urging him to continue serving. The white doublet, symbol and badge of the boy's station, once stained in Barbary (the barbarous and heathen world to which he must flee as an outlaw), will no longer have the value of unsullied white. Purity is without price. Francis has been tested as have the "undecided" in "The Hollow Men." As they recite the

21. See the Arden footnote to this passage. Kittredge, A. R. Humphreys, and an unidentified eighteenth-century commentator find the Prince's words "incoherent nonsense" or "totally in the humbug style."

paternoster, "For thine is the kingdom," the tedium of existence breaks their resolve: "Life is very long." Eliot's Hollow Men waver until time runs out. Francis, under duress, chooses right action. But a final exchange displays a poignant human frailty:

PRINCE
> What's o'clock, Francis?

FRANCIS
> Anon, anon, sir.
> (96–97)

The test is not over until life itself is unwound; as long as life tarries, the weak human will attempts to dally the inevitable summons. But one must be made aware of the time. Francis is fortunate to have a Prince to ask him, "What's o'clock?" In such wise has Hal become one of the weak, in order to save some.

That the Prince's purpose with the outlaws is the same seems indisputable. Instead of arresting strictly their errant course, the Prince upholds their idleness. He joins them, becomes one without law, so that "in the perfectness of time"[22] he might save some. For dramatic purposes these efforts are focused in Falstaff. At first appearance for both, before we learn through the Prince's first soliloquy the Prince's intentions, this priest/heir-apparent works for the redemption of the vagrant knight. Tagged, labeled, and marked as glutton, drunkard, lecher, and idler, Falstaff doesn't know the time of day; notably old, he seems unaware of the lateness of the hour, the time left him "to patch up [his] old body for heaven" (*II Henry IV*, II.iv.230–31). In the only words to which Falstaff will listen, Hal attempts to redirect the fat knight's wayward steps by unrelenting references to the gallows. Falstaff, moved momentarily by some deep-buried contrition within him, entertains briefly thoughts of repentance—"I must give over this life, and I will give it over. By the Lord, an I do not, I am a villain. I'll be damn'd for never a king's son in Christendom" (I.ii.94–96). But virtuous life for a lord of misrule is too long by far for even half a day: "Where shall we take

22. See footnote 18 above.

a purse tomorrow, Jack?" (or indulge in any sin?): "'Zounds, where thou wilt, lad, I'll make one" (97–98).[23]

Ultimately Hal is to fail with most of the outlaws and their women. Bardolph and Nym are cut off in *Henry V* for stealing. Doll Tearsheet and Mistress Quickly would appear to die in prison or in hospital, the first guilty of rolling and murdering a drunk, the second succumbing to the "malady of France."[24] We do not follow Poins, Peto, Gadshill, and Pistol to their ends; but in the gross and scope of opinion it looks bad for them since not one of them shows the least inclination toward reform or repentance. But emphasis must be upon the successes of the "mirror of all Christian kings" (*Henry V*, II.prologue.6), not upon his failures. Falstaff, perhaps partly as a result of the labors by the Prince, dies in the odor of sanctity, even if the vigil candles smell a little of flap-dragons. But the outlaw who submits finally to reason[25] is redeemed in time.

The two remaining Pauline roles assumed by Hal—under the law and Jew—are enacted in ways that smack of literary trickery, but enacted nevertheless in order that apostleship be fulfilled. As I have argued, the Prince is constant under the law, any apparent aberrancy being only an antic disposition, put on so as to become weak with the weak and outlaw with the outlaws. Coming under the law, then, is only a seeming-so, much as Paul's; for Paul stresses, parenthetically, "I am not without Law as perteining to God, but am in the Law through Christ" (I Cor. 9.21). Four scenes establish glowingly Hal's "glitt'ring reformation": the Prince's two

23. Another Pauline echo pertinent here is Falstaff's self-justification: "'Tis no sin for a man to labor in his vocation" (I.ii.102–3), a paraphrase of I Cor. 7.20: "let euerie man abide in the same vocation wherein he was called."

24. See pp. 279–80 and *Henry V*, V.i.79–80. I am, of course, accepting the emendation that reads *Nell* for *Doll*.

25. Ironically (if indeed Poins comes to the end predicted by Falstaff: "what hole in hell were hot enough for him?" [I.ii.105–6]), it is Poins who puts his finger on the cause of Falstaff's ultimate redemption: the whoreson round man will fight as long as "he sees reason" (I.ii.178–79).

reconciliations with his father (*I Henry IV*, III.ii.1–161; *II Henry IV*, IV.v.91–224), the very telling and symbolic submission to the law in the person of the Lord Chief Justice—

> My voice shall sound as you do prompt mine ear,
> And I will stoop and humble my intents
> To your well-practic'd wise directions—
> > (*II Henry IV*, V.ii.119–21)

and the portrait given by the bishops of *Henry V* (I.i.22–69). The public results of Hal's growing and open support of the laws and governors of England are a further reduction of chaos, a further move toward the harmony and order of a time when days are no longer evil.

Trickier still is Hal's becoming a Jew so that he might "winne the Iewes," but the very fact that the playwright is willing to reach so far for his effect is proof of its extreme importance to him. In the tavern inquisition, Falstaff adds some "Sixteen at least" to the eight or ten travelers reported by Gadshill. Peto claims that the victims were left unbound, but Falstaff amends,

> You rogue, they were bound, every man of them, or I
> am a Jew else, an Ebrew Jew.
> > (II.iv. 176–77)

Although the original eight to ten travelers were bound (II.ii.92), the "Sixteen at least" is a gross exaggeration. Falstaff's tale is riddled through with the most outrageous lies imaginable. By his own oath, the ancient ruffian has turned Jew. Hal, who has joined in these lies for the time being ("Prithee let him alone. We shall have more anon" [205–6]), becomes momentarily a Jew also. But Hal's purpose is to redeem the Jew Falstaff, "I'll be no longer guilty of this sin. . . . What trick . . . canst thou now find out to hide thee from this open and apparent shame?" (239, 260–62). Not off the point is Falstaff's response: "I shall think the better of . . . thee during my life . . . thou for a true prince" (270–72). Important to my argument throughout is the identification of Hal as true prince, true priest/king, in distinction to his father, a usurper, and chief cause of the cracks in the fabric of the realm. Hal is to be a true inheritor of the "kingdom" and as such its proper "redeemer."

The ultimate concern that all men have with time is how they use it on their journey to the heavenly city. I have already likened Henry IV to one of the late-repentant, believing him at the last to have worked out his salvation. Late as he is, he meets the minimum requisite: fixing finally in single-mindedness on the spiritual pilgrimage. As Henry nears his "worldly . . . period" (*II Henry IV*, IV.v.230), he advances toward the heavenly Jerusalem when his lords convey him to the lodging where he swooned, the earthly chamber called Jerusalem:

> bear me to that chamber; there I'll lie.
> In that Jerusalem shall Harry die.
> (*II Henry IV*, IV.v.239–40)

Hotspur has sputtered out his final seconds regretting loss of proud titles. Pride is his sin, the rewards of pride are his portion. His stilled-tongue of prophecy would seem to announce a time when he would be "clean forgot." Although Hal in his magnanimity would raise an epitaph of praise and wish him in heaven, Shakespeare allows his only remembrance on earth to be his ignominy, his treason, his *memento-mori* example: he is "dust / And food for—" . . . worms (V.iv.84–87).

But Falstaff is the major figure through whom the four last things are most closely pursued. Like Henry IV, one of the late-repentant, Falstaff is given an obituary by Mistress Quickly, who indicates that the old reprobate's penultimate words were "'God, God, God!' three or four times" (*Henry V*, II.iii.18–19). She is reasonably certain, as are most of us,

> Nay, sure, he's not in hell. He's in Arthur's bosom, if
> ever man went to Arthur's bosom.
> (9–10)

Not only did this most unlikely penitent cry out to his God but also

> 'A made a finer end, and went away an it had been
> any christom child.
>
> (10–12)

Mistress Quickly's punning redundancy, "finer end," is part of what has been an ongoing *memento-mori* motif,[26] traceable in Shakespeare as early as *The Comedy of Errors*.[27] In another earlier play extended grisly imaginings run through Juliet's head as she anticipates waking in the tomb before "Romeo / Come to redeem" her (IV.iii.31–32). She boasts to Friar Laurence what she would dare "to live an unstain'd wife":

> hide me nightly in a charnel house,
> O'er-cover'd quite with dead men's rattling bones,
> With reeky shanks and yellow chapless skulls;
> Or bid me go into a new-made grave
> And hide me with a dead man in his tomb.
>
> (IV.i.81–85, 88)

These thoughts, after the manner of *memento-mori* warning, should work in the girl to dissuade her from the death she contemplates, work to cause in her repentance for the sins she carries—filial

26. Lyric poems in the *memento-mori* genre often have for their titles the Latin tag *respice finem*. See, for example, the poem attributed to Thomas Proctor in *A Gorgeous Gallery of Gallant Inventions (1578)*, ed. Hyder E. Rollins (Cambridge, Mass., 1926), p. 99. For other ingredients of the *memento-mori* lyric, see the appendix.

27. The entire Pinch episode begins at IV.iv.41 with Dromio of Ephesus warning Adriana, "Mistress, 'respice finem,' respect your end" (fig. 30), and concludes with Antipholus of Ephesus's description of Pinch as a "living dead man" (V.i.242). See my article, "The Dance-of-Death motif in Shakespeare," *Papers on Language and Literature* 20 (1984): 15–28, in which I argue that Pinch figures symbolically as a skeleton in the Dance of Death.

disobedience and deception. The more should it work for Juliet since Friar Laurence inadvertently employs a strange vision to strengthen the girl's resolve to swallow the death-simulating potion:

> Now, when the bridegroom in the morning comes
> To rouse thee from thy bed, there art thou dead.
> (IV.i.107–8)

Strange it is for its purpose. That Juliet and the Friar do not find it so produces a heavy measure of irony. Laurence's image should bring to both their minds the parable of the wise and foolish virgins (see figs. 20, 22, and 23).[28]

Shakespeare continues to use the parable of the ten virgins in *I Henry IV*. At the beginning of II.i., the fourth consecutive scene to open and/or close with a time reference, the First Carrier notes the lateness of the hour: "An it be not four by the day, I'll be hang'd." His call for the hostler elicits a response we should remember later: "OSTLER [*Within*] Anon, anon" (II.i.1–4). The hostler's behavior is much like Francis's, except that the hostler never comes at all. Like Francis, and many another mere mortal, he means, no doubt, to come, but one thing leads to another, some more pressing demand captures his time, and, in fact, he fails altogether of his promise to come. In the meantime both carriers engage in a lengthy recital of service in the stable, fallen off dreadfully and best summed up with the Second Carrier's charge that "This house is turn'd upside down since Robin Ostler died" (II.i.10–11). The topsy-turvy world is a familiar condition in all those plays— *Hamlet, Lear, Macbeth*, to name three—in which usurpation of one sort or another takes place. Until the times of Henry IV are redeemed, a topsy-turvy world exists, from the court at Windsor, where a servant of the King "doth deny his prisoners," to the meanest stable between Rochester and London, where "there is ne'er a king christen could be better bit" than the First Carrier has

---

28. See chap. 5, especially pp. 217–20, for the full treatment of the parable in combination with other *memento-mori* motifs.

been "since the first cock" (II.i.14–19). The last words addressed to the nonappearing hostler are, "Hast no faith in thee?" (31–32).

When Gadshill appears, the Carrier, who has complained about the hostler's tardiness, lies himself, reading the stars at two o'clock, hoping to hide the two hours the coach lags behind schedule. These men are old hands. They lie not to hide their own indiligence. After all, they seem to be doing their best to get off, but they get absolutely no help at all from stable hands. They lie to mislead this unsavory character, who, if he knows their time of departure and the time they "mean to come to London," by some simple arithmetic can deduce the time they will pass Gad's Hill. Furthermore, these coachmen know the significance of the parable of the wise and foolish virgins. Gadshill, imitating the foolish maids, tries to borrow lanterns of the First and then the Second Carrier. Neither will give up his own lamp, the first refusing by oath: "i' faith" (33–43). Their answer to Gadshill's query of arrival time evokes to my ear again the parable "Time enough to go to bed with a candle" (44–45). They shall not be late to the doors of the city (London equaling the heavenly Jerusalem?), and will so have trimmed their candles (lanterns, lamps) as still to have light. With this assertion the carriers turn their backs on Gadshill, and, in effect, leave the neighborhood of evil. Shakespeare juxtaposes then the encounter between Gadshill and the false chamberlain in order that we may see the difference between one who consorts with evil and those who turn away. The larger Gadshill episode, which opened with the carriers' observations that things are topsy-turvy, closes with Gadshill's portrait of his "Troyan" companions, depicting an entire society as decayed morally as the "most villainous house in all London road": Gadshill is allied with "nobility and tranquillity, burgomasters and great oney'rs, . . . [who] pray continually to their saint, the commonwealth, or rather, not pray to her, but prey on her, for they ride up and down on her and make her their boots" (67–83).

We have observed an inordinate attention to time in the speeches of most of the major and many of the minor characters of the play: Henry IV's pausing "awhile," Hotspur's plea that "hours be short," Falstaff's "what time of day is it?" Hal's determination to redeem the "time," Francis and the hostler's "anon," and the carriers and Gadshill's maneuvering with the clock. We have observed the relationship of these matters to various Pauline roles, and we have found parabolic adornment to these themes. Perhaps the best way to sum up all is to quote the moral with which St. Matthew closes his tale: "Watche therefore: for ye knowe nether the day, nor the houre, when the Sonne of man wil come" (25.13).

In every way this tag to the parable of the ten virgins accords with the purpose of *memento-mori* verse: remember man that thou must die; "To whom, then, shall we sew, / For to haue rescew, / But to swete Jesu."[29] The *memento-mori* theme in the *Henry* plays runs in varying intensity, from the barest hint in Falstaff's first appearance, during which the Prince's gallows-jests remind Falstaff of death, and in a melancholy sweat, he breaks into a ten-minute fever of repentance, to the happy results of its work in Falstaff's last appearance, where, on his deathbed, he reaches toward God to wind up in "Arthur's bosom." Falstaff, then, that seemingly irrepressible vice, that universally scourged lord of misrule, is the figure in whom we observe *memento mori* ultimately to be salutary.

Falstaff thinks constantly of his end, if sometimes only to wish not to think of it. He will not be damned for any king's son (I.ii.95–96); he "doubt[s] not but to die a fair death" (II.ii.13–14). The Prince and Poins twit him, as though they were aware of a continual habit in him of talking to himself about last things: "how agrees the devil and thee about thy soul?" (I.ii.112). But the critical referent for *memento mori* is to be found once each in the two *Henry IV* plays. In Part I, Bardolph is perhaps the surprising agent of remembrance; his flaming "bubukles" substitute for the more usual skull. Falstaff makes "as good use of [Bardolph's face] as many a man doth of a death's-head or a memento mori. I never see thy face but I think upon hell-fire and Dives that liv'd in purple; for there he is in his robes, burning, burning [fig. 25]" (III.iii.29–33). In Part II, again, we have an unlikely minister, the prostitute

29. "Vppon a Deedmans Hed," *John Skelton: Poems*, ed. Robert S. Kinsman (Oxford, 1969), p. 9.

Fig. 25. West front, Lincoln Cathedral: (*top left*) Dives at table. (*top right*) Lazarus borne to heaven by flights of angels, Dives cast into hell. (*bottom*) Souls in Abraham's bosom. By permission of the Dean and Chapter of Lincoln Cathedral.

Doll Tearsheet: "Peace, good Doll, do not speak like a death's-head; do not bid me remember mine end" (II.iv.232–33).

Immediately prior to Bardolph's appearance as a death's-head, Falstaff finds himself "in some liking" to repent (III.iii.4–7); thus he is ripe for responding as he does to his servant's flaming face. He is put into readiness by comparing himself to a graft of that first fruit: "I am wither'd like an old apple-john" (3–4). The apple-john is Falstaff's own peculiar *memento mori*. Although the skull almost invariably is the reminder of death within the *memento-mori* genre, any object that carries imagery of decay and brings an observer to thoughts of death and repentance becomes in fact a *memento-mori* object. The generic requirement of repentance is met by Falstaff's sudden resolution, made the split second after he thinks of apple-johns: "Well, I'll repent" (4). The adjectives *wither'd* and *old* help, of course, to bring to Sir John visions of dissolution and death, but more significantly apple-johns received their name from association with St. John's Day (June 24).[30] St. John's Day is the nominal Midsummer Day, even though actual solstice occurs usually two or three days earlier. The solstice, of course, marks the sun's turnabout, after which it starts its journey toward the antipodes and heralds the advent of winter. As a symbol of man's life, the sun's seeming diminishment in heat and vigor presages man's ultimate winter and death. That such awareness was present in contemporary religious thought is clear from the epistle appointed to be read in the 1562 Book of Common Prayer on St. John the Baptist's Feast Day: "all fleshe is grasse. . . . The grass is withered, the floure falleth awaye. Even so is the people as grasse."

Not surprisingly, apple-johns appear also in Part II, where our old friend Francis, the drawer, scolds his fellow servant for setting a dish of the withered fruit upon Falstaff's table: "Thou knowest Sir John cannot endure an apple-john" (II.iv.2–3). The Second Drawer attributes Falstaff's loathing of the shriveled fruit to a jest of Hal's in which

30. *OED*. See also the importance of St. John's Day in *A Midsummer Night's Dream*, chap. 6, pp. 236–39.

The Prince once set a dish of apple-johns before him,
and told him there were five more Sir Johns, and putting off his hat, said "I will now take my leave of these
six dry, round, old, wither'd knights."

(4–8)

The Prince's purpose was the same as when he jested about the gallows: to bring the old man to remembrance of his end.

As for the remainder of Part I, *memento-mori* elements that
close out the play include the Prince's advice to Falstaff shortly
prior to the battle of Shrewsbury that he say his prayers, that he
owes God a death (V.i.124, 126). Falstaff, again in a mood to repent, wishes it were bedtime and all well. Yet, he irrepressibly determines to seek life rather than pay God beforehand. The lesson
of *memento mori*, however, remains with him as Part I ends. A final
image is "such grinning honor as Sir Walter hath" (V.iii.59), and
Falstaff's last words sound like the curtain speech of a redeemed
sinner—although, being Falstaff, he would still prefer to strike a
bargain with the redeemer—

If I do grow great, I'll grow less; for I'll purge,[31] and
leave sack, and live cleanly as a nobleman should do.[32]

(V.iv.161–63)

In Part II, where confrontation with old age is a more prevalent theme, Shakespeare envelops the play with two extended reminders to Falstaff that he cannot live forever. At Sir John's first
appearance in the second play, the Lord Chief Justice sets the fat
rogue up a glass wherein he may see his true portraiture; it is an

31. *purge*: repent. See note in Arden Shakespeare: "cf. *Iacke
Drums Entertainment* . . . Old wretch, amend thy thoughts, purge, purge,
repent!" (p. 163).

32. A Falstaff reformed permanently at this point is a strong argument for those who maintain that Part I and Part II are separately conceived compositions.

image of decay, comparable to Jaques's picture of the seventh age
of man:

> are [you not] written down old with all the characters
> of age? Have you not a moist eye, a dry hand, a yellow
> cheek, a white beard, a decreasing leg, an increasing
> belly? Is not . . . every part about you blasted with
> antiquity?
>
> (I.ii.178–83)

At Falstaff's last appearance in the second play, Prince Hal assails
the old man in *memento-mori* terms more conventional: "Know
the grave doth gape / For thee thrice wider than for other men"
(V.v.53–54) (fig. 26). His age is stressed; his white hairs mentioned; his vices both specified and generalized; he is a profane,
surfeit-swelled fool and jester, tutor and feeder of the Prince's sim-
ulated riots. For the last time Harry urges him to his prayers, to
seek grace. That Falstaff on his deathbed does so we have already
noted, and much credit should be given the Prince, this apostle to
his people, who by consorting with outlaws has saved at least one.
If Hal has sometimes seemed to play the fool in his efforts at
Falstaff's redemption, he has explained, and perhaps justified in
advance, the program he has followed. He tells us why he consents
to don leather jerkin and apron to catch Falstaff with his whore:

> From a God to a bull? A heavy descension! It was
> Jove's case. From a prince to a prentice? A low trans-
> formation! That shall be mine, for in every thing the
> purpose must weigh with the folly.
>
> (II.ii.165–68)

A "purpose" the Prince has, and it must be something other than
the mere "folly" of that riotous tavern scene. The purpose is then
as it has always been in all the Prince's encounters with Falstaff:
to show that "globe of sinful continents, what a life" he leads
(II.iv.284–85).

Fig. 26. Old man, Dance of Death, Hans Holbein.
Les simulachres & historiees faces de la mort. Lyon, 1538.

In such a light the "infamous" rejection scene (V.v.47–71) is reinterpreted much in the same spirit as Antonio's insistence that Shylock become a Christian. The newly crowned King purposes only Falstaff's salvation, and, as a generous Prince, now wholly under the law and intent to redeem all subjects, he allows the reprobate knight "competence of life . . . / That lack of means enforce [him] not to evils" (V.v.66–67).

In between these alpha and omega appearances of the aged sinner, and in addition to the apple-john and death's-head passages, other eschatological considerations are plentiful: "The fiend hath prick'd down Bardolph irrecoverable, and his face is Lucifer's privy-kitchen, where he doth nothing but roast malt worms";[33] the "devil blinds" the Page; Doll is "in hell already, and burns poor souls"; Mistress Quickly may or may not "be damn'd" for anything Falstaff knows, though he suspects she will "howl" for running a bawdy house ("suffering flesh to be eaten in [her] house") (II.iv.331–44). One more unnumbered time the repentant old man undergoes the briefest of reformations, brought on as much, perhaps, by the Prince's own chagrin "So idly to profane the precious time" (361) as by thoughts of his end. In any case, though "Now comes in the sweetest morsel of the night" (366–67), Falstaff determines to leave it unpicked—at least long enough to get outside the tavern. Once out, his resolution breaks down, and Bardolph rushes back to "Bid Mistress Tearsheet come to my master" (386–87).

Although many small notices of this somber theme of *memento mori* might be made, the last major employment we need consider brings in the Gloucestershire justices to set a melancholy mood before Sir John arrives:

SHALLOW
> . . . Jesu, Jesu, the mad days that I have spent!
> And to see how many of my old acquaintance
> are dead!

SILENCE
> We shall all follow, cousin.

SHALLOW
> Certain, 'tis certain, very sure, very sure.
> Death, as the Psalmist saith, is certain to all, all
> shall die [fig. 27].

> (III.ii.33–39)

These sobering reflections continue as Shallow dwells on the death of old Double. At the farcical recruitment, in the middle of which Shallow harks back to days long past, Falstaff regretfully reminds

33. *malt worms*: topers, a pointed reminder to the eulogist of sherris-sack.

Fig. 27. All shall die. *The boke named royall.* Press of Wynkyn de Worde, London, 1507.

him that the days of joy, the daughters of the game are at the verge of gone forever. The chimes they heard at midnight are a ghostly tinkle; and the bona-roba, Jane Nightwork, is "Old, old, Master Shallow" (193–215). Feeble adds his commentary, which takes us back remorselessly to Hal's words to Falstaff at the end of Part I: "A man can die but once. We owe God a death" (*I Henry IV*, V.i.126; *II Henry IV*, III.ii.235–36).

Thus we return to the death of Falstaff yet once more, and one other thing needs still be said about it. Because the old reprobate winds up improbably in "Arthur's bosom," we remember his recurrent evocations of the parable of Dives and Lazarus. In his first reference, he ties it to the *memento mori* of Bardolph's "salamander" face (figs. 28a, b):[34] "I never see thy face but I think upon

34. The salamander itself increases the force of the *memento-mori* warning. One of those symbols that may work in opposite directions, the salamander is iconologically identified with the children in the fiery fur-

Fig. 28. (a) Salamander, Garden of Eden. Hugo van der Goes, ca. 1470.
By permission of the Kunsthistorisches Museum, Vienna.

Fig. 28. (b) Salamander poisoning fruit tree. *Queen Mary's Psalter.* B. M. Royal MS 2 B. vii, fourteenth century. By permission of the British Museum.

hell-fire and Dives" (*I Henry IV*, III.iii.31–32). A mere two scenes later, Falstaff describes his conscripts as "slaves as ragged as Lazarus in the painted cloth, where the glutton's dogs lick'd his sores" (IV.ii.24–26). On the fat sinner's appearance in Part II, he drags once more the old tapestry out of the closet. To his "security"-minded tailor, Falstaff awards Dives's seat in hell: "Let him be damn'd, like the glutton! Pray God his tongue be hotter!" (*II Henry IV*, I.ii.34–35).

The parable of Dives and Lazarus appears only in Luke (16.19–31). We may see from Falstaff's own usage that Dives, in

<hr />

nace (who are thus, anagogically, able to escape hellfire), and is also a type for Satan (destined to burn eternally in hellfire). As either symbol, the salamander should have a salutary effect on Falstaff. It should either move him to emulate the faith of the Hebrews in Babylon or warn him to shun the bondage of Satan. For the salamander as iconological identification of the Hebrew youths, see Louis Réau, *Iconographie de L'Art Chrétien* (Paris, 1958), III.i, p. 70. For salamander as Satan, see Robert A. Koch, "The Salamander in Van der Goes' *Garden of Eden*," *Journal of the Warburg and Courtauld Institutes* 28 (1965): 323–26 (see fig. 28).

scriptural gloss, became the archetype of the glutton. Lazarus, of course, stands for the unfed, unwelcomed, unclothed wretched of the world. Dives gives him no succor,

> And it was so that the begger dyed, and was caryed by
> the Angels into Abrahams bosome.
>
> (16.22)

Few parables are more frequently met in the general iconography of apocalyptic art. Greatest and fullest treatment is probably to be found at Moissac, where in a separate panel on the left side of the porch that frames the south portal of St. Peter's, a high-relief sculpture renders the parable in stone as fully as one could wish. Plate 77 of Herrad of Landsberg's *Hortus Deliciarum* presents an enormous Abraham on a great throne with something like fifteen souls in his bosom (fig. 29).[35] The parable translates generally, in many of the great Gothic churches, into the form of this patriarchal figure, sometimes included in the tympana, but often to the right side of Christ in one of the archivolts that frame the judgment portals.[36] Not surprisingly, Dives is one of the catalogue of the famous dead in the prototype *memento-mori* poem attributed to St. Bernard of Clairvaux: "vel Dives splendidus totus in prandio."[37] The parable in stone was prominently available to Englishmen in a rather full sculptural treatment in low relief among the tableaux stretched across the west front of Lincoln Cathedral, the same edifice that has on its south transept a judgment portal accompanied by an elegant set of wise and foolish virgins (fig. 25).

Falstaff's constant recourse to the parable verifies the opinion of the Lord Chief Justice, who is "well acquainted with [his]

35. Ed. and trans. Aristide D. Caratzas (New Rochelle, N.Y., 1977).
36. Judgment portals at Reims and Bourges, for example, show prominent Abraham figures in their tympana. Chartres relegates the patriarch to the second innermost archivolt. An unusual variation in England is the sculpture surmounting the Percy chantry in Beverley Minster. Several art historians believe the soul of Lady Percy to rest in the bosom of God the Father rather than that of Abraham (see fig. 31).
37. *Latin Poems Commonly Attributed to Walter Mapes*, ed. Thomas Wright (London, 1841), p. 148.

Fig. 29. Souls in Abraham's bosom. *Hortus Deliciarum.*
Herrad of Landsberg (d. 1195). Florida State University Library.

manner of wrenching the true cause the false way" (*II Henry IV*, II.i.107–9), that the fat knight usually attributes his own worst faults to others. Surely the most noticeable feature about the physical Falstaff is his girth, and, surely, his foremost vice is gluttony; thus, he is quick to call the victims of Gadshill "Bacon-fed" and "gorbellied knaves" (*I Henry IV*, II.ii.84, 88). The comforting irony but also the certain proof of the efficacy of Hal's efforts and those of the others, witting and unwitting, who put before Falstaff such

Fig. 30. *Respice finem.* Heinrich Aldegrever, 1529. Florida State University Library.

Fig. 31. Soul in the bosom of God/Abraham. Percy chantry, Beverley Minster, Beverley, Humberside.

telling images of *memento mori* is the death of the glutton, who, unlike Dives, winds up himself in "Arthur's [Abraham's] bosom."

The Prince, then, has filled well his role. A deputy for his father, a true priest/king, even before he ascends the throne, chosen perhaps because his father had not the purity for the call-

287

ing, Harry V is for his lifetime a completely successful apostle to the gentiles. Through a variety of ways—becoming all things to all men, upholding the law, lessoning, catechizing, exhorting—he saves some, supports others, and defeats the rest; in short, he redeems the time.

As subthemes to this great example of spiritual leadership, Shakespeare adds several motifs, often found elsewhere in his plays: an overwhelming consciousness of time, with the need to know that man's life is short, that delay is sometimes fatal (Hotspur), and sometimes dangerous (Henry IV and Falstaff), but that time can be redeemed (Hal); a use of the parable of the ten virgins; and a wide-ranging employment of various *memento-mori* devices. All these matters merge in the parable: "Watche therefore: for ye knowe nether the day, nor the houre, when the Sonne of man wil come." Prince Hal's commandment to one of the least of his subjects is his call to all. As surrogate for the bridegroom, he bids, "Be with me betimes in the morning" (*I Henry IV*, II.iv.542–43).

8. *As You Like It:*
Et in Arcadia Ego

ome recent commentators have emphasized those features of *As You Like It* that stand as healthy correctives to the too-readily, too-often applied adjectives of *gay, bright, happy,* or *golden.*[1] And yet little critical acumen is required to notice that Jaques monitors an injection of melancholy, a forest gloom, into the sunshine glade of Arden, and that Touchstone, as his name denotes, holds up measurable quantities of the real world against which we must judge those yearned-after serenities and beatitudes of an Eden man was believed to have forfeited, of a paradise not yet regained.

What is lacking in these views is an awareness of the degree to which Shakespeare carried the somber counterpoint that underlies the joyous vitality of the world's best garden. *Garden* is the word, for in Shakespeare's greatest pastoral play, Arden stands for

1. Note especially Harold Jenkins, "*As You Like It,*" *Shakespeare Survey* 8 (1955): 40–51, and Helen Gardner, "*As You Like It,*" in *More Talking of Shakespeare,* ed. John Garrett (London, 1959), pp. 17–32.

Eden, even as Virgil's Arcadia stands for the Golden Age. But Shakespeare must contradict the very myth he perpetuates. Arden may stand for Eden, but, unfortunately, Arden is, ultimately, only Arden. Others have seen that Shakespeare's "mature comedy . . . permits . . . criticism of his ideal world in the very centre of it."[2] Others have noticed that Shakespeare "dares to speak in Arcadia, where one can never grow old, of Time's inevitable processes of maturity and decay."[3] But the degree of that decay has not been perceived to go beyond a "description of man's final decrepitude."[4] To date, the view we have of *As You Like It* is a composite of two of the most famous pastoral lyrics of the sixteenth century, themselves correctives to each other, but each, by itself, a half-view that Shakespeare is able to avoid in the balanced vision that he brings to *As You Like It*. I have in mind Marlowe's passionate shepherd who will all pleasures prove on an unending succession of May-mornings, and Ralegh's cautious nymph who knows that "flowers doe fade," youth does not last, love does not regenerate unfailingly, joys have their termination, and age has its need. Ralegh's nymph knows that "Time driues the flocks from field to fold."[5] But I would like to go one step further to observe the presence of death in the Forest of Arden.

Pertinent to my argument is that Harold Jenkins, like other writers, substitutes for Arden Arcadia: Shakespeare "dares to speak in Arcadia . . . of Time's . . . decay."[6] Clearly many of us believe that Shakespeare made the same substitution. Surely Arcadia was in his mind when he gave to Touchstone his answer to the

2. Jenkins, "*As You Like It*," p. 45.
3. Jenkins, "*As You Like It*," p. 49.
4. "As has often been observed . . . the seven ages speech ends with a description of man's final decrepitude—'sans teeth, sans eyes, sans taste, sans everything'" (Jenkins, "*As You Like It*," p. 49). But in using this quotation to illustrate decrepitude Jenkins errs, as it is the labor of this chapter to prove.
5. *The Poems of Sir Walter Ralegh*, ed. Agnes Latham (London, 1951), pp. 16–17.
6. Jenkins, "*As You Like It*," p. 49.

magical utterance of Rosalind: "Well, this is the forest of Arden" (II.iv.13). As her words cast spells about us—spells of shallow rivers, melodious birds, and a thousand fragrant posies—Touchstone, on the instant, sounds the counternote: "Ay, now am I in Arden" (14).

If we exchange Arcadia for Arden and read, "Ay, now am I in Arcadia," there comes to us the echo, the cadence, the translated words *et in Arcadia ego.*

We are reasonably familiar with shepherds and their Arcadian contentment through Theocritus, Bion, and Moschus, through Virgil, Mantuan, Sannazaro, Sidney, and Spenser.[7] We are perhaps less familiar with the elegiac notes that sound in the motto *et in Arcadia ego.* Unfortunately, the phrase has not been discovered earlier than the 1620s, when the Bolognese painter Giovanni Guercino used it in a canvas shown to be a forerunner of Nicolas Poussin's famous painting (fig. 32; see also fig. 33).[8] Shakespeare wrote *As You Like It* no later than 1600, leaving us with approximately a quarter-century in which we cannot prove the existence of the phrase. But for the words to find such ready employment in the sister art of painting, where it appears as a more appropriate piece of tombstone verse, argues an earlier existence. At least we may hypothesize that many a tomb now crumbled carried the legend borrowed by both Guercino and Poussin within approximately ten years of each other.[9]

Present in the Poussin painting are shepherds stopped in their pastoral joys by coming upon the tomb of an earlier inhabitant of their pleasant garden, an experience that casts them into somber contemplation. Present is the phrase upon the tomb: *et in Arcadia ego.* Present surmounting that tomb is the *memento-mori*

7. The classic treatment of the history of pastoral is W. W. Greg, *Pastoral Poetry and Pastoral Drama* (London, 1906).

8. Erwin Panofsky, "Et in Arcadia Ego," in *Philosophy and History,* ed. R. Klibansky and H. J. Paton (Oxford, 1936), p. 233.

9. See Panofsky, "Et in Arcadia Ego," pp. 224, 233, and 236 for the dates of the canvases under discussion.

Fig. 32. Et in Arcadia Ego. Giovanni Francesco Guercino, ca. 1622. Florida State University Library.

icon, a skull.[10] In the Guercino painting are all these elements plus one lacking in Poussin's: Erwin Panofsky calls our attention to a mouse gnawing the skull that the shepherds, fresh from their country matters, gaze upon, "a time-honoured and very well-known symbol for all-devouring time."[11]

10. Poussin treated the subject twice: one of his canvases is in the Louvre, the other in the collection of the Duke of Devonshire. Only the Devonshire painting exhibits the skull. Anne Barton has also linked *As You Like It* to the two Poussin paintings but reaches none of the conclusions offered here. See her essay, "*As You Like It* and *Twelfth Night*: Shakespeare's Sense of an Ending," in *Shakespearian Comedy*, ed. David Palmer and Malcolm Bradbury, Stratford-upon-Avon Studies, no. 14 (London, 1972), pp. 164–65.

11. Panofsky, "Et in Arcadia Ego," p. 233.

We have, then, in a painting coming some twenty-odd years after the composition of *As You Like It*, a pastoral setting of great loveliness, peopled by youths of great beauty. The youths may be presumed to be leading idyllic existences, yet they have been brought to a moment of harsh reality by a tomb, a skull, and a symbol of time which tell them that their youth, beauty, and love will not last forever, that underneath the stone pile lies a dead shepherd who was once also in Arcadia. To quote Panofsky, "Death himself . . . stops the shepherds and sets them thinking with the awful warning: 'I hold sway, even in Arcadia.'" [12] If we can believe that the *memento-mori* elements, as put together by Guercino and Poussin, were commonly available before 1623, in fact before 1599, and thereby ready to Shakespeare's hand, we can show a thread that runs through *As You Like It* enforcing the theme found in the Italian painting, the theme found in the French.

"Ay, now am I in Arden." If in these words of Touchstone we hear echoed *et in Arcadia ego* and believe death introduced consequently into the pastoral landscape, we should expect to find thereafter the other elements of the Guercino and Poussin paintings: all-devouring time, the *memento-mori* image, the dead shepherd who once, like the others, lived in Arcadia, and finally the somber meditation that youth, beauty, and love must fade, even as men themselves.

But to find these dark ingredients in *As You Like It*, we must do more than rehearse well-known features of the play such as Jaques's role as a conventional Elizabethan stage-malcontent or as a classic case of the Burtonian melancholic; we must do more than point out the very real enemies to joy, such as the double attempt at fratricide in which Oliver tries to dispatch Orlando first through the offices of Charles the wrestler, and that failing, through the torching of the hovel where Orlando sleeps; more than indicate that Duke Frederick marches upon Arden with a host, "purposely to take / His brother here and put him to the sword" (V.iv.156–57). We must do more than show that not every Jack gets his Jill in this bright, gay comedy which concludes with as many marriages as

12. Panofsky, "Et in Arcadia Ego," pp. 233–34.

any play in Shakespeare. But William does not get his Audrey, Phebe does not get her Ganymede; and I do recount these matters before moving on, for it is an important part of the argument that the *et-in-Arcadia-ego* theme includes distresses other than death in the lovely garden-world. Unreciprocated love such as William's and Phebe's is one of the chief of these.[13]

Since Touchstone initiates the death-in-Arcadia motif, he is the appropriate agent of time. He emerges as the contradiction to Orlando's claim that "There's no clock in the forest" (III.ii.296–97). In allegory that makes of Arcadia either a golden age or an Eden, a feature of these prelapsarian worlds must be the insignificance of time. Where there is no death, time has no sting. Not only Orlando is deluded. Report has reached even one of the entertainers at court that Arden carries all the features of Arcadia, that there the sands of time are meaningless:

> They say [the Duke] is already in the forest of Arden,
> and a many merry men with him. . . . They say many
> young gentlemen flock to him every day, and fleet the
> time carelessly, as they did in the golden world.
>
> (I.i.110–14)

Thus early Arden is equated with the "golden world" wherein inhabitants are young, happy, and undisturbed by time. When the Duke corroborates Charles the wrestler's "news," he translates the age of Saturn into that of Adam, an Adam before the fall:

> Are not these woods
> More free from peril than the envious court?
> Here feel we not the penalty of Adam.
>
> (II.i.3–5)

Though the seasons change—apparently a postlapsarian imposition—the season ordinarily punitive to man, winter, is no such

13. See Panofsky, "Et in Arcadia Ego," pp. 228–29.

thing. The Duke extracts only good from the cold as he does from all else provided in the Arden-Eden world: he and his followers "Find tongues in trees, books in the running brooks, / Sermons in stones, and good in every thing" (6–17). The general ambiance in Arden is such that even as one enters, time loses all significance. We know that Orlando tosses away his dial, and Celia, speaking, perhaps, for herself and Rosalind only, likes the "place, / And willingly could waste [her] time in it" (II.iv.90–91).

But clearly she does not speak for Touchstone who has not only retained his "dial" but also consults it tellingly; for with it, he gives the lie direct to all young lovers who would have time stand still in order that their love, youth, and beauty remain always at the golden moment:

> "It is ten o'clock.
> Thus we may see . . . how the world wags.
> 'Tis but an hour ago since it was nine,
> And after one hour more 'twill be eleven;
> And so, from hour to hour, we ripe and ripe,
> And then, from hour to hour, we rot and rot;
> And thereby hangs a tale."
>   (II.vii.22–28)

The hours are those of midmorning, those working toward maturation of the day, the last one tolled being eleven, even as the lovers are in the morning of their lives, just prior to the high-noon maturation of marriage. But the clock will not stop, not even in Arden; and the real impact, the shock that brings us up short, is not the image of maturation, the riping and riping, but the image of decay, the rotting and rotting. We should begin to envisage the *memento-mori* image of the skull beneath the rotting flesh.

Jaques, who retells these musings of Touchstone, was so charmed by their wit and wisdom that he "did laugh sans intermission / An hour by his dial" (II.vii.32–33), joining for once in the prevailing mood of Arden, or Arcadia, joining in the supposedly unbroken joy of the Golden Age. But Jaques records for us also the passing of one more hour, to show that merriment too eats up the minutes that haste man toward decay.

The playwright's concern with time is not limited to these speeches, themselves among the most oft-quoted lines of the play, but may be found throughout. The noun *time* appears on 43 occasions in *As You Like It*. Only two other nouns occur more frequently. One of these is, quite significantly, *man* (80 times); the other, perhaps insignificantly, is *Rosalind* (71 times). The 43 uses of *time* do not include such other nouns as *hour[s]* (18), *[o']clock* (7), *minute* (4), *day[s]* (21), *months* (1), *week* (1), and *year* (11), which are measurements of time and would swell the word count by 63, for a total of 106.[14]

Jaques's laughter "sans intermission" provides a word link (*sans*) with the next passage at which we need look, a passage which produces an unmistakable *memento-mori* image: Jaques's seven-ages-of-man speech. Time is the vehicle that carries man to his seventh condition, for "one man *in his time* plays many parts" (II.vii.141, my italics); and time carries man *out of his time* as well, for Jaques does not end this account with "second childishness":

> Last scene of all,
> That ends this strange eventful history,
> Is second childishness and mere oblivion,
> Sans teeth, sans eyes, sans taste, sans every thing.
> (II.vii.162–65)

Glosses on this passage have always indicated that the final line is a description of advanced decrepitude,[15] the lack of teeth and taste to be regarded as literal, but the lack of eyes and every thing to be regarded as metaphorical. But if we read the line as modifying "mere oblivion" rather than "second childishness," the description may be regarded as literal throughout. Lack of teeth, of eyes, and of all things else then presents the charnel-house skull (see figs. 18

14. These figures come from the *Oxford Shakespeare Concordances: As You Like It* (Oxford, 1969).
15. See note 4 above.

and 37). Once again we invoke Skelton's *memento-mori* lyric, "Vppon a deedmans hed," for purposes of comparison:

> Deth holow eyed,
> With synnews wyderyd,
> With bonys shyderyd,
> With hys worme etyn maw,
> And his gastly jaw.[16]

Skelton emphasizes the missing eyes and teeth and gives the general impression that all else is lacking, including a tongue with which to taste. Shakespeare's image is also like Southwell's:

> I often looke upon a face
>   Most ugly, grisly, bare, and thinne,
> I often view the hollow place,
>   Where eies, and nose, had sometimes bin.[17]

As You Like It falls, of course, in date of composition between both parts of the *Henry IV* plays on the fore side and *Hamlet* on the aft. All these plays, as well as many others, show the playwright altogether familiar with the *memento-mori* lyric and the effect that might be gained from it in dramatic presentation.[18] The final image of Jaques's seven-ages-of-man speech is clearly in this tradition.

To this point we have produced the elements of time and decay as well as the *nemento-mori* images that Panofsky has shown to be the ingredients of the *et-in-Arcadia-ego* theme. It remains to discover the tomb and the dead shepherd who lies under it.

The question of the dead shepherd, because of treatment

16. *The Poetical Works of John Skelton*, ed. Alexander Dyce (London, 1843), 1:18.

17. *The Poems of Robert Southwell, S.J.*, ed. J. H. McDonald and Nancy P. Brown (Oxford, 1967), p. 73. The editors maintain (pp. lxxxi–lxxxii) that Southwell is not the author of the poem.

18. See the chapters on *Hamlet* and the *Henry* plays especially, as well as the appendix and many pages passim.

accorded it by Panofsky, needs some clarification. Panofsky argues that a dead shepherd under the tombstone "could lead to considerations of almost opposite nature, depressing and melancholy on the one hand, comforting and assuaging on the other" (pp. 239–40). For a person to have lived and died in Arcadia "not only warns the readers of the merciless future, but also opens a vision of the beautiful past in that it evokes the thought of a former fellow being who enjoyed the pleasure of life in the same place and under similar conditions" (p. 239). Panofsky appears to accept further a view that interprets the dead shepherd as saying, "'You, who are now happy, are doomed to die' but also 'I, who am now dead, was happy in my day'" (p. 239). And, somewhat strangely in my view, he concludes, "The very idea of death could fade . . . [so that] 'Even in the jaws of death, there may be Arcadian happiness'" (p. 240).

Panofsky's logic (as well as that of his source, for he takes over these views directly from André Félibien [pp. 237–40], a biographer of Poussin) escapes me. I do not see the dead shepherd under the tomb as different in any way from the skull on top of it: mouldered body like bleached cranium says very simply, "Remember man thou art but dust" (fig. 33, see also fig. 32). A dead shepherd is not required to authenticate the joy and happiness of Arcadia, which is evident in the idyllic surroundings and in the youth, beauty, and love of the shepherds who live. For a rotted corpse to proclaim that "Even in . . . death there may be Arcadian happiness" works against the whole purpose of the *memento-mori* object, which is to put its observer into a frame of mind which we might represent best through Southwell's concluding stanza:

> If none can scape deaths dreadfull dart,
>   If rich and poore his becke obey,
> If strong, if wise, if all do smart,
>   Then I to scape shall have no way.
> Oh grant me grace O God that I,
>   My life may mend sith I must die.[19]

19. Southwell, *Poems*, p. 74.

Fig. 33. (a) Et in Arcadia Ego. Nicolas Poussin, ca. 1630. Devonshire Collection, Chatsworth. Reproduced by permission of the Chatsworth Settlement Trustees.

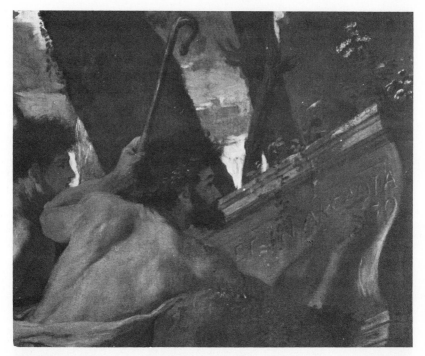

Fig. 33. (b) Detail of Fig. 33 (a).

Any suggestion that removal from Arcadia to paradise is merely a transfer from one perfect place to another, no matter how true that may prove to be, defeats and thwarts the purpose of *memento-mori* art, which is to turn the mind away from earthly felicity to sober meditation on the possibility exactly opposite: the possibility that the unprepared sinner may find himself transported from pleasant meads to plains of horror. Furthermore, the very message that *et in Arcadia ego* itself has to make is much the same as that of *memento mori*. The entire pastoral tradition had suggested to man that the joys of heaven were available on earth, so much so that Arcadia became the anagogical type for Eden and/or paradise. *Et in Arcadia ego* is the corrective to that idea. Paradise grants life eternal; and however much the poets and painters might like to play with the thought that Arcadia is a satisfying substitute, they are wrong insofar as they seek immortality on earth. Although the artist may find some form of everlasting existence in fame and remembrance, he will not find it in the body. Panofsky's is a Romantic idea that was alien to both the Middle Ages and the Renaissance, out of which *memento mori* and *et in Arcadia ego* come.

For Shakespeare, then, to add a dead shepherd to the skull suggests strongly some link between *As You Like It* and the *et-in-Arcadia-ego* motif, for both the skull and the shepherd are parts of the Guercino/Poussin pictorial iconography. And in the choice of his dead shepherd, Shakespeare is perfect:

> Dead shepherd, now I find thy saw of might,
> "Who ever lov'd that lov'd not at first sight?"
> (III.v.81–82)

By quoting from *Hero and Leander*, Shakespeare glances at Christopher Marlowe, thus employing a brilliant device; for Marlowe, as pastoral poet, lived in Arcadia, but Marlowe as murdered poet died in the real world. The playwright from Canterbury ties together all the themes of melancholy in the play. As Marlowe, Shakespeare's "Dead shepherd" reminds us that bucolics, poets, and playwrights "all must / As chimney-sweepers, come to dust." As pastoral poet he reminds us that golden lads and golden girls, all famous lovers, rich in youth and beauty, will have only the briefest span of life.

With his inclusion of the dead shepherd, Shakespeare completes all the ingredients of the *et-in-Arcadia-ego* theme, his contradiction to that pastoral allegory which identifies Arcadia as Eden or paradise. But Shakespeare, as is frequently his wont, has things both ways. He employs traditional typologies with one hand while he takes them away with the other. Such was his technique in *A Midsummer Night's Dream*, for instance,[20] and such it is in *As You Like It*. Although the idea that death is present in Arden preempts its identification as either prelapsarian Eden or paradise, Shakespeare suggests strongly that Arden symbolizes both. Surely any man,

20. See chap. 6.

such as Orlando, who accompanies into a garden world a companion named Adam enters, at least for the moment, a world something like it was before the fall of man. In fact, Arden has been established as a place very different from the court of Duke Frederick—and all its environs, as far as to the estate of Oliver de Boys—first by Charles the wrestler and Duke Senior, as we have seen, but more especially by Rosalind and her runaway fellows. As Touchstone and the two girls stand just outside the verges of Arden, even as Rosalind cries out, "Well, this is the forest of Arden," each of the travelers expresses great weariness:

> ROSALIND
> O Jupiter, how weary are my spirits!
> TOUCHSTONE
> I care not for my spirits, if my legs were not weary.
>
> . . . .
>
> CELIA
> I pray you, bear with me; I cannot go no further.
>
> (II.iv.1–9)

The forest boundaries provide something almost like an invisible barrier that separates a life desperately mortal from one of renewed vigor and grace. The forest, standing for both Eden and paradise, cannot be entered by the purely mortal, and Celia undergoes the merest hint of dying for them all before they may receive the joys they clearly partake of once in the forest: she "faint[s] almost to death" (II.iv.62). Once in, she loses that sense of time which only mortality gives us: "I like this place, / And willingly could waste my time in it" (90–91).

A brief scene interrupts in which Amiens sings a pastoral song, emphasizing the traditional content (*otium*) of Arcadia and echoing Duke Senior's observations that winter is only one of the sweetnesses of adversity. Following this pleasant interlude, Orlando and Adam arrive at those same limits of Arden so recently passed through by Rosalind, Celia, and Touchstone. The casting off of mortality so fleetingly expressed at Celia's entrance into Arden is treated fully in Orlando's companion, and perhaps more tellingly since we witness an apparent death of the old Adam immediately prior to his resurrection, so to speak, in Arden/paradise:

> Dear master, I can go no further. O, I die for food!
> Here lie I down, and measure out my grave. Farewell,
> kind master.
>
> (II.vi.1–3)

But exactly as these episodes establish the mystical qualities of Arden, its freedom from time and, presumably, from death, Shakespeare also inaugurates his countertheme with Jaques's report of his encounter with Touchstone and his dial.

The efficacy of the *et-in-Arcadia-ego* theme in all its fullness is great in its corrective value to a fairy-tale promise of happily ever after. Nevertheless, it will be difficult for some to accept the Guercino/Poussin treatment because of the failure to appear in art, letters, or on tombstone the formulaic *et in Arcadia ego* early enough to provide a source for Shakespeare. But at least two separate pictorial traditions supply material in plenty to support the *memento-mori* aspect of the Arcadian dirge. As early as 1490–1500 may be found a distinct variation of *memento-mori* iconography that Horst Janson has called "The Putto with the Death's Head" (fig. 34).[21] Shown by Janson to be in wide imitation throughout the fifteenth and sixteenth centuries, the Putto with the Death's Head may be described broadly as a pictorial representation that has as its minimum components a childlike figure (the Putto, more often depicted without wings than with them, suggesting the human child rather than cherub [fig. 35]), a *memento-mori* skull, and an hourglass. Frequently an inscription of horrifying import is present, drawing the viewer into an awareness of the brevity of life and of his own imminent decay and death. A German woodcut, dated guardedly by Janson at about 1520–30, includes a sar-

21. Horst Janson, "The Putto with the Death's Head," *The Art Bulletin* 19 (1937): 423–49.

Fig. 34. Putto with a death's head (Three Ages of Man). Vicenzo Cartari. *Immagini dei Dei degli Antichi.* Venice, 1580. Florida State University Library.

cophagus which might prove intermediary in the development of the Guercino/Poussin scene, for the background in this print from Saxony is quite bucolic or Arcadian, and the Putto is presented unnaturally deep in contemplation just as are the shepherds of the death-in-Arcadia canvases.[22]

22. Janson, "Putto," pp. 434, 438.

The significance of these materials for *As You Like It* may be discerned readily in their full use by Jaques in his two speeches central to this essay and to the play. From the seven-ages-of-man declension we get the Putto itself, rendered in Shakespeare's "infant, / . . . in the nurse's arms," and proceed all the way to the skull

Fig. 35. Putto with death's head. Tomb of Thomas Taylor (d. 1689). Church of St. Thomas of Canterbury, Clapham, Bedfordshire.

305

in Shakespeare's "mere oblivion." From Touchstone's dial we get the all-important infusion of time, dial being Shakespeare's substitute for hourglass. And from the fool's formulaic pronouncement—"from hour to hour, we rot and rot"—we get a variation on all the inscriptions in the pictorial tradition which range from "*L'hora Passa*" in the earliest woodcut adduced by Janson through Latin and German inscriptions ("*Hodie mihi cras tibi*," "*Heite mir morgen dir*") to relatively complex *memento-mori* statements such as a 1570 version in an Antwerp print: "*Vigilate quia nescitis diem neque horam.*"[23]

An interesting addition to the conventional theme is the appearance in some versions of a young man about whom Janson says, "Obviously suggested to the Northern mind by the figures of putto, youth and skull was the idea of the Three Ages of Man, childhood, adult age, and death, just as they had been represented since the late fifteenth century" (see fig. 34).[24] Samuel Chew has shown that the ages-of-man motif was so popular and so widely varied that one may find expansion from three ages of man to as many as twelve, with every number in between suggested by one artist or another.[25] The most famous treatment in seven ages, prior to Shakespeare's, was by Giorgio Vasari in 1554. Executed in fresco in an exposed location, the design quickly disintegrated, a decay expected by Vasari who left a detailed description. The "'conclusion of the whole invention' was Death on a lean horse."[26] Shakespeare's seven ages end also with death. Readily available to the playwright was the illustration, complete with skeleton, in *Bat-*

---

23. Janson, "Putto," pp. 433–45. Note that "*Vigilate . . . horam*" is the Vulgate Latin for Matthew 25.13: "Watche therefore: for ye knowe nether the day, nor the houre, when the Sonne of man wil come," the tag to the parable of the wise and foolish virgins. Shakespeare's interest in this parable and its moral have been demonstrated in chaps. 5 and 7, pp. 217–21 and 272–73, respectively.

24. Janson, "Putto," p. 443.

25. Samuel C. Chew, *The Pilgrimage of Life* (New Haven, 1962), pp. 153–73.

26. Chew, *Pilgrimage of Life*, p. 164.

Fig. 36. The seven ages of man. *Batman vppon
Bartholome*. Press of Thomas East, London,
1582.

man vppon Bartholome (1582, fig. 36). Chew's study exhibits clearly
that, whatever the number of ages in any given design, the final
age is either death, as Janson found it, or old age (decrepitude) in
conjunction with death. Sometimes the ancient figure holds in his
hands the *memento-mori* skull; sometimes the stooped decay points
to some other of the *memento-mori* devices; sometimes Death, with
one of his implements of destruction—dart, scythe, or flail—indicates the imminent demise of the wretched mortal. Shakespeare's
skull is in the tradition dead center, and, therefore, with or without an *et-in-Arcadia-ego* complement, puts death itself in the very
heart of Arden.

Fig. 37. *Memento-mori* skull. Geffrey Whitney. *A choice of emblemes.* Leyden, 1586.

A second pictorial tradition eminently available to Shakespeare was the emblem book. Again, if we cannot accept in *As You Like It* the full Guercino/Poussin treatment, we must recognize the minimal *memento-mori* tradition symbolized by the skull alone. The final print in Geffrey Whitney's *A choice of emblemes* (1586) displays the skull underpropped by a single large bone. The emblematic tag that surmounts the woodblock—*Ex maximo minimum*—is Whitney's variation for all the inscriptions that take man through a time sequence all the way to the corruption of the grave. But more to our aid are the verses appended:

> Where liuely once, Gods image was expreste,
> Wherein, sometime was sacred reason plac'de,
> The head, I meane, that is so ritchly bleste,
> With sighte, with smell, with hearinge, and with taste,
>   Lo, nowe a skull, both rotten, bare, and drye,
>   A relike meete in charnell house to lye. [fig. 37][27]

27. Geffrey Whitney, *A choice of emblemes* (Leyden, 1586), p. 229.

The similarity between Shakespeare's lost teeth, eyes, taste, and every thing and Whitney's sight, smell, hearing, and taste smacks of that closeness that can be found in two writers employing the same tradition, the second of whom engages in those variations that keep him from being a mere copyist. But we should note Whitney's series, each item prefaced by the English preposition *with*, and Shakespeare's series, each item prefaced by the French *without*.

With the reminders before them all, not only Jaques at play's end but all characters, all actors, theatergoers, and readers should think upon last will and testament, should think upon last things: "All lovers young, all lovers must / Consign to death and come to dust."

Appendix
The *memento-mori* Lyric

The prototype for the *memento-mori* lyric need be looked for no earlier than the Latin poem sometimes attributed to St. Bernard of Clairvaux, the *Cur mundus militat*, which was much translated into English in the fourteenth through the sixteenth centuries, and in which may be found most of the identifying components of the genre.[1] Briefly, the conventions of the poem are as follows: fear of death is implied or stated:[2]

1. For the Latin text and arguments of attribution, see Thomas Wright, *Latin Poems Commonly Attributed to Walter Mapes* (London, 1841), pp. 147–48. Wright cites the Latin poem in seven MSS. R. T. Davies, *Medieval English Lyrics* (London, 1964), p. 339, lists seven translations for the fifteenth century. Carleton Brown argues that at least one may come from the fourteenth century; he shows further that there still exist ten MSS. for *Cur mundus militat* and contends that therefore the poem must have circulated widely. *Religious Lyrics of the XIV*ᵗʰ *Century*, 2d ed. (Oxford, 1952), p. xii.

2. When the refrain *timor mortis conturbat me* is employed, the fear is, of course, stated explicitly. C. Brown and R. H. Robbins, *The Index of Middle English Verse* (New York, 1943), and R. H. Robbins and John L.

311

Quam breve festum est haec mundi gloria!
   ut umbra hominis sunt ejus gaudia,
     quae tamen subtrahunt aeterna praemia,
   et ducunt hominem ad rura devia.
(Wright, p. 148)

The 1577 translation of Thomas Tusser is a convenient English version that provides also the flavor of the poem as it might have seemed to Shakespeare.

How short a feast (to count) is this same worlds
   renowne?
Such as mens shadowes be, such ioies it brings to
   towne.
Which alway plucketh vs from Gods eternall blis:
And leadeth man to hell, a iust reward of his.[3]
(stanza 7)

Present in imagery or diction is the reminder of death, most often a fleshless skull (see fig. 18) but sometimes other imagery the purpose of which is to remind the reader of the end to which his body must come. Worms and rotting flesh are, of course, encountered almost as commonly as the skull itself:

O esca vermium! o massa pulveris!
   o ros! o vanitas! cur sic extolleris?
(Wright, p. 148)

Cutler, *Supplement to the Index of Middle English Verse* (Lexington, Ky., 1965), list seven and two poems, respectively, in which the Latin refrain is present.

   3. Thomas Tusser, *Fiue Hundred Pointes of Good Husbandrie*, ed. W. Payne and Sidney J. Herrtage, for the English Dialect Society (London, 1878), pp. 202–4, hereafter cited in the text by stanza number.

Appendix

O thou fit bait for wormes! O thou great heape of
   dust!
O dewe! O vanitie! why so extolst thy lust?
                                        (stanza 6)

Present also is either the intended reformation of the speaker or
an exhortation to the reader to prepare for salvation by giving
over evil ways:

   ignoras penitus utrum cras vixeris:
   fac bonum omnibus quamdiu poteris.
                        (Wright, p. 148)

   Thou therefore ignorant, what time thou hast to
      liue,
   Doe good to erie man, while here thou hast to giue.
                                        (stanza 6)

Along with repudiation of sin is reaffirmation of faith and/or as-
piration to higher things:

   Nil tuum dixeris quod potes perdere;
      quod mundus tribuit intendit rapere;
      superna cogita, cor sit in aethere,
      foelix qui poterit mundum contempnere.
                        (Wright, p. 148)

(Tusser omits this stanza.) Skelton captures the sense of the Latin
in his typically direct language:

   To whom, then, shall we sew,
   For to haue rescew,
   But to swete Jesu. . . ?
   Then be oure shylde!
   That we be not exyld
   To the dyne dale

Of boteles bale,
Nor to the lake
Of fendys blake.
   But graunt vs grace
To se thy face,
And to purchace
Thyne heuenly place . . .
Aboue the sky,
That is so hy.[4]

(pp. 19–20)

Exhortation to the reader is achieved through Skelton's French tag:
"*Myrres vous y*" (p. 20).

An outgrowth of the common *memento-mori* images of skull,
bones, and worms but often quite distinct is a succession of dark
and grisly visions, dwelling with insistent horror upon further corruption of the body, terrors of the grave (including implements
and furniture of burial [fig. 38]), and punishments of that greater
pit into which an unprepared or unrepentant soul might fall.
Later poets, taking their cue from St. Bernard's worms and dust,
develop almost infinite variations in lines such as Skelton's:

No man may hym hyde
From Deth holow eyed,
With synnews wyderyd,
With bonys shyderyd,
With hys worme etyn maw,
And his gastly jaw
Gaspyng asyde,
Nakyd of hyde. . . .
Oure eyen synkyng,
Oure bodys stynkyng,

4. *The Poetical Works of John Skelton*, ed. Alexander Dyce, 2 vols.
(London, 1843), hereafter cited in the text by page number. All quotations are from vol. 1.

Oure gummys grynnyng,
Oure soulys brynnyng.
                    (pp. 18–19)

Two other rhetorical devices found almost always in later derivatives of the *Cur mundus militat* are a catalogue of the famous dead and the *ubi-sunt* motif. Often these two items are merged:

Dic ubi Salamon olim tam nobilis?
    vel Samson ubi est dux invincibilis?
    vel pulcher Absolon vultu mirabilis?
    vel dulcis Jonathas multum amabilis?
Quo Caesar abiit celsus imperio?
    vel Dives splendidus totus in prandio?
    dic ubi Tullius clarus eloquio?
    vel Aristoteles summus ingenio?
                    (Wright, pp. 147–48)

(Tusser again)

Tell where is *Salomon*, that once so noble was?
Or where now *Samson* is, in strength whome none
    could pas?
Or woorthie *Ionathas*, that prince so louely bold?
Or faier *Absolon*, so goodlie to behold?

Shew whither is *Cesar* gone, which conquered far
    and néere?
Or that rich famous *Carle*, so giuen to bellie chéere:
Shew where is *Tullie* now, for eloquence so fit?
Or *Aristoteles*, of such a pregnant wit?
                    (stanzas 4–5)

Other than fourteenth- and fifteenth-century translations of the putative Bernardine verses, earliest lyrics exhibiting features of the *Cur mundus militat* but probably not yet to be under-

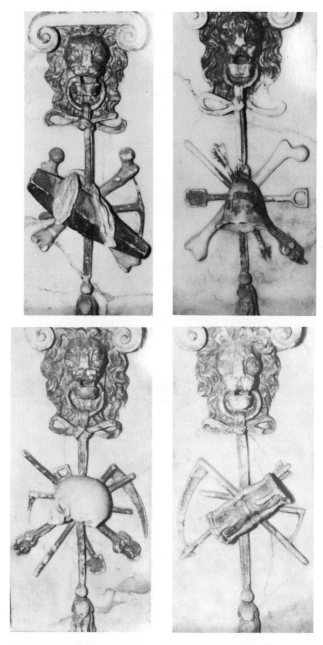

Fig. 38. *Memento-mori* iconography of death and implements of burial. (a–d) Funeral monument of Sir Anthony Mildmay (d. 1617), St. Leonard, Apethorpe, Northamptonshire.

Fig. 38. (*continued*). (e) Funerary wall monument, Grey-
friars Kirk, Edinburgh.

stood as *memento mori* are various pieces by John Lydgate.[5] "As A
Mydsomer Rose" combines a catalogue with *ubi-sunt* poignance
and concludes with an exhortation to the reader that he put his
reliance on Christ. The poem is devoid completely of the imagery
of corruption that seems the very epitome of the lyric we are at-

5. The famous passage in *Piers Plowman* (c. 1370–c. 1390) contains images and ideas suggestive of several of the lateral developments of

tempting here to define, but Lydgate's catalogue is instructive in itself. It borrows from St. Bernard's list, includes the nine worthies,[6] and throws in for measure other heroes of history and romance: Pyrrhus, Nebuchadnezzar, Sardanapalus, Chrysostom, Homer, Seneca, the Paladins ("Dozepeers"), and undifferentiated heroes of Troy, Colchis, Rome, Carthage, and Thebes, as well as a host of ten thousand unnamed knights and martyrs. In one of Lydgate's finest lyric moments, the poem closes with a mystical

---

memento-mori art: the *Vado mori*, the Triumph of Death, the Dance of Death, and, of course, the *Cur mundus militat*:

> Deeþ cam dryuynge after and al to duste passhed
> Kynges and knyghtes, kaysers and popes.
> Lered [ne] lewed he leet no man stonde,
> That he hitte euene, þat euere stired after.
> Manye a louely lady and [hir] lemmans knyʒtes
> Swowned and swelted for sorwe of [deþes] dyntes.
>
> (B-Text, Passus XX)

Piers Plowman, ed. George Kane and E. Talbot Donaldson (London, 1975), p. 665.

6. The catalogue in *Cur mundus militat* contains eight names: Solomon, Samson, Absalom, Jonathan, Caesar, Dives, Tully, and Aristotle. Of these only Caesar is one of the nine worthies. Dives is an ambiguous figure. Sandwiched between Caesar and Tully, Dives is intended probably as M. Licinius Crassus, whom antiquity surnamed Dives. Later writers, perhaps the author of *Cur mundus militat* himself, seem to have merged this third member of the first triumvirate with the unnamed rich man in St. Luke's parable. The Vulgate translated *rich man* as *dives* and thus was he named ever after. That both Crassus and the glutton of the parable were addicted to the table helps in the confusion: "vel Dives splendidus totus in prandio?" (Wright, p. 148). A *memento-mori* lyric in *The Paradise of Dainty Devices* (1576), under the oft-encountered title *Respice finem*, further muddies the waters by listing "Cresus." The poet (the verses are signed with the initials D. S.) has in mind Croesus, King of Lydia, apparent from the refrain of the poem: "The happy ende exceedeth all" (ed. Hyder Rollins, [Cambridge, Mass., 1927], p. 25). The burden is a paraphrase of the famous utterance given to Croesus by Solon.

transformation in which the transitory rose of summer becomes
the eternal savior:

> Ther bloody suffraunce was no somyr roose.
> It was the Roose of the bloody feeld,
>> Roose of *Iericho*, that greuh in Beedlem;
> The five Roosys portrayed in the sheeld,
>> Splayed in the baneer at Ierusalem.
> The sonne was clips and dirk in euery rem
> Whan Crist *Ihesu* five wellys lyst vncloose,
>> Toward Paradys, callyd the rede strem,
> Off whos five woundys prent in your hert a roose.[7]

In at least three other poems,[8] Lydgate combines a catalogue
with sentiments that evoke an *ubi-sunt* quality. "That Now Is Hay
Some-Tyme Was Grase" is the earliest poem to include women in
the catalogue. The men are the traditional nine worthies—Joshua,
David, Judas Maccabaeus (three Jews); Hector, Caesar, Alexander
(three pagans); Arthur, Charlemagne, Godfrey of Bouillon (three
Christians)—but the six women are from widely divergent sources:
Greek myth, Polyxena, Cressida, Helen; Roman epic, Dido; Old
Testament, Esther; and story, Griselda. Lydgate eschews graveyard

---

7. *The Minor Poems of John Lydgate*, Part 2, ed. Henry Noble Mac-
Cracken, EETS, vol. 192, original ser. (Oxford, 1934), p. 785, hereafter
cited in the text by page number. "As A Mydsomer Rose" provides in the
stanza quoted above another example of the rose equated with Christ
rather than with Mary. See chap. 3, p. 138 and the appertaining footnote,
number 19.

8. Still a fourth poem, not amongst the minor lyrics, is *The Assembly of the Gods*. A lengthy allegory, *The Assembly* contains an extended passage of seven rhyme-royal stanzas in which Atropos functions as the
death figure in a *memento-mori* set piece. An elaborate catalogue begins with the nine worthies but added are the following famous dead:
Nebuchadnezzar, Pharaoh, Jason, Hercules, Cosdras, Hannibal, Scipio,
Cyrus, and Achilles (ed. Oscar Lovell Triggs, EETS, vol. 64, extra ser.
[London, 1896], pp. 14–15).

imagery still but balances the transitory nature of this world's blessings with those of the next:

> Bydde folke not trust this worlde at all,
> Bydde theme remembre on þe cite
> Which is a-bove celestiall.
> > (*Minor Poems*, pp. 810–13)

"A Thoroughfare of Woe" includes but six of the nine worthies (dropping the Christian heroes) and three of St. Bernard's eight— Solomon, Absalom, and Samson. But in "Thoroughfare" Lydgate presents for the first time recent contemporaries, men whom he knew better than the ordinary commoner knows the great, men whose entire life spans were encompassed within his own: Henry V (1387–1422), Thomas, Duke of Clarence (1388–1421), Thomas Beaufort, Duke of Exeter (1375–1427), and Thomas Montacute, Earl of Salisbury (1388–1428). Following these specific persons, Lydgate launches into a general procession of the dead, looking backward toward Langland's "passhed / Kynges & knyghtes, kayseres and popes" and perhaps borrowing also from his own *Dance of Death* (*The Daunce of Machabree*), copied from the walls of Holy Innocents, probably in 1426:

> For deth ne sparith emperour ne kyng . . .
> > He castith downe princes from Fortunes
> > > wheele. . . .
>
> God sent aforn ful oft his officers,
> > To dukes, erles, barouns of estate,
> Sommoneth also by his mynisters
> > Surquidous people, pompous and elate,
> > Ageyns whos somons they dare make no debate,
> Obey his preceptis and may nat go ther fro,
> > To signifie to pope and to prelate,
> How this world is a thurghfare ful of woo.
> > > (*Minor Poems*, pp. 824–26)

Appendix

Interesting in its associations with the Dance of Death is this passage:

> Of his [God's] bedils the names to expresse,
>   And of his sergeauntis, as I can endite,
> To somowne he sendith langour and sikenesse,
>   And som with povert hym list to visite;
>   To iche estate so wele he can hym qwyte,
> Markyng his seruauntis with tokens where they goo.
>
> (p. 827)

Shakespeare uses both sergeant and beadle[9] in his own abbreviated Dances. Although the "fell sergeant" is not a representative of death in the traditional Dance, he is often one of those tapped by death. Lydgate, however, making the sergeant a servant of God and death in these lines, supplies for Shakespeare the famous image in *Hamlet*.

Lydgate's final effort in the genre we are describing, one which builds a bridge to the earliest practitioners of the archetypal poems of Skelton and Dunbar, is the Monk of Bury's "Timor Mortis Conturbat Me." In this poem, Lydgate adds to other patriarchs from the Old Testament the three Jews commonly found among the nine worthies. He again borrows Samson and Jonathan from the *Cur mundus militat*; and, for the second time, he includes a catalogue of women. Among the eight he garners from scripture, myth, and history, the two we meet most often in later *memento-mori* verses are Helen and Dido. Yet, even in this final lyric, where he employs a refrain from the Office of the Dead—Peccantē me quotidie & non penitētē timor mortis cōturbat me. Quia ī inferno nulla est redēptio: miserere mei deus & salua me[10]—not one worm,

9. See *Hamlet*, V.ii.338, *II Henry IV*, V.iv.1–28, and *Henry V*, IV.i.168–84. See my treatment, "The Dance-of-Death Motif in Shakespeare," *Papers on Language and Literature* 20 (1984): 15–38.

10. These lines are from the Responsio to Lectio VII in the *Vigilie mortuorum*. See *Portiforium seu Breviarum* [Sarum] (Paris, 1556), folio 70.

not one skull, not one fleshless bone is to be found, neither pickaxe nor spade. The closest he comes to later imagery is his picture of decrepitude: "crookyd age / Slak skyn, and many a wery boon" (p. 831). Thus it is Skelton who introduces to the English *memento-mori* lyric the horrors of the grave and inaugurates the full equivalent to St. Bernard's *Cur mundus militat.*

Transitional is Skelton's elegy "Of the Death of the Noble Prince, Kynge Edwarde the Fourth." General emphasis in this poem is on the transitory quality of life and grandeur. Very much in the tone of Lydgate's "mydsomyr roose," King Edward's grass has turned to hay, his life become a thoroughfare of woe. But in this elegy we have a touch of the corruption of the grave. The poem's refrain, "*Et, ecce, nunc in pulvere dormio!*" puts the body underground, and another line develops an image of moldering flesh (13). In this poem's catalogue—three figures from St. Bernard, one from the nine worthies—there seems a new insistence on horror that, later, expanded to the limits of black imagination, becomes a mainstay of sixteenth-century English *memento-mori* verse:

> Sainct Bernard . . .
> Seyth a man is but a sacke of stercorry,
>   And shall returne vnto wormis mete.
>   Why, what cam of Alexander the greate?
> Or els of stronge Sampson, who can tell?
>   Were not wormes ordeyned theyr flesh to frete?
> And of Salomon, that was of wyt the well?
> Absolon profferyd his heare for to sell,
>   Yet for al his bewte wormys ete him also.
>
>   (p. 4)

The body has so decayed that it is likened to excrement and is pictured thrice on its way through the guts of worms. In *Hamlet,* Shakespeare adds two intermediaries, and in the eternal cycle levels king with beggar, a glance at the procession of the dead that numbers all degrees, from pope to parish priest, from emperor to

Appendix

ploughman, familiar to us in another of the forms of *memento mori* that we call the Dance of Death:

> A man may fish with the worm that hath eat of a king, and eat of the fish that hath fed of that worm . . . to show . . . how a king may go a progress through the guts of a beggar.
>
> (IV.iii.27–32)

Skelton employs the *ubi-sunt* motif in the catalogue but also evokes the snows of yesteryear as Edward remembers glory and joy faded, now that he sleeps in dust:

> Where is now my conquest and victory?
>   Where is my riches and my royal aray?
> Wher be my coursers and my horses hye?
>   Where is my myrth, my solas, and my play?
>
> (p. 4)

In "Vppon a deedmans hed" the catalogue disappears and, with it, the *ubi sunt*. Perhaps we have an entirely different genre, but I think rather that "deedmans hed" is merely a divergent but correlative form. The imagery of the grave intensifies, centering on the skull, the chief object in *memento-mori* art, whether lyric or painting or sculpture. The skull is present in Skelton's "argument," for surely we are to assume that the "hed" sent him by the honorable "jentyllwoman" no longer has flesh upon it. Clearly, it serves well its purpose as reminder, as *memento*:

> Youre vgly tokyn
> My mynd hath brokyn
> From worldly lust; . . .
> We ar but dust,
> And dy we must.
>   It is generall
> To be mortall: . . .

No man may hym hyde
From Deth holow eyed.

       (p. 18)

Other quintessential ingredients—the speaker's intention to reform and the exhortation to the reader—are deftly inserted. Penitence and regeneration are clear in the lines cited; the French tag with which the poem concludes addresses the reader (although remembering that our poet is Skelton, we might wonder if he is not getting back somewhat at the lady by directing the tag to her): "*Myrres vous y*" (p. 20).

    Lord Vaux's poem illustrates the exhortation more forcefully. "I Lothe that I did loue," three stanzas of which are garbled by Shakespeare's gravedigger as he goes about his grim duties, rather harangues the reader:

> And ye that bide behinde,
> Haue ye none other trust:
> As ye of claye were cast by kinde,
> So shall ye waste to dust.[11]

Reaffirmation of faith takes various forms. "Vppon a deedmans hed" turns to the Son:

> To whom, then, shall we sew,
> For to haue rescew,
> But to swete Jesu?
>
>   (p. 19)

The elegy on Edward IV turns to the Father:

> *In manus tuas, Domine,* my spirite vp I yelde,
> Humbly beseching thé, God, of thy grace!
>
>   (p. 5)

11. *Tottel's Miscellany (1557–1587)*, ed. Hyder E. Rollins, 2 vols. (Cambridge, Mass., 1928), 1:166.

The grisly images that abound in "Vppon a deedmans hed" are sampled on pp. 314–15 above.

Skelton's contemporary, the Scots poet William Dunbar, perhaps takes his hint from Lydgate when, instead of the traditional catalogue of heroes of antiquity, he relies upon local and late poets:

> He has done petuously devour
> The noble Chaucer of makaris flour,
> The monk of Bery, and Gower, all thre:
> *Timor mortis conturbat me.*[12]

This trio is followed by the enumeration of twenty-one additional Scots poets of varying degrees of fame and obscurity. The catalogue, wherever it is found and however presented, serves always the same purpose: no hero so powerful, no thinker so wise, no creature so beautiful can defeat death. But Dunbar has also a *memento-mori* lyric with a traditional catalogue in which first line (*Memento homo quod cinis es*) and refrain (*Quod tu in cinerem revertis*) are from the Sarum missal Mass for Ash Wednesday. Achilles and Hercules are two new figures in the list.[13]

12. *The Poems of William Dunbar*, ed. James Kinsley (Oxford, 1979), p. 179. The earliest poem in English carrying this Latin refrain may or may not be the Lydgate piece cited above. Dating also from the fifteenth century is a carol with the same burden. Richard Leighton Greene gives the entire text in *The Early English Carols* (Oxford, 1935), p. 248. He prints also a second fifteenth-century carol in which the refrain is rendered in the following English: "The dred off deth do troble me" (p. 249). A bilingual Latin-English carol of the sixteenth century, reminiscent of macaronic verses, carries the refrain "Terribilis mors conturbat me" (pp. 249–50). Both the *timor-mortis* poem and the *terribilis mortis* were apparently popular still in mid-sixteenth century since versions occur in *Richard Hill's Common-Place Book*, ed. Roman Dyboski, EETS, vol. 101, extra ser. (London, 1907), pp. 3, 36.

13. Dunbar, *Poems*, pp. 176–77. *Richard Hill's Common-Place Book* contains several additional lyrics of considerable *memento-mori* interest. Based clearly on the Ash Wednesday refrain is the lyric "Erth owt of erth" (pp. 90–92), a poem found in numerous variations in other collections

Poets contemporary with Shakespeare imitate in their catalogues either the traditional Skelton or the imaginative Dunbar,

———

similar to Hill's. Interesting in this piece is an oblique reference to the
Dance of Death. Following a traditional listing of the nine worthies is
"William Conquerowr" and "Kyng Harry þe first," all obviously members
of a procession of the dead that reminds the anonymous author of the
famous frescoes at St. Paul's, where, according to John Stow (*A Survay of
London* [London, 1598], p. 264), "metres or poesie of this daunce, were
translated out of French into English, by John Lidgate, the Monke of
Bery, & with yᵉ picture of Death, leading all estates painted about the
Cloyster":

> & yf ye lyst of þe trewth to se a playn fugure,
> Go to seynt Powlis, & see þer the portratowr.
>   (Dyboski, p. 91)

In addition to "Erth owt of erth" is a four-stanza lyric worth reproducing here in light of my thesis concerning *As You Like It* (see chapter 8, pp. 305–7). Combined are a treatment of Four Ages of Man and a
conventional *memento-mori* finale, showing once again that decrepitude is
not the end of the story:

> In XXᵗⁱ yere of age, remembre we euerychon,
> þat deth will not be strange, to taste vs by on & on,
> With siknes grevous, which makith man to grone,
> Deth biddith beware, þis day a man, to-morow non.
>
> In XL yere of age, whan man is stowt & stronge,
> Trow ye þat deth dare stryk hym or do hym any wrong?
> Yes, for-soth, with worldly deth he vill not spare among,
> & seyth: "Man, beware! þou shalt not tary long."
>
> In LX yere of age, then tyme is cum to thynk—
> How he will cum to þe hows, & sit on þe bynke,
> Comaundyng man to stowpe toward þe pittis brynk;
> Than farewell, worldis joy, whan deth shall bid a man
>   drynk.
>
> The last age of mankynd is called 'decrepitus,'
> When man lakkith reason, than deth biddeth hym thus:
> Owt of þis world his lyf to pas with mercy of Jhesus;
> Deth strykith with sword / & seyth: "Man! it shal be thus."
>   (Dyboski, p. 93)

but all conclude similarly. Robert Southwell, the Jesuit priest, although but a few years older than Shakespeare, is completely medieval in his materials. His list has no surprises—Solomon, Samson, Alexander, Caesar—and its members provide the expected example:

> If none can scape deaths dreadfull dart,
>   If rich and poore his becke obey,
> If strong, if wise, if all do smart,
>   Then I to scape shall have no way.[14]

Thomas Nashe, a few years younger than Shakespeare, reduces his catalogue to one bright lady, Helen, and one pagan strongman, Hector. Other traditional types are represented generically as are two new figures, the physician and the artist:

> Rich men, trust not in wealth . . .
> Phisick himselfe must fade.
> All things to end are made. . . .
>
> Beauty is but a flowre,
> Which wrinckles will deuoure,
> Brightnesse falls from the ayre,
> Queenes haue died yong and faire,
> Dust hath closde *Helens* eye. . . .
>
> Strength stoopes vnto the graue,
> Wormes feed on *Hector* braue. . . .
>
> Wit with his wantonnesse
> Tasteth deaths bitternesse:
> Hels executioner
> Hath no eares for to heare
> What vaine art can reply.[15]

14. *The Poems of Robert Southwell, S.J.*, ed. J. H. McDonald and Nancy P. Brown (Oxford, 1967), p. 74. The editors maintain (pp. lxxxi–lxxxii) that Southwell is not the author of the poem.

15. *The Works of Thomas Nashe*, ed. R. B. McKerrow, repr. with supplementary notes by F. P. Wilson (Oxford, 1958), 3:282–84, hereafter

Nashe's "Song" is perhaps the most original poem—probably the finest also—in the entire range of medieval or Renaissance *memento-mori* poetry. Cast in the form of a litany, submitting to most of the requirements of a genre by Nashe's time some two hundred years old, heavily indebted for language and idea to a hack piece in *The Gorgeous Gallery of Gallant Inventions*, somehow Nashe's "Song" is the freshest of all its type. Not even placing it here in a long procession of its sister pieces can stale its magnificence:

> Haste therefore eche degree,
> To welcome destiny:
> Heauen is our heritage,
> Earth but a players stage,
> Mount we vnto the sky.
> I am sick, I must dye:
> > Lord, haue mercy on vs.
> > > (III, 283–84)

The *Cur mundus militat* itself continues to be copied in commonplace books and printed in miscellanies throughout the sixteenth century, thus remaining available to Shakespeare in numerous good and bad Latin redactions as well as in a variety of translations. Richard Hill copied an eleven-stanza Latin version into his commonplace book sometime before 1536,[16] and an anonymous poet, signing himself "My Lucke is losse,"[17] supplied an eight-stanza version to *The Paradise of Dainty Devices* as the initial poem in

---

cited in the text by page number. I am not aware that the similarities between Nashe's poem and the untitled anonymous lyric in *The Gorgeous Gallery of Gallant Inventions* (1578) have been noticed. The threefold Crassus-Croesus-Dives confusion recorded in footnote 6 above is fully present in the *Gallery* poem. The text is edited by Hyder E. Rollins (Cambridge, Mass., 1926), pp. 96–98.

16. Hill, pp. 93–94. See also footnotes 12 and 13 above.

17. Both George Gascoigne and Barnabe Riche have been suggested as authors.

the edition of 1576. His accompanying translation suffers from all the excesses of the period—extreme wordiness to pad out an alexandrine line and studious use of the devices of rhetoric—an overwhelming alliteration—to show that he has read his Quintilian. One year later, with admirable brevity and often happy phrasing, is the fine translation of Thomas Tusser, much of which is given in the early pages of this appendix. His rendering of the Dives line is among his best:

> Shew whither is *Cesar* gone, which conquered far
> and néere?
> Or that rich famous *Carle*, so giuen to bellie chéere?
> (stanza 5)

Independent of the *Cur mundus militat*, and flourishing still in the decade of the 1570s is the *memento-mori* lyric that developed out of Skelton's "Vppon a deedmans hed"—the lyric without catalogue or *ubi-sunt* motif. Representative are two pieces by George Gascoigne.[18] Clearly companion poems, both are written in fourteeners with midline rime, although the first is broken typographically into the familiar ballad stanza. "Gascoignes good morrow" and "Gascoygnes good night" represent this reprobate among poets as both waking and retiring with nothing but thoughts of his latter end. The "good morrow" likens the poet's bed to his grave and his nightgown to mold. His sleep is like "dreadfull death" (23–24). At this point—quite uncharacteristically for the genre—Gascoigne's poem turns upbeat. Actual awakening is compared to judgment day, but a happy judgment insofar that Gascoigne, heeding the warning of all *memento-mori* art, intends to keep his maker's visage constantly before him:

> Yet as this deadly night did laste,
> But for a little space,

18. Quotations from the works of Gascoigne are from *The Complete Works of George Gascoigne*, ed. John W. Cunliffe, 2 vols. (Cambridge, Eng., 1907, 1910), cited hereafter in the text by page number.

And heavenly daye nowe night is past,
Doth shewe his pleasaunt face:
So must we hope to see Gods face,
At last in heaven on hie. . . .

The daye is like the daye of doome,[19]
The sunne, the Sonne of man,
The skyes the heavens, the earth the tombe
Wherein we rest till than.

(I, 56)

"Gascoygnes good night," after a typically rambling eighteen-line introduction, becomes standard *memento-mori* fare, with an occasional spot of individuality in finding unlikely reminders:

The stretching armes, ye yauning breath, which I to
bedward use,

19. In view of the total orientation of this book, it seems appropriate to point out here that Gascoigne is also the author of a prose tract entitled *The Droomme of Doomes day* (1576). This lengthy document (240 pp. in its modern edition), eminently available to Shakespeare, incorporates many of the eschatological materials that we have observed in the spiritual encyclopedias of the Middle Ages (see introduction, pp. 3–8). For the full text, see Cunliffe, 2: 209–449. Christ's coming in judgment (p. 261) is followed by a prose *memento mori* that dwells with great horror on the decay of the flesh (p. 261). The *memento mori* is followed by an application of the parable of Dives and Lazarus (p. 263) and then a description of the torments of the damned (pp. 265–69). Again Dives and Lazarus are invoked (p. 266). Somewhat out of order, doomsday is described after the torments of the damned (pp. 269–71). The apocalyptic return of Elijah and Enoch is added (pp. 270–71), as well as the arrival of Antichrist along with other false prophets (p. 270). Amidst these events is scattered an imperfect version of the fifteen signs that precede doomsday (pp. 270–71). In a section called "The Needles Eye," Gascoigne admonishes his reader to constant meditation on the four last things in order to develop a *contemptu mundi*, beneficial if not absolutely necessary for the Christian who hopes for beatitude (pp. 388–96).

Are patternes of the pangs of death, when life will
    me refuse:
And of my bed eche sundrye part in shaddowes doth
    resemble,
The sūdry shapes of deth, whose dart shal make my
    flesh to trēble.
My bed it selfe is like the grave, my sheetes the
    winding sheete,
My clothes the mould which I must have, to cover
    me most meete:
The hungry fleas which friske so freshe, to wormes I
    can cōpare,
Which greedily shall gnaw my fleshe, & leave the
    bones ful bare:
The waking Cock that early crowes to weare the
    night awaye,
Puts in my minde the trumpe that blowes before the
    latter day.

(I, 58–59)

Although the *memento-mori* lyric will be with us always,[20] in a sense we see the dilution of the genre setting in about this same time, mostly in those pieces entitled generally "Respice finem." The stark imagery of pieces like Skelton's, Vaux's, Gascoigne's, and Southwell's has been muted and is consequently less terrifying. The effect created goes little further than the title itself, and in the case of the representative poem reproduced below, all is vitiated still further by the Latin tag—"Mors omnibus communis"—which serves this poem exactly in that way Claudius hopes it will influence Hamlet: "Thou know'st 'tis common, all that lives must die, / Passing through nature to eternity" (I.ii.72–73). When a reader finishes Proctor's poem, he may well respond as Gertrude, "Why seems it so particular with thee?" (75):

20. Book I of Evelyn Waugh's *Brideshead Revisited* (Boston, 1945) is entitled "Et In Arcadia Ego," and Muriel Spark's second novel carries for its title the phrase itself, *Memento Mori* (Philadelphia, 1958).

> Lo here the state of euery mortall wight,
> See here, the fine, of all their gallant ioyes:
> Beholde their pompe, their beauty and delight,
> Whereof they vaunt, as safe from all annoyes:
> To earth the stout, the prowd, the ritch shall yeeld,
> The weake, the meeke, the poore, shall shrowded lye
> In dampish mould, the stout with Speare and Sheeld
> Cannot defend, [*sic*] himselfe when hee shal dye.
>
> . . . .
>
> Your world is vayne, no trust in earth you finde,
> Your valyaunst prime, is but a brytle glasse:
> Your pleasures vade, your thoughts a puffe of winde,
> Your auncient yeres, are but a withered grasse.
>   Mors omnibus communis.[21]

Dromio of Ephesus seems to capture the pious platitudes with exactly the right disdain: "Mistress, 'respice finem,' respect your end; or rather, the prophecy like the parrot, 'beware the rope's end'" (*Comedy of Errors*, IV.iv.41–43).

Out of this entire tradition, Shakespeare fashioned the gravedigger scene in *Hamlet*. In other plays he called often upon various components of the *memento-mori* tradition as I trust this entire book witnesses. But it is upon *Hamlet*, V.i. that I shall focus to illustrate how Shakespeare translates a convention generally lyric into a dramatic one. As Hamlet first approaches the burial grounds where Ophelia is to be interred, he comes, in company with Horatio, upon a gravedigger delivering himself of some halting verses from Thomas Lord Vaux's "I Lothe that I did loue":

> "In youth, when I did love, did love,
>   Me thought it was very sweet,
> To contract—O—the time for—a—my behove,
>   O, methought there—a—was nothing—a—meet."
>
> . . . .
>
> "But age, with his stealing steps,
>   Hath claw'd me in his clutch,

21. *Gorgeous Gallery*, p. 99.

And hath shipped me into the land,
  As if I had never been such."

(61–64, 71–74)

At this point the gravedigger throws a skull up out of the pit he digs. After Hamlet comments to Horatio upon the scene they witness, the gravedigger concludes his vocal efforts with a third stanza:

"A pick-axe, and a spade, a spade,
  For and a shrouding sheet;
O, a pit of clay for to be made
  For such a guest is meet."

(94–97)

The gravedigger throws a second skull upon the ground and Hamlet comments further. To this point, few of the *memento-mori* materials presented take us further than the type-poem represented best by Skelton's "Vppon a deedmans hed." From the gravedigger's three stanzas we get a determination to prepare for death, a recognition that death is not far away, and some relatively mild graveyard imagery—pick, spade, winding sheet, and hollowed-out grave. But through action on stage and the running commentary that Hamlet provides, other ingredients of the genre are provided. Before he is finished, the gravedigger presents four skulls for us to meditate upon. Three are quite dramatically brought to our attention: "How the knave jowls it to the ground" (76). The fourth is forever famous and thus, of course, presented even more dramatically than the others: "Alas, poor Yorick! I knew him, Horatio" (183–84; fig. 39). Hamlet himself draws the most fearsome images: "That skull had a tongue in it, and could sing once . . . and now my Lady Worm's, chapless, and knock'd about the mazzard with a sexton's spade. Here's fine [note paradoxical pun] revolution, an we had the trick to see't. Did these bones cost no more the breeding, but to play at loggats with them?" (75–92).

Further corruption of the body is handled with grim humor—perhaps suggested to Shakespeare by the grinning jester that Holbein makes of his jigging skeleton in the most famous of all dance-of-death treatments:

333

Fig. 39. Fool, Dance-of-Death alphabet. Designs, Hans Holbein. Execution, Hans Lützelburger. Basle, ca. 1526.

HAMLET

How long will a man lie i' th' earth ere he rot?

FIRST CLOWN

Faith, if 'a be not rotten before 'a dies—as we have many pocky corses now-a-days, that will scarce hold the laying in—'a will last you some eight year or nine year. A tanner will last you nine year.

HAMLET

Why he more than another?

FIRST CLOWN

Why, sir, his hide is so tann'd with his trade that 'a will keep out water a great while, and your water is a sore decayer of your whoreson dead body.

(163–72)

Appendix

No lyric poet presents so detailed a picture of decay, and yet Shakespeare is not finished. The skull, evoked originally to compel meditation upon death, does its job well: "how abhorr'd in my imagination it is! My gorge rises at it. . . . Now get you to my lady's chamber, and tell her, let her paint an inch thick, to this favor she must come; make her laugh at that" (186–94; fig. 40).[22]

22. "Death and the Lady" is a distinct genre although elements from such a composition become a part of the traditional Dance of Death (see, for example, Holbein's panel which some captions identify as "The Nun"). But paintings such as Hans Baldung Grien's "Death and the Woman" (Charles D. Cuttler, *Northern Painting* [New York, 1968], p. 389) are clearly divorced from the seriatic nature of the dance. Dozens of wood-blocks take a common form which places the maiden before her mirror that reflects back to her a grinning skull (see fig. 40 for a variation on this composition). The following fifteenth-century poem shows a relationship both to the painter-illustrator composition and to Shakespeare's dramatic treatment quoted above:

Cest le myrroure pur lez Iofenes Dames a regardir
aud maytyne pur lour testes bealment adressere.

Maist thou now be glade, with all thi fresshe aray,
One me to loke that wyll dystene thi face.
Rew one thy-self and all thi synne vprace!
Sone shalte þu flytte and seche anoþer place,
Shorte is thy sesoun here, thogh thou go gay.

O maset wriche, I marke the with my mace.
Lyfte vp thy ieye, be-holde now, and assay!
Yche loke one me aught to put þe in affray;
I wyll not spare the, for thou arte my pray.
Take hede, and turne fro synne while þu hast space.

O þoughte, welthe heele to this, thaught ȝe say nay.
My tyme muste nedis comme as I manace;
Be lenghte one lyfe may lepe oute of my lace.
I smyte, I sle, I woll graunte no mane grace.
A-ryse! a-wake! amend here while thou may.

*Religious Lyrics of the XV*th *Century*, ed. Carleton Brown (Oxford, 1939), p. 241.

Fig. 40. "To this favor she must come." *Hore presentes ad vsvm Sarvm.* Press of Philippe Pigouchet, Paris, 1502.

For catalogue and *ubi-sunt* motif Shakespeare has gone to someone other than Vaux for his model:

HAMLET   Dost thou think Alexander look'd o' this
          fashion i' th' earth?
HORATIO   E'en so.

336

HAMLET   And smelt so? Pah! [*Puts down the skull.*]
HORATIO   E'en so, my lord.
HAMLET   To what base uses we may return, Horatio!
          Why may not imagination trace the noble
          dust of Alexander, till 'a find it stopping a
          bunghole?

(197–204)

If this were to consider too curiously, it does not stop Hamlet from a similar view of the Roman emperor:

Imperious Caesar, dead and turn'd to clay,
Might stop a hole to keep the wind away.
O, that that earth which kept the world in awe
Should patch a wall t' expel the winter's flaw!

(213–16)

For Caesar, Shakespeare might have gone to St. Bernard or any poet deriving from the Doctor; he might have gone to any poet citing the nine worthies for his catalogue; if so, there he would have found Alexander as well. But Shakespeare has a type list also, the sort of thing he would see as far back as Langland, as recent as Thomas Nashe. Of course, Shakespeare's list is his own. The playwright marshals hypothetical politician, courtier, and lawyer, as well as the known wit, Yorick. The politician "would circumvent God, might [he] not" (79–80)? But he has not. The courtier's courtesy has got him by with all lords but one, that lord who in Skelton's phrase is Lord of all. The lawyer cannot invoke the law against death, cannot order death to cease and desist in battery upon his body. And the wit cannot outgrin death, who laughs not with the jester Yorick, but at him now, and ironically with his own grinning skull. All in all, the larger lesson is spelled out for anyone who would put his trust in legal writs to keep off death: "They are sheeps and calves which seek out assurance in that" (116–17).

Shakespeare employs the *ubi-sunt* motif in the traditional manner; for the lawyer,

Where be his quiddities now, his quillities, his cases,
his tenures, and his tricks?

(99–100)

For the jester, the wit,

Where be your gibes now? Your gambols, your songs,
your flashes of merriment that were wont to set the
table on a roar?

(188–90)

All ingredients of the *memento-mori* lyric are then to be found
in V.i. of Shakespeare's *Hamlet* except perhaps the overriding purpose for the inclusion of such a scene, all but the overriding fear of
death unprepared for, of reliance upon the Lord as the only rescue from eternal death, all but the decision to give over evil ways in
order to inherit everlasting life. But for these very reasons I envisage the entire play as, among other things, an extended *memento-
mori* statement. Such a view helps us to understand one of the
main themes of the play and to deal with what has always been one
of the main problems in *Hamlet*.

An important thesis of the play is the response of a good
and virtuous man to an injunction to commit what appears to be
an evil act. Hamlet knows that private revenge is evil; his need to
find some way to kill Claudius without endangering his own soul
creates his delays, the chief problem of the drama. Hamlet is not a
sinner who must reform his life in preparation for death and in
hope for salvation; Hamlet is a good man who stands, except
for the daily venial sins, daily removed by penance, in a state of
grace—as much as any mortal can be in grace. When his father
dies, he wishes to die himself. He has no fear of death, then.
Where is the *timor mortis* required in the genre? For Hamlet, as is
implicit in this monitory verse, fear is fear of damnation, of that
second death, not mere mortality. Although Hamlet covets death, it
may not come through suicide. The "Everlasting" has "fix'd / His
canon 'gainst self-slaughter" (I.ii.131–32). When the ghost wafts

him to ground more removed and the others would prevent his going, Hamlet expresses disdain for his life but also acknowledges concern for his soul:

> I do not set my life at a pin's fee,
> And for my soul, what can it do to that,
> Being a thing immortal as itself?
> (I.iv.65–67)

All his acts, from this opening consideration until finally he rids the kingdom of its canker, are submitted to the scrutiny of sinless action. Hamlet cannot kill the false king until he knows himself fully to be the true king. He executes then—not murders—as flaming minister, as true king, not as scourge, not as private person in an act of private revenge. As true king, Hamlet must protect the common weal, must expunge all corruption that blights it. Hamlet is not damnable if he kills Claudius; contrariwise, he is damnable if he fails to act:

> is 't not to be damn'd
> To let this canker of our nature come
> In further evil?
> (V.ii.68–70)

The readiness is all; and Hamlet, by V.ii., is ready. In terms of the *memento-mori* poem, he will be in grace when he dies, though he commits what appears an evil act. He sees it finally not as evil but as required for the good of all, himself included; for he cannot remain in grace if he refrains from action.

Hamlet meets the *memento-mori* requirement of turning to God everywhere through the play. He must, in all his best, obey Gertrude because that is so commanded. He turns to "Angels and ministers of grace" (I.iv.39) for defense against what he must believe is an evil ghost. He repents sincerely for the rash and sinful murder of Polonius and "will answer well / The death [he] gave him" (III.iv.183–84). But the crucial utterance that asserts Hamlet's reliance upon his God is that same utterance in which he indicates clearly that he stands serene in grace:

> . . . we defy augury. There is special providence in the fall of a sparrow. If it be now, 'tis not to come; if it be not to come, it will be now; if it be not now, yet it will come. The readiness is all.
>
> (V.ii.217–220)

All conditions of the *memento-mori* poem are met, but they are met throughout the entire play, not solely in V.i. To reinforce his concept of the total play as a *memento-mori* statement, Shakespeare employs the devices of the lyric widely. The horror of the grave and hell are initiated in the first act. Apart from the general terror of the sentinels, of Marcellus and even of Horatio, Hamlet's description of the ghost is less that of some insubstantial essence than it is of a Lazarus, stinking and rotting from the tomb:

> . . . tell
> Why thy canoniz'd bones, hersed in death,
> Have burst their cerements; why the sepulcher
> Wherein we saw thee quietly interr'd
> Hath op'd his ponderous and marble jaws
> To cast thee up again. What may this mean,
> That thou, dead corse, again in complete steel
> Revisits thus the glimpses of the moon,
> Making night hideous, and we fools of nature
> So horridly to shake our disposition
> With thoughts beyond the reaches of our souls?
> (I.iv.46–56)

The ghost itself "could a tale unfold whose lightest word / Would harrow Hamlet's soul" (I.v.16–17).

All in all the first five scenes are riddled through with visions and statements from a grim other world that starts at the grave and moves with agony through judgment, punishment, fear, and anguish. Together with the fifth act, much of the entire first act wraps an envelope of *memento-mori* imagery, diction, and theme about the play. All scenes in between may be viewed, in part, in terms of Hamlet's concern for "readiness," in terms of an eschatological fear of going to death unprepared.

Perhaps in no other play has Shakespeare so thoroughly employed the *memento-mori* motif; yet scarcely a play in the rest of the canon lacks one element of the genre or another. The reading of any play of Shakespeare's, uncognizant of this dark element within, must assuredly suffer somewhat in understanding.

Index

Abraham, 156 and n.38, 157, 284
  and n.36, 287
"Abyde, gud men, & hald yhour
  pays," 160
Ages of man, 5, 306; four ages,
  326n.13; seven ages, 296, 297,
  305, 306; three ages, 306; twelve
  ages, 306
Anatomie of Abuses, 232
Anderson, Mary D., 9–10
Antichrist, 4, 7, 180
Apocalypse, 34, 37–38, 128, 129,
  152, 154, 155, 162, 178, 185, 192,
  284. *See also* Doomsday; Fifteen
  signs; Judgment day; Revelation
Apple-john, 276–77, 279
Arcadia, 236, 290–91, 293, 294,
  295, 298, 300, 301, 302, 303, 304.
  See also Eden; *Et in Arcadia Ego*;
  Paradise
Ars moriendi, 4, 5, 7, 202
Art of good lywyng & good deying, 5,
  29n.23
Arthur's bosom, 270, 274, 281, 287.
  See also Abraham
"As a Mydsomer Rose," 317–19, 322

As You Like It (excluding chap. on *As
  You Like It*), 236

Barber, C. L., 232, 234, 236
Bartholomaeus Anglicus, 5
Batman vppon Bartholome, 148n.28,
  306–7
Beaufort, Thomas, Duke of
  Exeter, 320
Bede, 178. *See also* Fifteen signs
Beggar and the rich man, 4. *See also*
  Dives and Lazarus
Bethell, S. L., 79, 85, 86
*Booke of Christian Praiers, A. See
  Queen Elizabeth Prayer Book*
Book of Common Prayer, The, 52,
  171, 237, 276
Bradley, A. C., 85, 86, 113
Brooke, Arthur, 207, 211, 224

Casanatensis manuscript, 5, 7, 8
Catalogue (of the famous dead),
  315–29, 336–37. *See also*
  memento mori
Caxton, William, 5, 9, 202
Celestine V, Pope, 115, 117

342

Chancel arch. *See* Stratford Guildhall Chapel

Chester cycle, 36, 180; play, 184, 185, 192; *Prophets and Antichrist, The,* 36, 180; XXII[d] play, 180

Chew, Samuel, 306, 307

Choice of emblemes, A, 308

Christ, 83, 84, 85, 88, 95, 96, 97, 108 and n.34, 110, 129, 138 and n.18, 147, 148–50, 151, 152, 154, 160, 162, 165, 178, 180, 184, 189, 192, 201, 217, 223, 224, 256 and n.5, 257–58, 284; Christ/angel, 91, 102, 106; Christ figure, 88, 96, 147, 256 n.5; Christ-God, 166; Christ-iconography, 143; Christ-like, 166, 257, 263 n.18; Christ ministrant, 152; Christological, 160; Christ triumphant, 152, 154. *See also* Comforter; God; Jesus; King of Kings; Savior; Son of Man

Christian Prayers and Meditations in English, French, Italian, Spanish, Greke, and Latine. See Queen Elizabeth Prayer Book

Chronicles, I, 167

Coleridge, Samuel Taylor, 193, 194

Colossians, 263–64, 265

Comedy of Errors, The, 271 and n.27, 332

Comforter, the, 147–48, 152. *See also* Christ; God; Jesus; King of Kings; Savior; Son of Man

Commandment, 48, 49, 50. *See also* Ten Commandments

Confessio Amantis, 10, 11

confiteor, 55, 58

Corinthians, I, 152, 154, 264–65, 268 and n.23

Council of Nicea, 239

Council of Trent, 171

Coursen, Herbert R., Jr., 160, 162

craft to liue well and to die well, The, 7, 36, 129, 180

Cur mundus militat, 311–13, 315, 321, 322, 328, 329

Curry, W. C., 176

Cursor Mundi, 178

Cymbeline, 247

Daemonologie, 20 n.11, 26–27, 176

Dance of Death, 4, 5, 7, 8, 10, 271 n.27, 320, 321, 323, 325 n.13, 333

Danse Macabre des Femmes, La, 7

Danse Macabre des Hommes, La, 7

Dante, 14, 22, 32, 78, 79, 115, 163, 165, 167–70, 176, 195, 196 n.36, 198, 200 and n.42, 204, 259

Daunce of Machabree, The, 10, 320

Day, John, 8, 123 n.7, 180

Deguilleville, Guillaume, 11

Despair, 112, 122–25, 146, 148, 152; *desperatio,* 123, 221. *See also Ira;* Patience; *Psychomachia;* Vices and virtues

Discouerie of Witchcraft, A, 20 n.11

Dives and Lazarus, 156 and n.39, 157, 274, 281, 283–84, 287, 318 n.6, 330 n.19. *See also* Abraham; Beggar and the rich man

Divine Comedy, The, 79, 163

Donne, John, 1, 80

Doomsday, 29 n.23, 34, 36, 37, 38 n.34, 187, 190, 193, 201, 206 n.1, 213, 223, 330 n.19; general doom, 212; great doom, 186. *See also* Apocalypse; Fifteen signs; Judgment day; Revelation

Dunbar, William, 11, 321, 325, 326

Duty, 19, 45, 48, 49, 51, 58, 59, 68, 89. *See also* Love

"Ecce Homo," 161

Eden, 92, 289, 290, 294, 295, 301, 302. *See also* Arcadia; Paradise

Edward the Confessor, 201

Edward IV, 322–23

Eliot, T. S., 266–67

Ephesians, 255, 256, 258, 260 n.16, 261, 263, 265

Epithalamion, 238, 239, 253 n.20

Eschatology, 3, 8 n.4, 9, 13, 15, 38, 44, 48, 69, 78, 105, 108, 125, 156,

Eschatology (*continued*)
176, 208, 211, 217, 251, 279, 330n.19, 341. *See also* Four last things; Last things
Et in Arcadia Ego, 236, 291–94, 297, 300–301, 303, 307. *See also* Arcadia; Eden; Paradise
Eworth, Hans, 227
"Exhortation de bien vivre & bien mourir," 7

Faerie Queene, The, 79–80
False appearances, 16–17, 89, 91, 100, 125, 145; disguise, 39; false-covering, 170; false king, 16, 39, 44, 47, 339; falseness, 47; false-seeming, 16; false witness, 49; seeming, 90. *See also* Identification
Faustus, 3, 78. *See also* Marlowe
Fifteen signs, 5, 7, 36, 178, 180, 184–86, 190, 192, 330n.19; "Fiffteen Toknys Aforn the Doom, The," 36, 180; fifteen tokens preceding judgment day, 7; "Les quinze signes," 7; *Signa quindecim . . .*, 180; signs that precede doomsday, 4–5; signs that precede judgment day, 8; "xv syngys or toknys that shal cum befor the iugement general of god, The," 7; xv tokens, 192. *See also* Apocalypse; Doomsday; Judgment day; Revelation
Four last things, 77, 270. *See also* Eschatology; Last things
Four Last Things, 11
Friar Alberigo, 32, 163, 168, 170

Gascoigne, George, 329, 331
"Gascoignes good morrow," 329–30
"Gascoygnes good night," 329, 330–31
Glutton, 284, 287
Gluttony, 29 and n.22, 260
God, 166, 207, 208, 227, 231, 251, 281; Godhead, 105, 155, 166; Godlike, 251. *See also* Christ; Comforter; Jesus; King of Kings; Savior; Son of Man
Golden Age, 290, 294, 295
Gorgeous Gallery of Gallant Inventions, The, 327n.15, 328
Gospel of St. John, 150, 152, 161, 217
Gospel of St. Luke, 83, 84, 137, 155, 156, 157, 283
Gospel of St. Mark, 83, 95, 151
Gospel of St. Matthew, 38, 118, 122 and n.6, 129, 138, 148, 149, 184, 187, 190, 217, 219, 274, 306n.23
Gothic cathedral portals, 156, 157. *See also* Judgment-day portals; Judgment porch
Gower, John, 10, 11
grant danse macabree des hōmes & des femmes, La, 7
Greene, Graham, 83
Gregorian calendar, 239
Gregory XIII, Pope, 239
Guercino, Giovanni, 291, 292, 293, 301, 303, 304. *See also Et in Arcadia Ego*

Hamlet (excluding chap. on *Hamlet*), 82, 85, 86, 120, 140, 141, 173, 197, 205, 206, 207, 219, 231, 250, 257, 272, 332–41
Hankins, John, 28 and n.21
Hebrews, Epistle to the, 257
Henry V, 320
Hero and Leander, 301
Herrad of Landsburg, Abbess of Hohenburg, 4, 5, 284
Hill, Richard, 328
Hoccleve, Thomas, 10, 11
Holbein, Hans, 333
Holinshed, 169
Holkham Bible Picture Book, 4, 178
"Hollow Men, The," 266–67
Holy Innocents, 4, 10, 320
Holy Trinity, Stratford, 9
Homilie agaynst disobedience and wylful rebellion, 118n.2
Hopkins, Gerard Manley, 83

Horn, 250. *See also* Trumpet
Hortus Deliciarum, 5, 7, 284

Identification, 17, 19, 125, 140–48,
154. *See also* False appearances
Idolatry, 207, 212, 217
"I Lothe that I did loue," 324, 332–33
Inferno, 14, 164, 166 and n.6, 168,
195, 200 n.42, 204
In paradisum, 53 n.41, 57 and
n.45, 68
"I often looke upon a face," 297,
298, 327
Ira, 221–22; choler, 221; wrath,
221. *See also* Despair; Patience;
Psychomachia; Vices and virtues
Isaiah, Book of, 237
Isidore of Seville, 4, 5

Janson, Horst, 303–6
Jenkins, Harold, 236, 290
Jeremiah, 83
Jesus, 129, 138, 210, 274, 280. *See
also* Christ; Comforter; God; King
of Kings; Savior; Son of Man
Job, 83; Book of, 122 and n.6
Johnson, Samuel, 232
Judgment day, 8, 29, 38, 128 n.10,
129, 152, 157, 178, 180, 186, 187,
201, 206, 211, 213, 250; end of
the world, 35; "general censure,"
29, 70, 206, 207; iugement general, 7, 29 n.23; Jugement generall, 129, 206 n.1; Judgment panel,
5; last days, 178, 184; last judgment, 5, 8, 9, 156, 223; "promis'd
end," 154. *See also* Apocalypse;
Doomsday; Fifteen signs; Revelation
Judgment-day portals, 156 n.38,
187 n.30, 224, 284
Judgment porch, 10, 224. *See also*
Lincoln cathedral
Julian calendar, 237, 239
Julius Caesar, 15

King James, 20 n.11, 25–27,
176, 196

King John, 12
King Lear (excluding chap. on
Lear), 12, 13, 15, 16, 24, 58,
192, 197, 272
King of Kings, 146. *See also* Christ;
Comforter; God; Jesus; Savior;
Son of Man
Kittredge, G. L., 50, 235
Knight, G. Wilson, 14, 164, 194

Lambert of St. Omer, 5
"Lament for the Makaris," 11, 325
and n.12. *See also* Dunbar
Langland, William, 320, 337. *See also*
Piers Plowman
Last things, 4, 204, 231, 309. *See also*
Eschatology; Four last things
Latini, Brunetto, 33
Lazarus (brother of Martha and
Mary), 340
Lazarus and Dives. *See* Dives and
Lazarus; *see also* Abraham; Beggar
and the rich man
Legenda Aurea, 178
Lerne to Dye, 11
"lerne you to dye when ye wyll,
To," 11
Lincoln cathedral, 9, 10, 224, 284
Lost coin, parable of the, 156
Lost sheep, parable of the, 156
Love, 19, 48, and n.37, 49, 58–59,
68, 69, 89, 140. *See also* Duty
Lydgate, John, 10, 36–37, 180, 184,
187, 192, 317–22, 325

Macbeth (excluding chap. on *Macbeth*), 12, 13, 14, 15, 16, 24, 80, 82,
120, 272
Marlowe, Christopher, 1, 3, 290, 301
Marriage/grave motif, 211, 214, 217
Measure for Measure, 70, 207, 237,
256, 258
memento mori (excluding appendix),
8, 11, 60, 65–66, 208–16, 219,
220, 236, 248 and n.18, 250, 253,
270–78, 280–81, 284, 287, 288,
291, 293, 295–97, 298–301, 303,
306, 307

Milton, John, 82, 105, 108
Minister, 33, 44, 60, 61, 66, 87, 339;
    ministerial, 33, 45, 47, 52, 75, 87;
    ministration, 74
Miracle, 125, 155
Mirour de l'Omme, 10
Moissac, 284
Montacute, Thomas, Earl of Salis-
    bury, 320
Moon, 232–36, 240–43, 242 n.16,
    247, 249 n.19, 252; moonbeam,
    235; moonlight, 234, 235, 241;
    moonrise, 241; moonshine, 235,
    242, 252; new crescent, 240;
    new moon, 233, 235, 240, 241;
    Phoebe, 241; waning crescent, 241
More, Sir Thomas, 1, 3, 10, 11
Much Ado About Nothing, 236
Muir, Kenneth, 164, 166 and n.6

Nashe, Thomas, 327–28 and
    n.15, 337
Newt, 148 n.28. *See also* Salamander;
    Wall-newt
Nicholas le Rouge, 7
Ninth circle (*Inferno*), 164–70, 176,
    196 n.36; Antenora, 164, 165,
    167; Brutus, 165, 166; Caesar,
    165; Caina, 164, 165, 167; Canto
    33, 168; Cassius, 165, 166; Cocy-
    tus, 168, 196; Judas Iscariot, 165,
    166; Judecca, 164, 165, 167;
    Ptolomaea, 164, 165, 167, 169,
    171, 176, 198
"Nou goð sonne vnder tre," 151

Office of the dead, 321
"Of the Death of the Noble Prince,
    Kynge Edwarde the Fourth,"
    322–23, 324
Othello (excluding chap. on *Othello*),
    12, 13, 15, 16, 17, 18, 24, 120,
    173, 206, 207, 231

Panofsky, Erwin, 292, 293, 297,
    298, 301
Paradise, 91, 92, 213, 289, 300–303.
    See also Arcadia; Eden

Paradise Lost, 82, 105, 108
Paradise of Dainty Devices, The,
    318 n.6, 328
Patience, 123, 221; *patientia*, 123,
    221. *See also* Despair; *Ira*; *Psycho-
    machia*; Vices and virtues
Pauline, 265, 268 n.23, 274. *See also*
    St. Paul
Pèlerinage de la Vie Humaine, Le, 11
Pelican, 149, 150 and n.29
Penance, 54–58 and n.42, 68, 74,
    202, 257, 338; absolution, 56, 57,
    58, 115, 162; confession, 52, 54,
    55, 56, 58, 72, 108, 115, 162, 202;
    contrition, 54, 55, 56, 58, 72, 162,
    202; penitence, 58, 111, 324; pen-
    itent, 22; penitential, 72, 74; re-
    pent, 56, 58, 75, 111, 221, 271,
    276, 339; repentance, 54 n.42, 60,
    108, 164, 202, 257, 259, 267, 268,
    271, 274, 276; repentant, 74, 115,
    280; repentant (late-), 259, 270;
    satisfaction, 54, 56, 58, 72, 74,
    115, 162, 202, 259
Pierre le Loyer, 20 n.11, 27, 86, 176
Piers Plowman, 317 n.5
Pilgrims Wish, 28
Poussin, Nicolas, 291–93 and n.10,
    298, 301, 303, 304. *See also Et in
    Arcadia Ego*
Priest/king, 54, 256–58, 270, 287
Proctor, Thomas, 331
Prodigal son, parable of the, 4, 145,
    156
Prophets and Antichrist, The, 36, 180.
    See also Chester cycle
Prudentius, 4
Prufrock, 72
Psalms, 52 and n.41, 55, 111
Psychomachia, 4, 10, 123 and n.7,
    221. *See also* Despair; *Ira*; Pa-
    tience; Vices and virtues
Putto with the Death's Head,
    303–6

IIII Livres des Spectres, 176
Queen Elizabeth Prayer Book, 8, 36,
    180, 184, 190, 192

Ralegh, Sir Walter, 1, 290
"Respice finem," 271 and nn.26 and 27, 331–32
Resurrection, 187, 231
Revelation, 152, 154, 162, 190. *See also* Apocalypse; Doomsday; Fifteen signs; Judgment day
Revenge, 21–22, 30, 33, 45, 49, 51–52, 53, 58, 59–61, 66, 69, 75, 81, 93, 250, 338, 339; avenge, 50; revenge code, 50, 58, 67; revengeful, 55; revenger, 59; revenger/scourge, 60; vengeance, 103; vengeful, 52–53
Richards, I. A., 83, 86
Richard II, 12, 256, 257
Richard III, 12, 15
Romeo and Juliet (excluding chap. on *Romeo and Juliet*), 69, 244, 245, 251, 271
Romeus and Juliet, 211
Rose, 108–9n.34, 138n.19, 391 and n.7. *See also* Rosemary
Rosemary, 138 and n.19
Rowe, Nicholas, 233, 243

St. Barnabas's Day, 238–39
St. Bernard of Clairvaux, 4, 284, 311, 314, 320, 322, 337
St.-Denis, 10, 223, 224
St. Jerome, 178
St. John's Day, 237, 276; Feast of St. John the Baptist, 232, 236–38, 239, 276; June 24th, 237, 239, 276; *Johannisnacht*, 232, 250
St. Paul, 255, 256n.5, 257, 258, 261, 263n.18, 264–65, 268. *See also* Pauline
St. Paul's (cloisters), 10
Salamander, 148n.28, 281 and n.34. *See also* Wall-newt
Sarum missal, 171, 325
Satan, 85, 108, 165, 201
Savior, 97, 106, 127, 155, 162, 319. *See also* Christ; Comforter; God; Jesus; King of Kings; Son of Man
Saxl, Fritz, 5, 7–8
Scot, Reginald, 20n.11, 27, 86, 176

Scourge and minister, 16 and n.8, 61, 339
Senses, 8, 118–27, 140, 147
Skelton, John, 10, 11, 210, 297, 313–14, 321, 322–25, 326, 329, 331, 333, 337
Smith, Henry, 28
Solstice, 237–238, 239, 241, 276
Song (Nashe's), 327–28
Son of Man, 137. *See also* Christ; Comforter; God; King of Kings; Savior
Southwell, Robert, 297, 298, 327, 331
Spenser, Edmund, 79–80, 238–39, 253n.20, 291
Spiritual encyclopedia, 3–9, 10, 11, 29n.23, 35, 129, 206n.1
Sponsus, 224
Stoppard, Tom, 68
Stratford Guildhall Chapel, 9, 157
Stubbes, Philip, 232
Suger, Abbot, 223

Tempest, The, 256
Ten Commandments, 150. *See also* Commandment
"That Now Is Hay Some-Tyme Was Grase," 319–20
Thomas, Duke of Clarence, 320
"Thoroughfare of Woe, A," 320
Three Living and the Three Dead, The, 5
timor mortis, 311n.2, 321, 325n.12, 338
Timor mortis conturbat me, 325 and n.12
"Timor Mortis Conturbat Me," 321
Toad, 148 and n.27, 152, 153n.33
Topsy-turvy, 16, 38, 39, 41, 42, 56, 60, 63, 89, 100, 104, 117, 119, 120, 127, 133, 136, 137, 140, 272; overturning of order, 134; overturned world, 121; universal upheaval, 127, 133; upside-down, 16, 38, 41, 67, 109, 117, 120, 127, 135 and n.17
Treatise of Specters, A, 20n.11

True king, 339. *See also* False appearances; Identification
Trumpet, 150 n.31, 152–53, 157, 187, 193, 212, 250–51
Tusser, Thomas, 312–13, 315, 329
Twelfth Night, 82, 236
XXII^d play (Chester cycle), 180. *See also* Chester cycle

ubi sunt, 315, 317, 319, 323, 329, 336–37
Unjust steward, parable of the, 156
"Vppon a deedmans hed," 11, 210, 274, 297, 313–15, 323–24, 325, 329, 333

Vasari, Giorgio, 306
Vaux, Thomas, Lord, 219, 324, 331, 332, 336
Veni Creator Spiritus, 171–72

Vérard, Antoine, 5, 7, 9
Vices and virtues, 4, 8, 123 n.7, 221. *See also* Despair; *Ira*; Patience; *Psychomachia*
Vincent of Beauvais, 4, 5, 178

Wall-newt, 148 and n.28. *See also* Salamander
Wellcome manuscript, 5, 7–8
Whitney, Geffrey, 308–9
Wilson, John Dover, 44, 46, 65, 233–34, 245
Winter's Tale, The, 240
Wise and foolish virgins, parable of the, 4, 10, 217–24, 227, 272–73, 274, 284, 306 n.23
Works of charity, 8 and n.4
Wynkyn de Worde, 5, 7, 9, 36, 180, 184, 185, 192–93